# CUTTING EDGE

## THIRD EDITION

**ELEMENTARY**

**STUDENTS' BOOK**

WITH DVD-ROM

**SARAH CUNNINGHAM PETER MOOR
AND ARAMINTA CRACE**

# CONTENTS

| Unit | Grammar focus | Vocabulary | Skills |
|------|---------------|------------|--------|
| **01** <br> **PEOPLE AND PLACES** <br> page 06 | *be*: positive forms <br> *be*: positive and negative short forms <br> Articles with jobs <br> *be*: personal questions | Countries and nationalities <br> Jobs | **Reading and listening:** What do you know? Test your knowledge of countries, languages and nationalities |
| **02** <br> **PEOPLE AND THINGS** <br> page 16 | *this/that, these/those* <br> Possessive *'s* <br> *have got* | Everyday objects <br> Family | **Reading:** Family connections |
| **03** <br> **YOUR LIFE** <br> page 24 | Present simple: positive and negative (*I, you, we, they*) <br> Present simple: questions and short answers (*I, you, we, they*) | Common verbs <br> Telling the time <br> Places in a town | **Reading:** Brits at home ... and abroad <br> **Listening:** Life on a Scottish island |
| **04** <br> **LIKES AND DISLIKES** <br> page 34 | Present simple: positive and negative (*he/she/it*) <br> Present simple: questions and short answers (*he/she/it*) | Activities <br> Phrases for time and frequency | **Listening:** A typical pop star? <br> **Reading:** Some people are life's winners! |
| **05** <br> **FROM A TO B** <br> page 42 | *can/can't*: possibility and ability <br> Articles: *a/an*, *the* and no article | Transport <br> Travelling | **Reading:** Nine things you didn't know about world travel |
| **06** <br> **FOOD AND DRINK** <br> page 52 | *there is* and *there are*; *some* and *any* <br> *how much* and *how many* | Food: countable and uncountable nouns <br> Food pairs | **Reading:** Healthy diets around the world |
| **07** <br> **LIFE STORIES** <br> page 60 | Past simple: *was/were* <br> Past simple: regular and irregular verbs | Life events <br> Past time phrases | **Reading:** An ordinary man ... an extraordinary business <br> **Listening:** Jackie Kennedy Onassis |

Study, Practice & Remember page 138, Audio scripts page 166, Irregular verb list page 175

| Pronunciation | Task | Language live/ World culture | Study, Practice & Remember |
|---|---|---|---|
| Word stress<br>Short forms – *am, are, is*<br>Stress in questions and short answers | Find information from documents<br>**Preparation:** Reading<br>**Task:** Speaking | **World culture**<br>**Video and research:**<br>Life in the Arctic | Study and Practice 1, page 138<br>Study and Practice 2, page 138<br>Study and Practice 3, page 138<br>Study and Practice 4, page 138<br>Study and Practice 5, page 139<br>Remember these words, page 139 |
| Word stress<br>*this, that, these, those*<br>Short forms – *has/have got*<br>Vocabulary – family | Talk about your five favourite people<br>**Preparation:** Listening<br>**Task:** Speaking | **Language live**<br>**Writing:** Completing a form<br>**Speaking:** Answering questions | Study and Practice 1, page 140<br>Study and Practice 2, page 140<br>Remember these words, page 141 |
| Stress and weak forms – questions<br>Stress and weak forms – telling the time | Describe life in your favourite town<br>**Preparation:** Reading and listening<br>**Task:** Speaking | **World culture**<br>**Video and research:**<br>Indian railway | Study and Practice 1, page 142<br>Study and Practice 2, page 142<br>Study and Practice 3, page 143<br>Remember these words, page 143 |
| Verb forms – *he/she/it*<br>Strong and weak forms – *does* | Choose a holiday activity<br>**Preparation:** Reading and listening<br>**Task:** Speaking | **Language live**<br>**Speaking:** Meeting people<br>**Writing:** Introducing a friend | Study and Practice 1, page 144<br>Study and Practice 2, page 144<br>Study and Practice 3, page 145<br>Remember these words, page 145 |
| Weak forms – prepositions and articles<br>Strong and weak forms – *can/can't* | Do a transport survey<br>**Preparation:** Reading and listening<br>**Task:** Speaking | **World culture**<br>**Video and research:**<br>Race across London | Study & Practice 1, page 146<br>Study & Practice 2, page 146<br>Remember these words, page 147 |
| Linking in sentences<br>Stress on word pairs | Describe a favourite place to eat<br>**Preparation:** Listening<br>**Task:** Speaking | **Language live**<br>**Writing:** Describe a place to eat<br>**Speaking:** Ordering food and drink | Study and Practice 1, page 148<br>Study and Practice 2, page 149<br>Remember these words, page 149 |
| Strong and weak forms – *was/were*<br>Regular past simple forms – *-ed* endings | Tell a life story<br>**Preparation:** Listening<br>**Task:** Speaking | **World culture**<br>**Video and research:**<br>The Information Age | Study and Practice 1, page 150<br>Study and Practice 2, page 150<br>Study and Practice 3, page 151<br>Remember these words, page 151 |

# CONTENTS

| Unit | Grammar focus | Vocabulary | Skills |
|------|---------------|------------|--------|
| **08** **FACT OR FICTION?** page 70 | Past simple: negative form Past simple: question form | Adjectives to describe stories Entertainment | **Listening:** *We Will Rock You –* a song and a musical |
| **09** **BUY AND SELL** page 78 | Comparative adjectives Superlative adjectives | Describing objects Shops and services | **Reading:** Top five unusual shops |
| **10** **LOOK GOOD** page 88 | Present continuous Present simple or continuous? | Clothes Describing personality | **Listening:** Clothes at work |
| **11** **NATURE** page 96 | Question words Quantifiers: *a lot of, a little, a few, not any, not much, not many* | Animals and natural features Big numbers | **Reading:** Working animals **Listening:** Intelligent animals **Listening:** South Africa |
| **12** **GOOD TIMES** page 106 | *going to* for future intentions *would like to* and *want to* for future wishes | Celebrations and parties Weather and seasons | **Reading:** Celebrating the seasons |
| **13** **LIVE AND LEARN** page 114 | *have to* and *don't have to* *might* and *will* | School and university subjects Education and training | **Listening:** Two career paths **Reading:** From slates to iPads ... Language learning then, now and in the future |
| **14** **KEEP IN TOUCH** page 124 | Present perfect (unfinished time) Present perfect (with *ever*) | Ways of communicating Technology | **Reading:** Mind-blowing facts about modern communication |

Study, Practice & Remember page 138, Audio scripts page 166, Irregular verb list page 175

| Pronunciation | Task | Language live/ World culture | Study, Practice & Remember |
|---|---|---|---|
| Linking – *did you* | Talk about an evening in or out<br>**Preparation:** Listening<br>**Task:** Speaking | **Language live**<br>**Speaking:** Arranging an evening out<br>**Writing:** Arranging an evening out | Study and Practice 1, page 152<br>Study and Practice 2, page 152<br>Remember these words, page 153 |
| Stress – comparative adjectives | Choose souvenirs from your country<br>**Preparation:** Listening<br>**Task:** Speaking | **World culture**<br>**Video and research:** Famous markets | Study and Practice 1, page 154<br>Study and Practice 2, page 154<br>Remember these words, page 155 |
| Vocabulary – clothes | Analyse your personality<br>**Preparation:** Reading and listening<br>**Task:** Speaking | **Language live**<br>**Speaking:** Asking for goods and services<br>**Writing:** Describing people | Study and Practice 1, page 156<br>Study and Practice 2, page 156<br>Remember these words, page 157 |
| Vocabulary – numbers | Devise a general knowledge quiz<br>**Preparation:** Reading and listening<br>**Task:** Speaking | **World culture**<br>**Video and research:** Animals in danger | Study and Practice 1, page 158<br>Study and Practice 2, page 158<br>Remember these words, page 159 |
| Weak forms – *going to* | Plan a festival<br>**Preparation:** Reading<br>**Task:** Speaking | **Language live**<br>**Writing:** Information to promote a festival<br>**Speaking:** Suggestions and offers | Study and Practice 1, page 160<br>Study and Practice 2, page 160<br>Remember these words, page 161 |
| Weak forms and linking – *have to/don't have to* | Complete a careers questionnaire<br>**Preparation:** Reading<br>**Task:** Speaking | **World culture**<br>**Video and research:** A dream come true | Study and Practice 1, page 162<br>Study and Practice 2, page 162<br>Remember these words, page 163 |
| Strong and weak forms – *have* (Present perfect) | Take part in a game<br>**Preparation:** Reading and listening<br>**Task:** Speaking | **Language live**<br>**Speaking:** Telephoning<br>**Writing:** A text message | Study and Practice 1, page 164<br>Study and Practice 2, page 164<br>Remember these words, page 165 |

# 01

# PEOPLE AND PLACES

## IN THIS UNIT

- Grammar: *be*: positive forms; *be*: positive and negative short forms; Articles with jobs; *be*: personal questions
- Vocabulary: Countries and nationalities; Jobs
- Task: Find information from documents
- World culture: Life in the Arctic

## Speaking and listening

**1a** 🎧 **1.1** Listen to the conversation. Number the sentences in the order you hear them.

> **A:** Hi, I'm Teresa.
> **B:** Nice to meet you, Teresa.
> **B:** Hello, my name's Adam. What's your name?
> **A:** And you!

**b** Work in pairs. Practise the conversation using your own names.

**2a** Complete the conversations with the sentences in the box.

........................................................................

I'm fine, thanks.      Nice to meet you, May.
Where are you from?      Are you from the USA?

........................................................................

**Conversation 1**
**A:** Hi! How are you?
**B:** ¹_____ How are you?

**Conversation 2**
**A:** This is May. She's from Hong Kong.
**B:** ²_____
**C:** Nice to meet you, too.

**Conversation 3**
**A:** ³_____
**B:** No, no ...
**A:** ⁴_____
**B:** I'm from Sydney ... in Australia.
**A:** Oh, really?

**b** 🎧 **1.2** Listen and check your answers. Then practise the conversations.

## PRACTICE

**1a** Ask other students the questions below.

> What's your name?
>
> Where are you from?

**b** Tell the class about another student.

> This is … She's from …

**2** Work in pairs and take turns. Ask and answer questions about the people in the photos.

> Where's he from?
>
> He's from …

> Where are they from?
>
> They're from …

FRIENDS (291) ▼

Abed Arif    UAE

Luca Simone    Argentina

Adrian D.    Poland

Jo and Al Kelly    Australia

Alicia Cruz    Mexico

the Anderson family    USA

# Grammar focus 1
*be*: positive forms

### GRAMMAR

*be*: positive forms

**1** Complete the gaps with *are*, *am* or *is*.
  1 I _____ fine.
  2 _____ you from Mexico?
  3 He _____ from Ireland.
  4 Carla _____ from Italy.
  5 Ben and Emily _____ from Australia.

Question words: *what/where*

**2** Complete the gaps with *what* or *where*.
  1 _____ 's your name? (= what is)
  2 _____ are you from?

> Unit 1, Study & Practice 1, page 138

## Vocabulary
### Countries and nationalities

**1a** Complete the table below with the words in the box.

| British | American | Japanese | Chinese |
|---------|----------|------------|-----------|
| Polish | Italian | Vietnamese | Russian |
| Irish | Spanish | Brazilian | Australian |

| Country | Nationality |
|---------|-------------|
| Spain | |
| China | |
| the USA | |
| Brazil | |
| Italy | |
| Great Britain | |
| Poland | |
| Australia | |
| Japan | |
| Vietnam | |
| Ireland | |
| Russia | |

**b** 🎧 1.3 Listen and check.

### PRONUNCIATION

**1** 🎧 1.4 Listen to the stressed syllable.
Bri-tish   A-mer-i-can   Ja-pa-nese

**2a** Look at the nationalities in exercise 1a. Mark the stressed syllable.

**b** 🎧 1.5 Listen and check. Practise saying the nationalities, paying attention to the stressed syllable.

## Reading and listening

**1a** Work in pairs and do the quiz.

**b** 🎧 1.6 Listen and check your answers. Count your points.

IT'S A FACT!
300 = the number of languages spoken in London

# What do you know?
Test your knowledge of countries, languages and nationalities

**1** Match the stamps to the countries. (4 points)
Poland   China   Brazil   Egypt

**2** Match the currencies to the countries. (4 points)
Russia   Turkey   India   Argentina

rupee      rouble      lira      peso

**3** Which word is in: (5 points)
Russian?   Chinese?   Italian?   Arabic?   Spanish?
a 你好   b **ciao**   c **привет**   d **hola**   e مرحب

**4** Which of these companies is: (4 points)
Korean?   American?   Japanese?   British?

**5** What nationality are these singers? (3 points)

Andrea Bocelli   Delta Goodrem   Luis Miguel

# Grammar focus 2

## *be*: positive and negative short forms

**1a** Match sentences 1–15 with photos A–C.

1 Her name's Hanna.    C
2 His name's Gustavo.
3 Their names are Amy and Lucas.
4 He's from Brazil.
5 They're from Sydney, Australia.
6 She's from Kraków in Poland.
7 She's 33 and she's married.
8 They are both 26.
9 He's 19.
10 She's a businesswoman.
11 They're tourists.
12 He's a student at university.
13 He isn't married. He's single.
14 They aren't married. They are friends.
15 She isn't on holiday. She's on business.

**b** 🎧 **1.7 Listen and check.**

## GRAMMAR

1  Complete the table.

| + | Short form | – | Short form |
|---|---|---|---|
| I am | _____ | I am not | I'm not |
| you are | you're | you are not | _____ |
| he is | _____ | he is not | _____ |
| she is | _____ | she is not | _____ |
| it is | it's | it is not | _____ |
| we are | we're | we are not | we aren't |
| they are | _____ | they are not | _____ |

## PRONUNCIATION

**1a** Look at audio script 1.8 on page 166. Notice the short forms.

**b** 🎧 **1.8 Listen to the sentences.**

**2**  Listen again and practise saying the sentences.

## PRACTICE

**1a** Write four true sentences and four false sentences about the people in photos A–C.

*Hanna's from Poland.*

*Amy and Lucas are married.*

**b** Work in pairs and read your sentences. Are they true or false? Correct the false sentences.

> Amy and Lucas are married.

> False. They aren't married. They're friends.

**2a** Tick the sentences that are true for you. Correct the false sentences.

You're in an English lesson.  ✓
You're from Korea.   *I'm not from Korea. I'm from ...*
1 You're Italian.
2 Your school's in Los Angeles.
3 Your classroom's very small.
4 Your teacher's from Ireland.
5 Your teacher's married.
6 Your mother's a businesswoman.
7 Your parents are on holiday.
8 Your English lessons are in the evening.
9 You're 35 years old.
10 You're at work.

**b** Work in pairs and compare your sentences.

Unit 1, Study & Practice 2, page 138

# Vocabulary
## Jobs

**1** Match the jobs in the box with pictures A–L.

| | | |
|---|---|---|
| a footballer | a musician | an engineer |
| a lawyer | a police officer | a singer |
| a shop assistant | a doctor | an actor |
| a waiter | a businessman | a businesswoman |

# Grammar focus 3
## Articles with jobs

**1** Look at the two sentences. Which one is correct?

**1** He's actor.
**2** He's an actor.

### GRAMMAR

**1** With jobs we use the articles *a/an*.

| an + vowel (*a, e, i, o, u*) | He's **an** actor.<br>She's **an** engineer. |
|---|---|
| a + other letters | He's **a** waiter.<br>She's **a** doctor. |

## PRACTICE

**1a** Complete the sentences with *a* or *an*.

**1** He's _____ doctor.
**2** I'm _____ engineer.
**3** Susanna's _____ shop assistant.
**4** I'm not _____ teacher.
**5** Diego's _____ police officer.
**6** She isn't _____ actor.
**7** He's _____ lawyer.
**8** I'm _____ singer.

**b** 🎧 1.10 Listen and check your answers.

**2a** Write five sentences about people you know. Include two false sentences.

*I'm a teacher.    Daniel's an engineer.*

**b** Work in pairs and take turns. Say and correct your sentences.

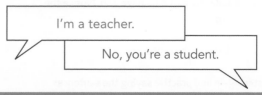

I'm a teacher.

No, you're a student.

Unit 1, Study & Practice 3, page 138

# Grammar focus 4
## *be*: personal questions

**1** Read the questions below and choose the correct answers.

**1** What's your full name?
  **a** My name's Will.
  **b** It's William Anthony Barker.
**2** What's your job?
  **a** I'm a musician.
  **b** She's a student.
**3** What's your email address?
  **a** It's 25 Manor Road, London SW10.
  **b** It's <u>willbarker@tlc.com</u>.
**4** Where are you from?
  **a** I'm from Ireland.
  **b** I'm on holiday.
**5** How old are you?
  **a** I'm 24.
  **b** I'm fine, thanks.
**6** Are you here on holiday?
  **a** No, I'm from Japan.
  **b** Yes, I am.

---

### GRAMMAR

#### Questions: *be*

**1 Notice the word order.**

| Question | Answer |
|---|---|
| Where **is he** from? | **He's** from Russia. |
| What**'s your** name? | **My name's** Ana. |
| How old **are you**? | **I'm** 24. |

**Short answers to *Yes/No* questions**

| | |
|---|---|
| *Are you here on holiday?* | Yes, **I am**. |
| | No, **I'm not**. |
| *Is she a musician?* | Yes, **she is**. |
| | No, **she isn't**. |

---

**2** Work in pairs and take turns. Ask and answer the questions in exercise 1.

## PRACTICE

**1** Complete the questions and answers.

**1 A:** What _____ his name?
  **B:** His name _____ Andrew Kerr.
**2 A:** What's his _____ ?
  **B:** He _____ an engineer.
**3 A:** _____ 's he from?
  **B:** He's _____ Scotland.

**2** Work in pairs and take turns. Ask and answer questions about the people in the photos. Use the questions and answers in exercise 1 to help you.

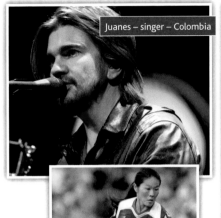
Juanes – singer – Colombia

Colin Firth – actor – Britain

Homare Sawa – female footballer – Japan

Hung Huang – businesswoman – China

**3a** Choose the correct answers.

**1** *Is / Are* you a student?
**2** *Is / Are* your teacher English?
**3** *Is / Are* you from Brazil?
**4** *Is / Are* you 21 years old?
**5** *Is / Are* your name Julian Mendez?
**6** *Is / Are* you here on holiday?

**b** Write answers to the questions and make them true for you.

---

### PRONUNCIATION

**1** 🎧 1.11 Look at audio script 1.11 on page 166 and listen to the stress in the questions and short answers.

1 A: Are you a student?  2 A: Is your teacher English?
  B: Yes, I am.               B: No, she isn't.

**2** Practise saying the questions and short answers.

---

**4** Work in pairs and take turns. Ask and answer the questions in exercise 3a.

> Are you a student?

> No, I'm not. I'm a businessman.

Unit 1, Study & Practice 4 and 5, page 138

# Task

## Find information from documents

### Preparation Reading

1 Read Deepa's personal information card. Are statements 1–9 true (T) or false (F)?

  1 Her first name's Deepa.
  2 Her surname's Zaman.
  3 She's 29 years old.
  4 She's from India.
  5 Her mobile number's 07866 332144.
  6 Her email address is ds82@hotmail.co.uk.
  7 Yamin Zaman is her husband.
  8 His work number is 020 7267 9952.
  9 Her doctor's name is Dr Highfield.

**EMPLOYEE PERSONAL INFORMATION**

| | |
|---|---|
| **Full name** | Deepa Samar Zaman |
| **Date of birth** | 24.10.82 |
| **Place of birth** | Mumbai, India |
| **Address** | 79 Nelson Road, London, N8 4TQ |
| **Home number** | 020 8348 9841 |
| **Mobile number** | 07733 342921 |
| **Email address** | dsz82@hotmail.co.uk |

| | |
|---|---|
| **Emergency contact** | Yamin Zaman (husband) |
| **Home number** | 020 8348 9841 |
| **Work number** | 020 7267 9952 |
| **Mobile number** | 07866 332144 |

**Doctor's name, address and telephone number**
Dr Jenny Henderson
Highfield Medical Centre, 10 Middle Road, N8 4RT
020 8348 3534

2a 🎧 1.12 Listen to two students asking questions about Deepa. Tick the questions and phrases you hear in the Useful language box.

  b Listen again and check.

### Task Speaking

1 Work in pairs. Student A: Look at Tom's documents on page 13. Complete the information about him below. Student B: Look at Michiko's documents on page 132. Complete the information about her below.

**PROFILE**

Full name _____
Age _____
Address _____
_____
_____
_____

Job _____
Where from? _____
Email address _____
Telephone _____

**PROFILE**

Full name _____
Age _____
Address _____
_____
_____
_____

Job _____
Where from? _____
Email address _____
Telephone _____

# THOMAS **BRIGGS**

## PERSONAL DETAILS

| | |
|---|---|
| **Phone** | 07744 345332 |
| **Email** | thomasb@yahoo.co.uk |
| **Date of birth** | 24.06.91 |
| **Nationality** | British |

## CORE SKILLS AND EXPERIENCE

I'm in my last year of an engineering degree and I'm now looking for a job in the electrical engineering industry. I'm a very hard-working person and I'm also very good at working to deadlines.

## HOBBIES

### Student card

**Name:** Tom Briggs
**Place of study:** University of Brighton
**Course of study:** Engineering
**Telephone number:** 07744 345332
**Email address:** thomasb@yahoo.co.uk

Mr Thomas J. Briggs
44 Preston Road
Brighton BN1 2PR

## USEFUL LANGUAGE

**a Questions**
What's his/her (name / surname / full name)?
How do you spell that?
Where's he/she from?
What's his/her (home/work/mobile) number?
How old is he/she?
What's his/her job?
Is he/she married or single?

**b Useful phrases**
I don't know.
Sorry, I don't understand.

2 Work in pairs. Student A: Ask Student B questions about Michiko. Complete the information about her on page 12. Student B: Ask Student A questions about Tom. Complete the information about him on page 12.

> Useful language a and b

3 Work in pairs and take turns. Ask and answer questions about your partner.

Hello, what's your name?

Hi, my name's João Carneiro.

## SHARE YOUR TASK

**Practise talking about you.**

**Film/Record yourself talking about you.**

**Share your film/recording with other students.**

# WORLD CULTURE

## LIFE IN THE ARCTIC

## Find out first

**1a** Work in pairs and discuss. What do you know about life in the Arctic? Try to answer the questions in the quiz below.

### Arctic life

1 **Which country is not in the Arctic?**
   a Canada
   b Chile
   c Greenland
2 **In winter, the temperature in the Arctic is:**
   a minus 40°C
   b 0°C
   c 2°C
3 **Inuits are the indigenous people of:**
   a the Antarctic
   b the Arctic
   c Iceland
4 **Which of these foods are in the Arctic?**
   a fruit
   b seafood (e.g. fish, mussels)
   c vegetables
5 **An igloo is:**
   a an animal
   b a fish
   c a house

**b** Go online to check your answers or ask your teacher.

**Search:** Arctic map / Inuit diet / Inuit / Arctic temperature / igloo

## View

**2a** You are going to watch a video about life in the Arctic. Before you watch, check you understand the meaning of the words/phrases in the box.

dangerous    the sun    snow    ice    igloo
plants       mussels    tea     trees  water

**b** ▶ Watch the video and tick the things that you see in the box.

**3** Read the text from the video below. Then watch again and complete the gaps with the words in the box.

cold   eat   food   friends   from   ice   is   it's

The Arctic in March: a place with no plants, no trees and no ¹_____ .

Lukasi ²_____ an Inuit. He's ³_____ north-east Canada.

'In the land of the Inuit, there is nothing to grow. We can't farm anything.'

Lukasi and his ⁴_____ travel a long way to find food.

It's very ⁵_____ .

They make an igloo.

Outside ⁶_____ minus 45 degrees Celsius. But in the igloo it's 16 degrees.

There is food under the ⁷_____ .

It's very dangerous.

But there is something good to ⁸_____ : mussels. 'These mussels are great!'

Lukasi and his friends are very hungry. But there is food for everyone.

## World view

**4a** Look at the statements about life in the Arctic below. Tick the ones that are true for your country.

- It is very cold in winter.
- There are no plants and no trees.
- It's in the Northern hemisphere.
- Fish is a popular food.
- Indigenous people live there.

**b** Work in pairs and compare your answers.

### 📶 FIND OUT MORE

**5a** Look at the names of other indigenous people in the box below. Do you know anything about them?

......................................................................

the Degar    the Tuareg    the Yanomami

......................................................................

**b** Go online to find out more about them and answer the questions.

1 Where do they live?
2 What is the weather like there?
3 What do they eat?

......................................................................

**Search:** Degar/Tuareg/Yanomani + weather/temperature/diet

......................................................................

## ▶ Write up your research

**6** Write about one of the indigenous people you researched. Use the example below to help you.

The Inuit are an indigenous people. They are from the Arctic: Greenland, Canada, the USA and Russia. It is very cold there! Their diet is fish and meat.

# PEOPLE AND THINGS

## IN THIS UNIT

- Grammar: *this/that*, *these/those*; Possessive *'s*; *have got*
- Vocabulary: Everyday objects; Family
- Task: Talk about your five favourite people
- Language live: Completing a form; Answering questions

## Vocabulary
### Everyday objects

**1** Work in pairs. Match the words in the box with the photos.

| | | | |
|---|---|---|---|
| a bottle of water | a camera | a wallet | tissues |
| an identity card (an ID card) | a credit card | keys | glasses |
| a mobile phone (a mobile) | a dictionary | photos | a bag |
| a packet of chewing gum | a memory stick | coins | a watch |

---

### PRONUNCIATION

**1** 🎧 2.1 Listen to the words in exercise 1. Mark the stressed syllables.

bottle of water    camera    wallet

**2** Practise saying the words, paying attention to the stressed syllables.

---

**2** Work in pairs and take turns. Ask and answer the questions.

1 Which things are in your bag now?
2 Which things are always in your bag?

**3** Close your book. Say all the objects you can remember.

## GRAMMAR

**this/that, these/those**

| this key | these keys | that key | those keys |

**Possessive 's**

*Tina's cat*
NOT *the cat of Tina*

*Bono's friends*
NOT *the friends of Bono*

## PRONUNCIATION

1 🎧 **2.3** Listen to the pronunciation of *this*, *that*, *these* and *those*. Practise saying the phrases.

this dictionary   that man   these children   those keys

2a 🎧 **2.4** Listen and write the eight sentences.

b Listen again and practise saying the sentences.

# Grammar focus 1
*this/that, these/those*; Possessive *'s*

1a Read about Ed Turner and choose the correct answers.

Hi, my name's Ed Turner. ¹***That / This*** is my wife Thelma ... and ²***these / those*** are my beautiful children, Ike and Tina, and ³***Tina / Tina's*** cat, Buddy.

And ⁴***that's / this is*** our dog Bono over there. That's his little house and ⁵***these / those*** are ⁶***Bono / Bono's*** friends!

b 🎧 **2.2** Listen and check.

## PRACTICE

1 Choose the correct answers.

1 **A:** Jerry, ***this / that*** is Mike.
**B:** Nice to meet you, Mike.
2 That's ***Paola / Paola's*** car.
3 Is ***that / this*** your friend over there?
4 ***John / John's*** has got a new phone.
5 Are ***these / those*** your keys here?
6 What's your ***friend / friend's*** name?
7 Look at ***these / those*** birds over there!
8 My ***sister / sister's*** new flat is really beautiful.

2 Work in pairs and take turns. Point to objects in the classroom. Ask and answer questions.

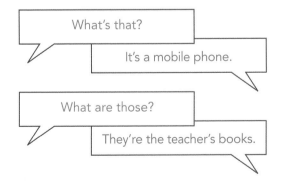

What's that?

It's a mobile phone.

What are those?

They're the teacher's books.

Unit 2, Study & Practice 1, page 140

17

# Grammar focus 2
*have got*

**1** 🎧 2.5 Look at the photo. Listen and complete the conversation with the words in the box.

I've got    I haven't got    Have you got

**A:** Look, that's beautiful! ¹_____ my camera with me. ²_____ one?
**B:** No, but ³_____ my mobile phone with me. Here you are.
**A:** Oh, thanks!

## GRAMMAR

**1 Complete the gaps.**

| + | I've *got* my mobile phone with me.<br>He's/She's _____ his/her credit card.<br>We've/They've _____ the bag. |
|---|---|
| – | I haven't _____ my watch with me.<br>He/She hasn't _____ his/her glasses.<br>We/They _____ the keys. |
| ? | Have you _____ a dictionary?<br>_____ he/she _____ a camera?<br>_____ we/they _____ a bottle of water? |

**2** 🎧 2.6 Listen and check.

**3 Notice:**
**He's** Japanese. (= he is)
**He's** got a Japanese car. (= he has)

## PRONUNCIATION

**1** Listen again to audio 2.6 in the grammar box.

**2** Practise saying the sentences.

## PRACTICE

**1** Complete the sentences with the correct form of *have got*. Use short forms where possible.

1 I _____ a new phone. It's really good!
2 Sorry, I _____ the photos with me.
3 Ask Pedro for the time. He _____ a watch.
4 We _____ a dog. Her name is Amber.
5 _____ you _____ a dictionary?
6 She _____ an identity card. It's number NA342115.
7 I think her parents are very rich. They _____ four cars.
8 _____ your brother _____ the keys?

**2a** Match the questions in A with the answers in B.

| A | B |
|---|---|
| 1 Have you got a car? | a It's a Honda. |
| 2 How old is it? | b It's about five years old. |
| 3 What colour is it? | c Yes, I have. |
| 4 What kind of car is it? | d It's red. |

**b** Work in pairs and take turns. Ask and answer questions about the things in the box.

| | | |
|---|---|---|
| a car | a mobile | a dog |
| a computer | a favourite bag | a cat |
| a dictionary | a TV in your bedroom | a camera |

> Have you got a mobile?

> Yes, I have.

> What kind is it?

> It's a Samsung.

Unit 2, Study & Practice 2, page 140

# Reading and vocabulary
## Family

## FAMILY CONNECTIONS

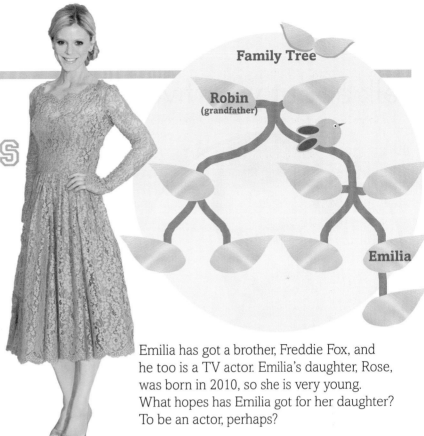

**Family Tree**

**Robin** (grandfather)

**Emilia**

Emilia Fox is from England and she is an actor (in films and on TV). Many people in her family are also actors. Both her parents are actors: her father is Edward Fox (a film actor) and her mother is Joanna David (a TV actor). Her grandmother, Angela Worthington, was an actor and her uncle, James Fox, is an actor. James Fox is in many films. In *WE*, he plays King George V. James's son, Laurence Fox, is in the same film – as King George's son! James's daughter, Lydia Fox, is also a TV actor.

Emilia has got a brother, Freddie Fox, and he too is a TV actor. Emilia's daughter, Rose, was born in 2010, so she is very young. What hopes has Emilia got for her daughter? To be an actor, perhaps?

**1a** Read about British actor Emilia Fox. Write the names in her family tree.

**b** Read the article again. How many people in her family are also actors?

**2** Complete the table with the words in the box.

| father | sister | grandparents | grandmother |
| son | uncle | granddaughter | cousin |
| niece | children | husband | girlfriend |

| Male | Female | Male and female |
|------|--------|-----------------|
| boyfriend | aunt | grandchildren |
| brother | daughter | parents |
| grandfather | mother | _____ |
| grandson | wife | _____ |
| nephew | _____ | _____ |
| _____ | _____ | |
| _____ | _____ | |
| _____ | _____ | |

**3** Answer the questions about Emilia Fox's family.

1 How many brothers has she got?
2 How many cousins has she got?
3 What is her grandmother's name?
4 What is her uncle's name?
5 What job does her uncle do?
6 Who is Edward Fox's nephew?
7 Who is his niece?
8 Who are Laurence Fox's uncle and aunt?

**4** Work in pairs and take turns. Ask and answer three of the questions below. Give more details in your answers.

1 How many brothers and sisters have you got?
2 How many cousins have you got?
3 How many uncles and aunts have you got?
4 How many nephews and nieces have you got?
5 How many children have you got?

> How many cousins have you got?
>
> I've got three. Their names are …

### PRONUNCIATION

1 🎧 2.7 Listen to six sentences. Notice the pronunciation of the family words (*nephew*, *son*, etc.).

2 Practise saying the sentences.

# Task

## Talk about your five favourite people

Anthony

Emily

Liz

### Preparation Listening

**1a** Look at the photos of Liz and her five favourite people. Which person do you think is:

    **1** her friend?
    **2** her niece?
    **3** her favourite fictional character?
    **4** her brother?
    **5** her favourite actor?

**b** 🎧 **2.8** Listen and check.

**c** Complete column A in the table below.

|  | **A Who is he/she?** | **B Other information** |
|---|---|---|
| Anthony | He's Liz's brother. |  |
| Emily |  |  |
| Elaine |  |  |
| George Clooney |  |  |
| Sherlock Holmes |  |  |

**2a** Listen again and complete column B with the information in the box.

| | |
|---|---|
| is 26 years old | is a really good friend |
| is lovely | is not a real person |
| is fantastic | has got a new job |
| is from the USA | has got two children |

**b** Work in pairs and take turns. Say two things about each person in the table.

> Elaine is a really good friend.
> She's got a new job.

**3** Listen again and tick the phrases you hear in the Useful language box.

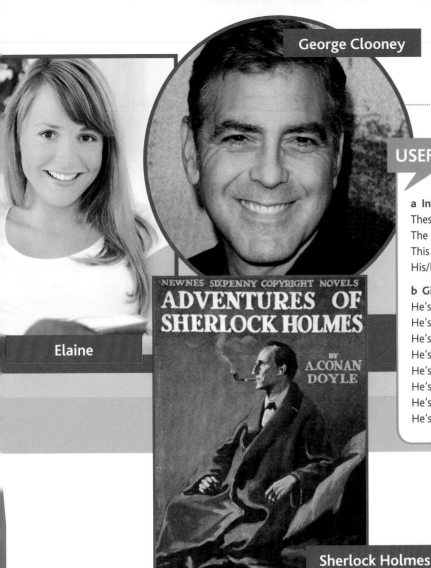

George Clooney

Elaine

ADVENTURES OF SHERLOCK HOLMES
NEWNES SIXPENNY COPYRIGHT NOVELS
BY A. CONAN DOYLE

Sherlock Holmes

USEFUL LANGUAGE

**a Introducing your favourite people**
These are my (five) favourite people.
The first person is my (sister, friend, ... ).
This is my (brother, niece, ... ).
His/Her name's ...

**b Giving details**
He's/She's (three) years old.
He's/She's a singer.
He's/She's (lovely, fantastic).
He's/She's got (a new job, two children).
He's/She's American.
He's/She's from (the USA).
He's/She's not a real person.
He's/She's my favourite (fictional character / actor).

# Task Speaking

**1a** Choose your five favourite people. For example:

- a family member
- a friend or colleague
- an actor, a singer, a writer, etc.
- a fictional character

**b** Look at the questions below. Make notes about your five favourite people.

1 Is he/she a real or fictional person?
2 What is your relationship to him/her?
3 How old is he/she?
4 Where is he/she from?
5 What's his/her job?
6 What other information can you give about him/her?

**2** Work in pairs and take turns. Practise talking about your five favourite people. Use your notes and photos (if you have any). Ask your teacher for any words/phrases you need.

> Useful language a and b

**3a** Work in groups and take turns. Talk about your favourite people.

**b** Ask other students questions about their favourite people.

**SHARE YOUR TASK**

**Practise talking about your five favourite people.**

**Film/Record yourself talking about your five favourite people.**

**Share your film/recording with other students.**

# LANGUAGE LIVE

Sign there ...

## Writing
### Completing a form

**1** Work in pairs. Look at the photo and discuss. Where are the people? What do you think they are doing?

**2** Match the words/phrases in A with the examples in B.

**A**
1 contact phone number
2 date
3 date of birth
4 email address
5 home address
6 first name
7 nationality
8 postcode
9 signature
10 surname
11 title

**B**
a Richard
b 07822 014873
c British
d Adison
e richardadison@yourworld.com
f 45a Elm Road, London
g 7.6.2014
h Mr/Mrs/Miss/Ms
i 22.1.93
j W8 9BG
k *Richard Adison*

**3** Complete the Student Record Form with information about you.

### Student Record Form

**PERSONAL DETAILS**
Title: _____     First name: _____
Surname: _____
Date of birth (DD/MM/YYYY): _____
Nationality: _____

**CONTACT DETAILS**
Address: _____
Telephone: _____
Email: _____

**DECLARATION**
The details here are true to the best of my knowledge.

Signature: _____
Date (DD/MM/YYYY) _____

# Speaking
## Answering questions

**1** ▶ Watch the video of people in a medical centre. Number the people in the order you first hear them speak.

- the receptionist
- the doctor
- the male patient
- the female patient

**2** Watch again and choose the correct answers.

1 Name:
  a James Alan
  b James Allan
  c James Allen
2 Address:
  a 13 Book Street
  b 30 Brook Street
  c 39 Brook Street
3 Postcode:
  a BS6 7AH
  b BS7 6HA
  c BS8 67A
4 Contact phone number:
  a 07229 895700
  b 07529 280703
  c 07259 298730
5 Age:
  a 23
  b 28
  c 33

**3a** Look at the questions from the video below. Who asks each question? Write J (James), R (the receptionist) or D (the doctor).

1 What's your name?   *R*
2 How do you spell that?
3 What's your address?
4 What's your postcode?
5 Have you got a contact phone number?
6 How old are you?
7 Can you say that again, please?
8 Have you got any questions?

b ▶ Watch and listen to the key phrases and check your answers.

**4** Work in pairs and take turns. Ask and answer the questions in exercise 3a. Use information about you or the information below.

| Name | Lee Sung |
|---|---|
| Address | 86 Hospital Road, Oxford |
| Postcode | OX2 ISP |
| Telephone | 01865 591243 |
| Age | 25 |

| Name | Christine Wilson |
|---|---|
| Address | 21a John Street, Belfast |
| Postcode | BT2 7AG |
| Telephone | 02895 413019 |
| Age | 19 |

### AFTER UNIT 2 YOU CAN ...

Say short sentences about everyday objects.

Ask and answer questions about people and things.

Talk about your family and favourite people.

# 03

## YOUR LIFE

### IN THIS UNIT

- Grammar: Present simple: positive and negative (*I, you, we, they*); Present simple: questions and short answers (*I, you, we, they*)
- Vocabulary: Common verbs; Telling the time; Places in a town
- Task: Describe life in your favourite town
- World culture: Indian railway

> My parents live in a small fishing village 100 km south of Bangalore

My name is Amrita and I live in Bangalore in India. It's a big city with about 8.5 million people. I live in a flat with my friend Geeta. We study computer studies at the same university. We get up at 7.30 a.m. and we go to university by bus. We start classes at 9.00 a.m. and then finish at 4.30 p.m. In the evenings, we go out a lot. We don't have dinner at home – we go to a restaurant with friends.

My parents are Jairam and Sanjula. They live in a small village 100 km south of Bangalore. They don't live in a flat – they live in a house. They get up very early – at 5.30 a.m. My father and his friends are fishermen. They work for a small company, and they work very long hours. They don't go to work by bus – they walk to the river. In the evenings, they have dinner at home with their families.

Amrita

## Vocabulary
### Common verbs

**1a** Work in pairs and look at the photos. Where do you think Amrita is from? Can you describe the places in the photos?

**b** Read the text about Amrita. Which of the people in the box does she talk about?

her friend   her sister   her father   her mother   her grandparents

**2a** Read the text again. Are statements 1–8 true (T) or false (F)? Correct the false statements.

1 Amrita and Geeta live in a house in Bangalore.
2 They study at school in Bangalore.
3 They go to university by train.
4 They have dinner in a restaurant.
5 Jairam and Sanjula live in a small city.
6 Jairam and his friends get up very early.
7 They work for a big company.
8 They have dinner in a restaurant with their families.

**b** 🎧 3.1 Listen and check.

**c** Work in pairs. Practise saying the correct sentences.

# Grammar focus 1
## Present simple: positive and negative (*I, you, we, they*)

**1** Read the text again and find three negative verbs.

### GRAMMAR

**1 Complete the gaps.**

| + | I *live* in a flat.<br>You _____ to work by bus.<br>We _____ dinner in a restaurant.<br>They _____ in an office. |
|---|---|
| – | I *don't* live in a flat<br>You _____ go to work by bus.<br>We _____ have dinner in a restaurant.<br>They _____ work in an office. |

## PRACTICE

**1** Complete the sentences and add more information to make them true for you.

I *don't live* (live) in a house. *I live in a flat.*
**1** I _____ (get up) very early.
**2** I _____ (have) breakfast with my family.
**3** I _____ (go) to work by bus.
**4** I _____ (have) lunch in a café.
**5** I _____ (go) out a lot in the evenings.
**6** I _____ (study) in the evening.
**7** I _____ (go) to bed early.

**2a** Write six sentences about you using the ideas in the box.

| | |
|---|---|
| live in a small town | get up late at the weekend |
| go to restaurants a lot | study a lot at the weekend |
| have a big meal for lunch | work very long hours |
| live on my own | get up before 6.00 a.m. |
| go to bed after midnight | study English after work/school |
| have a big family | work at home |

**b** Work in pairs and compare your answers. Find six things you have in common.

*We live in a small town.*

*We don't have a big meal for lunch.*

Unit 3, Study & Practice 1, page 142

**3** Work in pairs. Complete gaps 1–5 with the words in the box.

go   get up   have   ~~live~~   study   work

I *live*
— in a house/flat.
— in a big city / in a small town.
— with my parents/friends.

1 I _____
— to work/school by car/train/bus.
— to bed early/late.
— out a lot.

2 I _____
— breakfast at home.
— lunch/dinner in a restaurant/café.
— a shower/bath in the morning/evening.

3 I _____
— very hard.
— English/economics.
— at university.

4 I _____
— in an office / in a school/hospital.
— at home.
— for a big company.

5 I _____
— early on weekdays.
— at 7.30 a.m.
— late at the weekend.

# Grammar focus 2

## Present simple: questions and short answers (*I, you, we, they*)

**1a** 🎧 3.2 Niall is a student in Dublin, Ireland. Listen to him talking to another student. Tick the questions you hear.

1 Do you live in a big city?
2 Do you live with your family or friends?
3 Do you get up early?
4 Do you have breakfast at home?
5 Do you have a shower in the morning or in the evening?
6 Do you go to university?
7 Do you have lunch in a café?
8 Do you have dinner early?
9 Do you study a lot in the evening?
10 Do you go to bed early?

**b** Listen again and write Niall's answers.

---

### GRAMMAR

**1** To make questions and short answers we use *do/don't*.
A: *Do you have breakfast at home?*
B: *Yes, I do.*
A: *Do you work in an office?*
B: *No, I don't.*

**2** Complete the questions and short answers.
1 A: _____ you live in a city?
  B: Yes, I _____ .
2 A: _____ you go to bed early?
  B: No, I _____ .

---

## PRACTICE

**1a** Complete the questions and answers.

1 A: _____ you live in a house?
  B: No, I _____ . I live in a flat.
2 A: _____ you go to English classes?
  B: Yes, I _____ . I study very hard.
3 A: Do you _____ out a lot in the evening?
  B: Yes, I _____ . I have dinner in restaurants a lot.
4 A: _____ you have a shower in the evening?
  B: No, I _____ . I have a shower in the morning.
5 A: Do you _____ in an office?
  B: No, I _____ . I work in a hospital.
6 A: _____ you get up early?
  B: No, I _____ . I get up at about 8.30 a.m.

**b** 🎧 3.3 Listen and check.

**2** Work in pairs and take turns. Ask and answer the questions in exercise 1a.

---

Unit 3, Study & Practice 2, page 142

## Vocabulary
### Telling the time

**1a** Match times 1–6 with pictures A–F.

1 five o'clock
2 two fifteen
3 one thirty
4 seven forty-five
5 ten twenty
6 eight fifty-five

**b** Match times 2–6 with the times in the box.

half past one    twenty past ten    quarter to eight
five to nine    quarter past two

**IT'S A FACT!**
On average, people in Britain get up at 6.57 a.m. and go to bed at 10.39 p.m.

**2a** Write the times.

9.55 (nine fifty-five) _five to ten_
1 7.15 (seven fifteen) _____
2 9.30 (nine thirty) _____
3 8.40 (eight forty) _____
4 6.45 (six forty-five) _____
5 12.05 (twelve o-five) _____
6 2.20 (two twenty) _____
7 4.00 (four) _____

b 🎧 3.5 Listen and check.

## PRONUNCIATION

**1** Listen to the times again. Notice the stress and weak forms of *to* and *o*.

● /tə/ ●          ●        ●
five to ten       four o'clock

**2** Practise saying the times.

**3** Work in pairs and take turns. Look at the clocks in different cities around the world. Ask and answer questions about the time in each city.

> What's the time in Hong Kong?

> It's seven thirty in the morning.

▶ Unit 3, Study & Practice 3, page 143

**4a** Write four more questions (5–8), starting with 'On weekdays ...'.

On weekdays, what time do you:
1 get up?
2 have breakfast?
3 go to work/school/university?
4 have lunch?
5 _____ ?
6 _____ ?
7 _____ ?
8 _____ ?

b Work in pairs and take turns. Ask and answer questions 1–8.

c Now ask and answer the questions again, starting with 'At weekends ...'.

> At weekends, what time do you get up?

> I get up at half past eight on Saturdays, because I play football. On Sundays, I get up at ten o'clock ...

06:00 Berlin
10:10 Istanbul
15:40 Paris
13:45 Rio de Janeiro
21:55 San Francisco
06:15 Canberra
07:30 Hong Kong

## Reading and vocabulary
### Places in a town

**1a** Match the words in the box with pictures A–J.

| | |
|---|---|
| a beach | a block of flats |
| a park | a supermarket |
| a shopping centre | small shops |
| a street market | a swimming pool |
| a restaurant | a cinema |

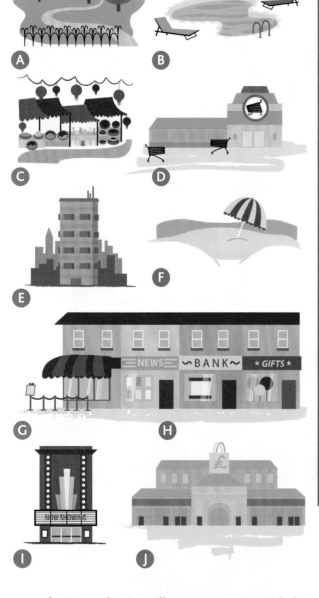

**b** Do you live in a village, town or city? Tick the things you've got where you live. Cross the things you haven't got.

**c** Work in pairs. Tell your partner the things you've got and haven't got where you live.

> In my town, we've got restaurants.

> We haven't got a beach in my village.

# Brits at home ...
## and abroad

**Dawn, David, Sam and Julie**
My husband and I live in Dubai, a big city in the United Arab Emirates. Our children, Sam and Julie, go to the International School. They start at 8.00 a.m. and finish at 2.30 p.m. They don't go to school on Friday and Saturday, but Sunday's a school day. We live in a modern block of flats with a swimming pool, and we've got really good beaches not far away.

> " We live in a modern
> block of flats with
> a swimming pool

**2a** Work in pairs. Look at the photos and discuss. Which three countries do you think the photos show? Do they show a village, town or city?

**b** Read the article and check your answers.

**3** Match sentences 1–6 with the places in the article. Write A (Aurignac), S (Southwold) or D (Dubai).

1 People buy their food at a street market.   *A*
2 Children go to school on Sunday.
3 Shops close at half past five.
4 People go to the beach or swimming pool.
5 They've got a 24-hour supermarket nearby.
6 People eat in the park.

**n and Andrew**

live in a house in Aurignac, a small village in
South of France. Food is very important here.
ryone buys their food at the street market every
urday. When the weather's good, we have a
nic with friends in the local park. And we've got
e really good restaurants in the village centre.

**nry**

e in a small town called Southwold. We haven't
a big shopping centre – just small shops in the
n centre. The shops open at nine. They don't
e at lunchtime, but they do close at 5.30 p.m.
st shops don't open on Sunday, but we've got
4-hour supermarket a few kilometres away.

**4a** Read the article again. Underline two things
that are the same where you live. Circle two
things that are different.

**b** Work in pairs and compare your answers.

> Food is important in Aurignac. Food is
> important in my town, too. We've got
> good restaurants in the town centre …

> We haven't got good restaurants
> in my village.

# Listening
## Life on a Scottish island

**1** 🎧 **3.6** Sheena lives in Stornoway, a town on the Isle of Lewis
in Scotland. Listen and tick the things she talks about.

- the journey from Ullapool to Stornoway
- the languages on the Isle of Lewis
- the shops in Stornoway
- summer sunsets
- weekends

**2** Listen again and choose the correct answers.

**1** Ullapool to Stornoway is:
  **a** two hours 40 minutes by ferry.
  **b** four hours 20 minutes by ferry.
**2** The supermarket in Stornoway is open:
  **a** until 5 o'clock.
  **b** until midnight.
**3** On Sunday, all the shops are:
  **a** open.
  **b** closed.
**4** In summer, it is:
  **a** dark at 10.30 in the evening.
  **b** light at 10.30 in the evening.
**5** People on the Isle of Lewis speak:
  **a** only Gaelic.
  **b** English and Gaelic.

**3a** Complete the sentences.

**1** Stornoway is very different from my town because …
**2** Stornoway is an interesting place to visit because …

**b** Work in pairs and compare your sentences.

# Task

## Describe life in your favourite town

### MELBOURNE: MUST-KNOW FACTS!

- Capital of the state of Victoria
- Average temperature: January 25°C, July 13°C
- Languages: English (91%), Italian (4%), Greek (3%), Chinese (2%)
- Population: 3.5 million

## Life in Melbourn

**1 Where do most people live?**
a in houses
b in flats
c other

**2 What time do children start and finish school?**
a 7.30 a.m. and 2.30 p.m.
b 8.30 a.m. and 3.00 p.m.
c 9.00 a.m. and 3.30 p.m.
d other

**3 Where do most people have lunch?**
a at home
b in a restaurant
c in their office or outside
d other

**4 Do shops open late?**
a no
b yes, on Thursday and Friday
c yes, on Friday and Saturday
d other

**5 Do shops close at lunchtime?**
a yes
b no
c other

**6 Do shops open on Sunday?**
a yes
b no
c other

**7 What time do peop have dinner at hom**
a about 6.00 p.m.
b about 7.00 p.m.
c about 8.00 p.m.
d other

**8 What time do most restaurants close?**
a 9.30–10.00 p.m.
b 10.30–11.00 p.m.
c 11.00–11.30 p.m.
d other

## Preparation Reading and listening

1 Work in pairs. Look at the photos and read the facts about Melbourne, Australia. Do you think Melbourne is a nice place to live? Why / Why not?

2a 🎧 3.7 Mike lives in Melbourne with his family. Listen to him answering the questionnaire about life in Melbourne. Tick the correct answers.

b 🎧 3.8 Listen to the second part of the interview and check your answers.

3a Listen again to the first part of the interview. Tick the questions you hear in the Useful language box (part a).

b Listen again to the second part of the interview. Tick the phrases you hear in the Useful language box (part b).

## USEFUL LANGUAGE

**a Asking about life in a village, town or city**
Do most people live in houses or flats?
What time do children start school?
Where do most people have lunch?
Do shops close at (lunchtime)?
Do most people have dinner at home?
What time do restaurants close?
Do shops open on (Sunday)?
What time do people have dinner?

**b Describing life in a village, town or city**
Most people live in houses.
Most people live in the city centre.
Children start/finish school at ...
Most people don't go home ...
Most shops open/close at ...
Most people have lunch/dinner at ...
Restaurants/Pubs open/close at ...

# Task Speaking

**1a** Think of your favourite village, town or city. Look at
questions 1–8 in the questionnaire and make a note of your
answers. Ask your teacher for any words/phrases you need.

**b** Work in pairs and take turns. Ask and answer questions 1–8.
Make a note of your partner's answers.

> Useful language a

**2** Work in groups and take turns. Describe your favourite
place or your partner's favourite place.

> Useful language b

## SHARE YOUR TASK

**Practise describing your
favourite place or your
partner's favourite place.**

**Film/Record yourself describing
the place.**

**Share your film/recording with
other students.**

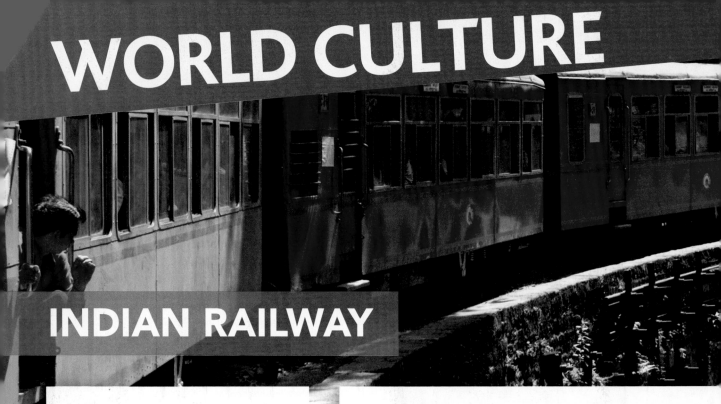

# WORLD CULTURE

## INDIAN RAILWAY

## Find out first

**1a** Work in pairs and discuss. How much do you know about India? Try to answer the questions in the quiz.

### What do you know about India?

1 What is the capital city of India?
   a Delhi
   b Kolkata
   c Mumbai
2 Shimla is in the _____ of India.
   a centre
   b north
   c south
3 What is the average temperature in Delhi in June?
   a 20°C
   b 30°C
   c 40°C
4 How many kilometres of railway are there in India?
   a 640
   b 6,400
   c 64,000
5 Do you see snow in India?
   a No, never
   b Yes, sometimes
   c Yes, all the time

**b** Go online to check your answers or ask your teacher.

Search: India capital / Shimla map / Delhi temperature / India railway / India snow

## View

**2a** You are going to watch a video about a family in India. Before you watch, check you understand the meaning of the words/phrases in the glossary.

GLOSSARY
*colonial times*   the time when the British governed India
*station master*   the manager at a railway station
*porter*           a person who helps passengers with their bags
*prediction*       a guess about the future

**b** ▶ Watch the video. Number the people (1–5) in the order you see them.

- Sanjay Geera
- a British tourist on the train
- a porter
- Satna (Sanjay's wife)
- Sanjay's son

**3** Read the sentences. Then watch again and choose the correct answers.

1 Shimla is a **big** / **small** city.
2 In colonial times, the British came to Shimla because of the **weather** / **railway**.
3 **Five** / **Six** trains come to Shimla every day.
4 Sanjay is **a porter** / **the station master** at Shimla Station.
5 About **fourteen** / **forty** porters work at Shimla Station.
6 Sanjay and his wife Satna live in **Shimla** / **Summerhill**.
7 Satna's job is in a **office** / **school** in Shimla.
8 Her train is at **8.00** / **8.30** every morning.
9 Their children go to **school** / **university** in Shimla.

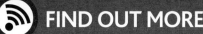

# World view

**4a** Look at the statements below. Write SN (Sanjay), ST (Satna), C (their children) or A (all of them) next to each statement.

> I am serious about my job – it's important.

> My day is very long.

> We live in a big house.

> I work in an office.

> I catch a train to work in the morning.

> We go to a private school.

**b** Read the statements again and make them true for you.

*I don't live in a big house. I live in a small apartment.*

**c** Work in pairs and compare your sentences.

## FIND OUT MORE

**5a** Read the text about UNESCO World Heritage Sites.

> UNESCO World Heritage Sites are places of special importance around the world: old cities, national parks, nature reserves. There are nearly 1,000 World Heritage Sites in more than 150 countries.

**b** Look at the World Heritage Sites in the box below. What do you know about them?

| | | |
|---|---|---|
| Great Barrier Reef | Angkor Wat | Rapa Nui |
| Grand Canyon | Stonehenge | Historic Cairo |

**c** Go online to find out more about three of the World Heritage Sites and answer the questions.

1 Where is it (country/region)?
2 What is it (city / nature reserve, etc.)?

**Search:** Great Barrier Reef / Angkor Wat / Rapa Nui / Grand Canyon / Stonehenge / Historic Cairo

## Write up your research

**6** Write about the three World Heritage Sites you researched. Use the prompts below to help you.

The _____ is a UNESCO World Heritage Site in _____ (country).

It is in _____ (state/region).

It's a _____ (what it is).

### AFTER UNIT 3 YOU CAN ...

**Ask and answer questions about your daily routine.**

**Ask and answer questions to tell the time.**

**Describe life in a village, town or city (e.g. what people do, where they live).**

**Research World Heritage Sites online.**

# 04

## LIKES AND DISLIKES

### IN THIS UNIT

- **Grammar:** Present simple: positive and negative (*he/she/it*); Present simple: questions and short answers (*he/she/it*)
- **Vocabulary:** Activities; Phrases for time and frequency
- **Task:** Choose a holiday activity
- **Language live:** Meeting people; Introducing a friend

## Vocabulary
### Activities

1   Work in pairs and look at the photos. Which of the activities in the box can you see?

| | |
|---|---|
| going for walks | spending time with friends |
| dancing | playing computer games |
| cycling | watching sport |
| reading | spending time on the internet |
| cooking | swimming |

2   Work in pairs and take turns. Ask and answer questions about what you like and don't like. Use the activities in exercise 1 and your own ideas.

> Do you like cooking?

> No, I don't. I hate it!

# Listening

## A typical pop star?

**1a** 🎧 **4.1** Work in pairs. Listen to the first part of a podcast about Adele. Answer the questions.

1 Is Adele from the UK or the USA?
2 Is she a singer or an actor?

**b** 🎧 **4.2** Listen to the second part of the podcast. Tick the things you hear them talk about.

- her house
- her boyfriend
- her friends
- her concerts
- her clothes
- her plans for the future

**2** 🎧 **4.3** Listen to the whole podcast about Adele and choose the correct answers.

1 Adele is from *London* / *Edinburgh*.
2 Her house is in *America* / *England*.
3 She has a pet *cat* / *dog*.
4 Penny is her *mother* / *sister*.
5 She is nervous about *big concerts* / *meeting people*.
6 She likes *simple* / *crazy* clothes.
7 Her favourite colour for clothes is *blue* / *black*.

**3** Work in pairs and discuss. Adele isn't a typical pop star. Why not?

# Grammar focus 1

## Present simple: positive and negative (*he/she/it*)

**1** Look at audio script 4.2 on page 168 and underline the verbs. Which are positive? Which are negative?

---

### GRAMMAR

**Present simple: *he/she/it* form**

1 Complete the gaps.

| + | She **lives** in a big house. <br> She _____ simple black clothes. |
|---|---|
| – | She **doesn't like** doing big concerts. <br> She _____ **have** lots of crazy clothes. |

2 Notice these *he/she* forms.

have　　She **has** some close friends.
go　　　She **goes** to restaurants.
do　　　She **does** some big concerts.

**Likes/dislikes with nouns and *-ing***

*She likes **comfortable clothes**.*　　*She doesn't like **flying**.*
*She hates **the food** on aeroplanes.*　　*She loves **singing**.*

---

### PRONUNCIATION

1 🎧 **4.4** Look at audio script 4.4 on page 168. Listen to the *he/she/it* form of the verbs in the sentences. Count the number of syllables in the verbs.

likes = 1　　　watches = 2

2 Practise saying the sentences.

---

### PRACTICE

**1a** Write four true and four false sentences about what Adele likes and doesn't like. Use the ideas below.

go to restaurants　*She hates going to restaurants.*
1 go for walks with her dog
2 fly
3 her dog
4 her mother
5 spend time with friends
6 do big concerts
7 black clothes
8 the food on aeroplanes

**b** Work in pairs and take turns to say your sentences. Are your partner's sentences true or false?

Unit 4, Study & Practice 1, page 144

# Reading and vocabulary
## Phrases for time and frequency

**1a** Read the article below about life's winners. Match statements 1–5 with the pictures.

**b** Work in pairs and discuss.

- Which statement in the article do you like most?
- Which of the winning habits do you have?

**2a** Complete the phrases with the correct preposition.

1. _____ the morning
2. _____ the afternoon
3. _____ the evening
4. _____ the weekend
5. _____ weekdays (Monday–Friday)

**b** Read the article again and check your answers.

**3** Put the adverbs in the box in the best place on the line.

| often | sometimes | usually | not often |
| --- | --- | --- | --- |

**100%** ←—————————————→ **0%**
always _____ _____ _____ _____ never

**4a** Complete the sentences with *always*, *never*, *often*, *sometimes* or *usually* to make them true for you.

1. I _____ go shopping at the weekend.
2. I _____ check my email in the morning.
3. I _____ watch sport on television in the evening.
4. I _____ go out without my mobile phone.
5. I _____ go to sleep in the afternoon.
6. I am _____ late for class.
7. I _____ read computer magazines.
8. I _____ do my homework in the evening.

**b** Work in pairs and compare your sentences.

Unit 4, Study & Practice 2, page 144

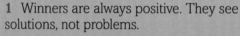
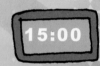

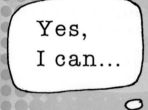

# Some people are life's winners!

Are you one of life's winners? Are you a winner in your job, in a sport or in life? If so, which of these winning habits do you have?

1 Winners are always positive. They see solutions, not problems.

2 Winners never, never, never say, think or do negative things!

3 Winners are usually early birds. In the morning, on average, successful people get up two hours before the rest of us. But only on weekdays, because at the weekend it's time to relax in bed.

4 Winners often have a rest in the afternoon. And in the evening, they make time to relax with friends and family.

5 Winners sometimes make mistakes. But they learn from their mistakes, and they never make the same mistake again!

05:30

Yes, I can...

ONE WAY

15:00

ZZZZZ

No, I can't...

# Grammar focus 2
## Present simple: questions and short answers (*he/she/it*)

**1** Read about Olympic athlete Denise Lewis and choose the correct answers.

1 She does **seven** / **nine** sports in her Olympic event.
2 She lives in **Birmingham** / **London**.

### DENISE LEWIS

Olympic athlete Denise Lewis comes from Birmingham, England's second city. She was a gold medal winner in the heptathlon – seven different athletic events – at the 2000 Olympic Games in Sydney. Now she often appears on British TV and radio as an athletics commentator. She also works for a charity, helping young people to play sport. In her free time, she likes dancing and she plays tennis and golf. She lives in London with her husband, Steve, and their three children.

**2a** Complete the questions about Denise Lewis with the words in the box.

| come | does | have | live |
|------|------|------|------|
| play | where | who | like |

1 Does Denise Lewis _____ from England?
2 _____ she appear on TV?
3 _____ does she work for?
4 Does she _____ in Birmingham now?
5 Does she _____ dancing?
6 What other sports does she _____ ?
7 _____ does she live now?
8 How many children does she _____ ?

**b** Read the text again and answer the questions.

---

**Questions and short answers with *he/she/it***

**1 Complete the question and answer below.**
A: **Does** Denise Lewis **live** in London?
B: Yes, she **does**.
A: _____ she **live** in Birmingham?
B: No, she _____ .

***Wh-* questions**
***Where does*** Denise Lewis live?   ***What*** sports ***does*** she **do**?

---

**1** 🎧 **4.5 Listen to the questions in exercise 2a. How is *does* pronounced? Is it the strong form /dʌz/ or the weak form /dəz/?**

**2** Practise saying the questions.

---

## PRACTICE

**1** Match questions 1–6 with the answers in the box.

| | |
|---|---|
| Yes, she does. | No, she doesn't. |
| Her family. | She likes dancing. |
| From Birmingham. | She also does charity work. |

1 Where does Denise come from?
2 Does she work on TV?
3 What other work does she do?
4 What does she like doing in her free time?
5 Does she live in Birmingham?
6 Who does she live with?

**2** Complete the questions.

1 _____ 's his/her name?
2 Where _____ he/she come from?
3 _____ does he/she live now?
4 _____ he/she work or study?
5 Where _____ he/she work/study?
6 _____ he/she like his/her job/studies?
7 _____ does he/she like doing in his/her free time?
8 _____ he/she play a sport?

**3** Work in pairs and take turns. Student A: Turn to page 133. Student B: Turn to page 134. Ask and answer the questions in exercise 2.

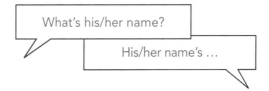

What's his/her name?

His/her name's …

---

**Unit 4, Study & Practice 3, page 145**

# Task

## Choose a holiday activity

### Preparation Reading and listening

**1a** Work in pairs. Match the activities in the box with photos A–D.

| | |
|---|---|
| sailing | playing music |
| preparing dinner | taking a photograph |

**b** Read the advert. Match holiday courses 1–4 with photos A–D.

**2** Read the advert again. Which course is good for people who:

1 want to meet new people?    *1, 3*
2 like singing?
3 love cooking?
4 like art?
5 like to be in the open air?
6 love the sea?
7 like eating with friends?
8 play a musical instrument?

▷ ## Are you always bored in the holidays?

**Choose one of our fantastic holiday courses – have fun, learn something new and make friends. All our courses are five days.**

**Course 1: Join a band**
Do you love playing music, but you haven't got anyone to play with? This course is for you! Bring musical instrument … your guitar, your violin … or just your voice! Meet other musicians and star a band. Learn how to make music together.

**Course 2: Picture perfect**
This course teaches you how to take fantastic photographs using modern digital cameras. But it not just photography … we also help you with you painting skills. Use your photos to paint personal pictures of people and scenery.

**Course 3: Plain sailing**
All you need to know about sailing. Don't bring equipment; we have everything you need. We ta you to a beautiful area – only a 30-minute drive and we sail in every type of weather. You learn to sail in groups of five … so you make friends, too!

**Course 4: A taste of Italy**
Do you like Italian food? Do you want to learn how to prepare it? This course shows you how to make three simple tasty dishes. We have all the ingredients for delicious traditional Italian food. Have an amazing dinner party for your friends at the end of the course!

**3** 🎧 **4.6** These four people want to do a holiday course. Listen and make a note of what each person likes and doesn't like.

> **❝** I love being in the fresh air.
> Lucy, 28, Australia

> **❝** I like being alone sometimes.
> Juan, 20, Spain

> **❝** I think I'm a very creative person.
> Cassia, 22, Brazil

> **❝** I'm a professional musican.
> Tom, 35, Great Britain

**USEFUL LANGUAGE**

**a  Giving and asking for an opinion**
Maybe the (painting) course is good for …
What do you think?
I think the (sailing course) is good for her …

**b  Giving reasons**
… because she likes being outside.
… he/she says he likes eating.

**c  Agreeing and disagreeing**
No, I don't think so.
I'm not sure.
Yes, you're right.
Yes, I agree.
I don't agree.

**4a** 🎧 **4.7** Listen to two students talking about the holiday courses. Work in pairs and answer the questions.

  **1** Which person are they talking about?
  **2** What do they decide?

**b** Listen again and tick the phrases you hear in the Useful language box.

# Task Speaking

**1a** You are going to decide on holiday courses for the other three people. Read the advert again and look at the information about each person. What do you think is the best course for each person?

**b** Work in groups and agree on the best holiday course for each person. Ask your teacher for any words/phrases you need.

> Useful language a–c

**2** Report back to the class. Say which holiday course you chose for each person and why.

**SHARE YOUR TASK**

**Practise talking about which holiday courses you chose and why.**

**Film/Record yourself talking.**

**Share your film/recording with other students.**

# LANGUAGE LIVE

Nice to meet you.

## Speaking
## Meeting people

**1a** Work in pairs and discuss. How do you feel about meeting people for the first time?

**b** ▶ Watch the video. How does Robert feel?

**2** Read statements 1–8 and watch again. Are the statements true (T) or false (F)?

1 Mr and Mrs Wicks don't know Robert.
2 Robert gives Kate some flowers.
3 Mrs Wicks makes some tea for Kate and Robert.
4 Kate likes tea.
5 Robert doesn't like coffee.
6 Robert likes his job.
7 Mr Wicks likes motorbikes.
8 Robert would like to see Mr Wicks's motorbike.

**3a** Choose the correct answers.

1 Lovely **see** / **to see** you.
2 **That** / **This** is Robert.
3 Nice **to meet** / **meet** you.
4 **These** / **This** are for you.
5 Thank you. They're **lovely** / **love**.
6 **Do** / **Would** you like some tea?
7 Yes, **please** / **pleasure**.
8 No, thanks. I'm **fine** / **very well**.
9 Do you like **work** / **working** in a supermarket?

**b** ▶ Watch and listen to the key phrases and check your answers.

**4** Complete the conversation between three people at a dinner party with the words in the box.

| | | | |
|---|---|---|---|
| drink | these | meet | running |
| Scotland | fine | love | lovely |

**A:** Hello, Barney. ¹_____ to see you.
**B:** Hello, how are you?
**A:** I'm ²_____ . This is Charlie – he's from ³_____ .
**C:** Hello, Barney. Nice to meet you.
**B:** Nice to ⁴_____ you, too. ⁵_____ are for you.
**A:** Thank you! They're lovely. Please sit down. Barney, would you like a ⁶_____ ?
**B:** Yes, please.
**A:** Charlie, would you like something to drink?
**C:** Yes, please.
**A:** So, Charlie ... do you like ⁷_____ ?
**C:** Yes, I ⁸_____ it!

**5a** Work in groups of three. Rewrite the conversation using your own names and ideas.

**b** Practise your conversation.

# Writing
## Introducing a friend

**1** Look at the photos. Match the questions about Takashi in A with the answers in B.

**A**
1 What's his name?
2 Where does he come from?
3 Where does he live now?
4 What does he do?
5 Where does he work?
6 What does he like about life in London?
7 What doesn't he like about life in London?
8 Does he like the people in London?

**B**
a He's a musician.
b In a bar called East and West.
c His name's Takashi.
d Yes, he does. They're very nice when you know them.
e The weather!
f He lives in London.
g From Okinawa in Japan.
h He likes the international atmosphere.

**2** Use the information in exercise 1 to complete the email about Takashi.

> **To:** Anna
> **Subject:** Your visit to London
>
> **Message:** Draft
>
> Hello, Anna!
> When you go to London, phone my friend Takashi! He loves having visitors. Takashi comes from ¹_____ but now he lives in ²_____ . He's a ³_____ and plays the piano. He likes ⁴_____ in London, but he doesn't like ⁵_____ ! He thinks the people in London are ⁶_____ .
>
> Have a great time!
>
>
> Love,
> Mimi

**3** Think of someone you know (or invent someone). Look at the questions in exercise 1 and complete the notes below.

> His / Her name's _____ .
> He / She comes from _____ in _____ .
> Now he / she lives in _____ .
> He's / She's a / an _____ . (job)
> He / She works / studies in / at _____ .
> He / She likes _____ .
> He / She doesn't like _____ .
> He / She thinks the people in _____ are _____ !

**4** Write a description of the person. Use the description of Takashi in exercise 2 and your notes from exercise 3 to help you.

> **AFTER UNIT 4 YOU CAN ...**
>
> Ask and answer questions about someone's routine.
>
> Talk about things you like and don't like doing.
>
> Express your opinion, agreement and disagreement.

# 05

# FROM
# A TO B

## IN THIS UNIT

- Grammar: *can/can't*: possibility and ability; Articles: *a/an*, *the* and no article
- Vocabulary: Transport; Travelling
- Task: Do a transport survey
- World culture: Race across London

## Vocabulary and reading
### Transport

**1** Look at the photos. Which types of transport in the box can you see?

| | | | | | |
|---|---|---|---|---|---|
| a car | a bus | a train | a tram | a bicycle | an underground train |
| a plane | a taxi | a scooter | a ferry | a motorbike | |

**2a** Put the types of transport in order, from fast to slow.

*1 plane*

**b** Work in pairs and compare your answers.

**3** Work in pairs and discuss. How do these people usually travel in your town?

- schoolchildren
- students
- business people
- old people
- police officers

Schoolchildren usually go on foot, but they sometimes go by bus or by car.

# 9 things you didn't know about world travel
## Did you know that ...

1 In the USA, 74% of people drive a car. In Japan, it's 59%; and in Germany, it's _____ %. The average American family owns 1.9 cars.

2 More than 100 million people in the world ride a bicycle. About a third of these people are in China. In the Netherlands, about 30% of people choose to ride a bicycle. But in the USA, it's only about _____ %.

3 In Italy, a country of 60 million people, _____ people have scooters. In Rome, 500,000 people ride scooters, so they can get about easily in the city traffic.

4 In Italy, the average journey to work is about 25 minutes; and in the USA, it's about 32 minutes. In Great Britain, it's about _____ minutes – that's nearly 200 hours a year travelling to and from work.

5 Every day, more than _____ people travel into the centre of London: 77% take a bus or train, about 20% drive and only 3% walk to work.

6 There are over _____ underground train systems in the world, including those in Paris, Shanghai, Mexico City, Seoul, Moscow, Madrid and Tokyo.

7 The London Underground, or the 'Tube', has _____ stations. Over 1,000 million passengers use the Tube every year.

8 The underground train system in Tokyo is very efficient: people usually wait no more than _____ minutes for a train. The only problem is that it's sometimes difficult to get on or off a train because they're often very crowded.

9 The two busiest international airports are Hartsfield–Jackson Airport in Atlanta, USA, with 71 million passengers every year, and Beijing Capital International Airport, with _____ . That means about 160 people fly to Atlanta every minute.

---

**4a** Work in pairs. Read the article and discuss. Which numbers go in the gaps?

.........................................................................................

| 2 | 5 | 53 | 160 | 45 |
|---|---|----|-----|----|
| 270 | 1 million | 9 million | 60 million | |

.........................................................................................

b 🎧 5.1 Listen and check.

**5a** Choose the correct answers.

1 *drive* / *ride* a car
2 *drive* / *ride* a bicycle
3 *drive* / *ride* a scooter
4 *take* / *go* a bus or train
5 walk *to* / *for* work
6 wait *to* / *for* a bus or train
7 get *on* / *in* a bus or train
8 get *out* / *off* a bus or train
9 fly *in* / *to* the airport

b Read the article again and check your answers.

### PRONUNCIATION

1 🎧 5.2 Listen to the phrases in exercise 5a. Notice the pronunciation of words with /ə/ (e.g. *a, the, to, for*).

2 Practise saying the phrases.

**6a** Look at the statements below. Which are true for your town or city? Correct the false statements.

1 Most people drive small cars.
2 People always wait in a queue to get on a bus.
3 People often fly from one city to another.
4 Not many people walk to the shops.
5 A lot of people ride bicycles to work.
6 Traffic is a problem all day.
7 Buses are very crowded.
8 Taxis drive very slowly.
9 Trains and buses are very cheap.
10 A lot of people ride scooters in the city centre.

b Work in pairs and compare your sentences.

# Vocabulary

## Travelling

**1** Work in pairs. Look at the photos of Hong Kong and discuss.

- What different forms of transport can you see?
- Do you think it is easy to travel about in Hong Kong?

**2a** Work in pairs and discuss.

- How often do you travel by plane?
- Do you like/dislike travelling by plane?
- Do you like/dislike spending time at airports?

**b** Read sentences a–j and put them in the correct order. Make sure you understand the words in bold.

**a** You **go through security**.
**b** You decide to **fly** somewhere for the weekend. *1*
**c** Finally, you **board** the plane.
**d** You **book your ticket online**.
**e** You go to the **check-in desk** with your **luggage**.
**f** Your **flight** is **delayed** so you wait in the **departure lounge**.
**g** They take your **luggage** and give you a **boarding pass**.
**h** You go to the airport and look for '**Departures**'.
**i** You arrive at your **destination** and **go through immigration control**.
**j** You look at the **screens** for your **flight** and **gate number**.

**c** 🎧 5.3 Listen and check.

**3** Work in pairs and discuss.

- How can you buy tickets for bus, train or plane travel? How often do you do this?
- What do you like/dislike about travelling on buses, trains and ferries?
- Can you travel to foreign destinations by bus or train from where you live? Which do you prefer? Why?

# Grammar focus 1

## *can/can't*: possibility and ability

**1a** Work in pairs and discuss. What do you usually do when you have a long wait for a bus, train or plane?

**b** Read the webpage below. Which of your ideas from exercise 1a does it mention?

SEARCH TRAVEL FORUM

### Travel forum – any questions

#### Question

**GiorgioX:** My girlfriend and I want some advice about our trip to Thailand via Hong Kong. Does anyone know about Hong Kong International Airport (HKIA)? We have a stopover of eight hours there.

#### Answers

**JJB99:** HKIA is really amazing! *Traveller* magazine says it's the world's number one airport, and I can see why. I love it! You can fly direct to more than 160 destinations worldwide from there. But also, it's got great facilities – you can go shopping in the many different shops and you can visit the huge number of restaurants. Some restaurants are open 24 hours. My advice is: enjoy your time shopping and eating!

**HarryH:** You have an eight-hour stopover, so you've got time for leisure, and maybe sleep! Take your computer, because you can use the free Wi-Fi 24-7. Also, you can play various sports, including golf at the nine-hole golf course near Terminal 1! With all the possibilities, you can't get bored. But, if you get tired, remember you can't sleep in Terminal 1 – but you can sleep in one of the special lounges for a small fee.

**TimeFlies:** Hi! I'm in HIKA now! This airport is really big and has everything you need. In most airports, you can't smoke … and there is no smoking in Terminal 1. But you can smoke in the special smoking lounges in Terminal 2.

**IT'S A FACT!**
Hong Kong has about 8,000 skyscrapers. New York has about 4,000.

## GRAMMAR

1 We use *can* for things it is possible to do or things we are able to do.
*You **can** fly direct to more than 160 destinations.*
*You **can** smoke in Terminal 2.*
*A: **Can** you play golf near the airport?*
*B: Yes, you **can**.*

2 We use *can't* for things it is not possible to do or things we are not able to do.
*A: **Can** you smoke in most airports?*
*B: No, you **can't**.*

## PRACTICE

**1a** Complete the sentences about Hong Kong International Airport with *can* or *can't*.

1 You _____ eat at all times of the day and night.
2 You _____ sleep in Terminal 1.
3 You _____ play golf near the airport.
4 You _____ smoke in Terminal 1.
5 A: _____ you smoke in Terminal 2?
   B: Yes, you _____ .
6 A: _____ you sleep in Terminal 1?
   B: No, you _____ .

b 🎧 5.4 Listen and check.

## PRONUNCIATION

1 Listen again. Notice the pronunciation of *can* and *can't*.

2 Practise saying the sentences.

2 🎧 5.5 Listen to Mei Ling talking about things you can and can't do in Hong Kong. Tick the things you can do. Cross the things you can't do.

- travel by tram
- eat and drink on the underground trains
- find a seat easily on the underground trains
- find a taxi quickly
- use a special travel card on all public transport
- buy food and drink with the special travel card

3 Work in pairs and take turns. Ask and answer questions about a town or city you know, using the ideas in exercise 2. Add two more questions of your own.

Can you travel by tram in your town?

No, you can't.

Unit 5, Study & Practice 1, page 146

My name is **Ignacio** and I'm 27 years old. I live with my family in **a house** in **Mexico City**, **the capital city** of **Mexico**. It's a fantastic city, but we have a real problem with traffic. Most people come to work **by car**, so it's very busy **in the morning** when they come into the city centre and in the evening when they go home. I'm **an engineer** and I work for an international company, from **nine to five**, Monday to Friday. I have a company car and my journey **to work** takes about 40 minutes. I also use my car **at the weekend** when I play football with my friends.

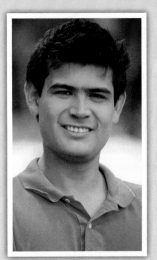

## Grammar focus 2
### Articles: *a/an*, *the* and *no article*

**1** Read about Ignacio and answer the questions.

**1** Where does Ignacio live?
**2** What's his job?
**3** What does he do at the weekend?

---

**GRAMMAR**

**1** Complete the rules about articles with *the*, *a/an* or – (no article). Look at the words in bold in exercise 1a to help you.

1 We use _____ :
  • with jobs.
  • with a singular noun to mean 'one'.
2 We use _____ :
  • when there is one of something (e.g. the capital city of Mexico).
  • with parts of the day (e.g. in the morning).
  • with names of some countries (e.g. the USA).
  • with some phrases (e.g. at the weekend, on the left).
3 We use _____ :
  • with names of people.
  • with most names of cities/countries.
  • with *by* and a type of transport (e.g. by car).
  • with some phrases (e.g. at home, to work, nine to five).

# PRACTICE

**1a** Choose the correct answer: *a*, *an*, *the* or –
(no article).

1 I live in **the** / – Dublin. It's **a** / **the** capital
city of – / **the** Ireland.
2 This is my cousin. Her name is **the** / – Lucia
and she's **a** / **an** actor.
3 I'd like to study English in – / **the** USA or
in – / **the** UK.
4 He goes to **the** / – work by **a** / – bus, from
– / **the** Monday to – / **the** Friday.
5 I work in **a** / – shop from **the** / – ten to
**the** / – four at **the** / – weekend.
6 She likes staying at **the** / – home in
**the** / – evening and watching TV.

b 🎧 **5.6** Listen and check.

**2a** Write full answers to the questions.

1 Where do you live?
2 Where does your family come from?
3 What is your job?
4 How do you travel to school or work?
5 What other ways can you travel to school
or work?
6 What is your favourite day of the week?
Why?
7 What is your favourite time of day? Why?
8 During the week, what do you usually do in
the morning, in the afternoon and in
the evening?
9 At the weekend, what do you usually do
in the morning, in the afternoon and in
the evening?

b Check your answers. Are the articles correct?

c Work in pairs and take turns. Ask and answer
questions 1–9.

**3a** Look at the quiz and complete the gaps with
*a*, *an*, *the* or – (no article).

b Work in pairs. Look at the words in bold in
the quiz. Are statements 1–7 true (T) or
false (F)?

c Check your answers on page 133. Which
information is the most surprising?

Unit 5, Study & Practice 2, page 146

# MEXICO QUIZ
## TRUE OR FALSE?

1 Mexico has got borders with three other countries:
\_\_\_\_\_ Guatemala, \_\_\_\_\_ **Costa Rica** and \_\_\_\_\_ USA.
2 The national language is \_\_\_\_\_ **Portuguese**, but
many people understand \_\_\_\_\_ English, especially
in tourist areas and near the borders.
3 The population of \_\_\_\_\_ Mexico City, including
the surrounding area, is about **18 million**.
4 There are \_\_\_\_\_ lot of traffic problems, so from
\_\_\_\_\_ Monday to \_\_\_\_\_ Friday you can only drive
your car into the city centre **four** times.
5 Many Mexicans travel around by \_\_\_\_\_ taxi.
The traditional colours for taxis in \_\_\_\_\_ city centre
are **green** and **gold**.
6 Offices are usually open in Mexico City from **7.00**
in \_\_\_\_\_ morning to 7.00 in \_\_\_\_\_ evening.
7 There are many famous Mexicans. For example:
• Thalía: she's \_\_\_\_\_ **businesswoman**.
• Carlos Slim Helú: he's \_\_\_\_\_ **singer**.
• Salma Hayek: she's \_\_\_\_\_ **actor**.

# Task

## Do a transport survey

### Preparation Reading and listening

**1a** Work in pairs and discuss.

- Which photo shows a cycle-sharing scheme?
- Which city does it show?

**b** Read the text below and answer the questions.

1. How many bicycles does London's cycle-sharing scheme have?
2. What is the popular name for the scheme?
3. Why do people call it that?
4. How much does it cost to use a bicycle for 30 minutes?
5. What is the record number of journeys in one day using the scheme?

London's cycle-sharing scheme started in 2010. The scheme covers a large area of London, with over 8,000 bicycles and 570 stations to keep them in. For a small amount of money, you can take a bicycle from one station and cycle to your destination. You then leave the bicycle in another station. The popular name for the bicycles is 'Boris Bikes', after Boris Johnson, who was the Mayor of London at that time.

One of the main aims of the scheme is to reduce the number of cars and buses on the roads. Every day, thousands of people use Boris Bikes to make short journeys around the city, especially as it is free for less than 30 minutes and £1 for one hour. The record number of journeys in one day is over 47,000 – during the London 2012 Olympics.

**2** Work in pairs and discuss.

- Would you like to use Boris Bikes as a tourist in London? Why / Why not?
- Do you know any other cities that have cycle-sharing schemes?
- Can you think of any disadvantages of schemes like this?

**3a** Look at the transport survey. Write full questions using the prompts in brackets.

**b** Write your own question 8, with possible answers a–e.

**4a** 🎧 5.7 Listen to a student answering the questions in the transport survey. Choose the correct answers in the survey.

**b** Listen again and tick the phrases you hear in the Useful language box (parts a and b).

## Task Speaking

**1** Look again at the questions in the survey. Make a note of your answer to each question. Ask your teacher for any words/phrases you need.

> Useful language a and b

# How do you travel ... ?

**1** _____
(How / travel / to school or work every day?)
**a** by bus                **b** by car
**c** by train              **d** on foot        **e** other

**2** _____
(How long / your journey / take?)
**a** 1–10 minutes          **b** 10–20 minutes
**c** 20–45 minutes         **d** 45 minutes +

**3** _____
(How far / walk / every week?)
**a** 0–5 km                **b** 6–10 km
**c** 10–15 km              **d** more than 15 km

**4** _____
(Which of these things / can / do?)
**a** drive a car           **b** ride a bike
**c** ride a scooter        **d** drive a van

**5** _____
(How often / travel by car?)
**a** every day             **b** once a week or less
**c** several times a week  **d** never

**6** _____
(How often / use public transport?)
**a** every day             **b** often, but not every day
**c** once a week or less   **d** never

**7** _____
(What / think of / public transport in your town?)
**a** excellent             **b** good
**c** OK                    **d** not good    **e** don't know

**8** _____
**a** _____              **b** _____
**c** _____              **d** _____    **e** _____

**2a** Work in pairs and take turns. Ask and answer the questions in the survey. Make a note of your partner's answers.

**b** Work in groups. Tell other students about your partner's answers to the survey.

> Useful language c

## SHARE YOUR TASK

**Practise talking about your partner's answers to the survey.**

**Film/Record yourself talking.**

**Share your film/recording with other students.**

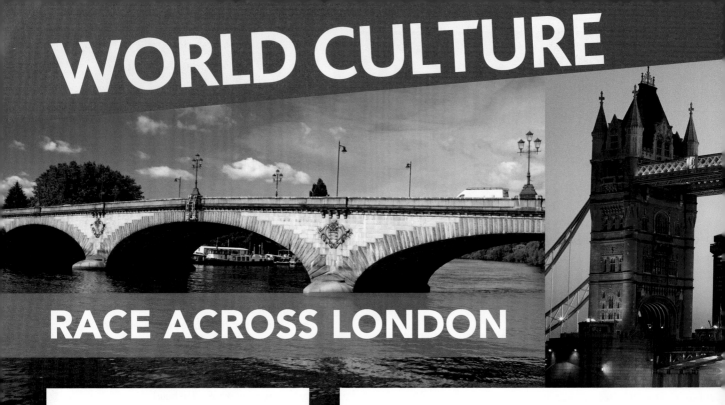

# WORLD CULTURE

## RACE ACROSS LONDON

## Find out first

**1a** Work in pairs. Look at the photos and discuss. Which famous places in the box can you see? Do you know any other famous places in London?

Canary Wharf          London City Airport
Tower Bridge          the River Thames
Kew Bridge

**b** Read about the famous places below. Try to guess the correct answers.

## London landmarks

- The River Thames goes from the west of England, through London and to the sea – a distance of **246 km / 346 km**.
- Kew Bridge is in West London. It's about **110 / 180** years old.
- Tower Bridge is a famous tourist attraction in London. It is next to the **Houses of Parliament / Tower of London**.
- Canary Wharf is an important **business centre / shopping centre** in East London.
- London City Airport is a **large / small** airport in East London.

**c** Go online to check your answers or ask your teacher.

Search: Thames length / Kew Bridge opened / London City Airport / Tower Bridge / Canary Wharf

## View

**2a** You are going to watch a video about a race across London. Before you watch, check you understand the meaning of the words/phrases in the glossary.

GLOSSARY
***rush hour*** the time when people travel to/from work
***speed limit*** the maximum kilometres per hour you can travel
***Top Gear*** a popular UK TV programme about cars

**b** ▶ Watch the video. Complete the table with the type of transport each presenter uses in the box below. Then number the presenters (1–4) in the order they finish the race.

bicycle          speedboat          car          public transport

|  | James | Richard | the Stig | Jeremy |
|---|---|---|---|---|
| Type of transport | | | | |
| Order in the race (1–4) | | | | |

**3** Watch again and complete the gaps with the numbers in the box.

| 14 | 20 ... 25 ... 18 | 28 | 80 |

1 The distance from Kew Bridge to London City Airport: _____ km
2 The speed limit on the River Thames in Central London: _____ kph
3 Jeremy's speed at Tower Bridge: _____ kph
4 James's speed in Central London: _____ kph

## World view

**4a** Look at the statements below. Tick the ones that are true for you.

> Cycling is a popular sport in my country.

> I like Formula One racing.

> Camel racing is a popular sport in my country.

> There is a marathon in my city every year.

> You can watch horse racing on TV in my country.

> Public transport is very cheap in my country.

> A lot of people use bicycles to get to work in my country.

**b** Work in pairs and compare your answers.

## 🔊 FIND OUT MORE

**5a** Look at the famous races in the box below. What do you know about them?

| | |
|---|---|
| Tour de France | University Boat Race |
| New York City Marathon | Dubai World Cup |
| Monaco Grand Prix | |

**b** Go online to find out more about each race and answer the questions.
1 What kind of race is it?
2 Where does it happen?
3 When does it happen?
4 Who was the last winner?

Search: [name of race] + date/winner

## ▶ Write up your research

**6** Write about one of the races you researched. Use the prompts below to help you.

The _____ (name of race) is a _____ (type of race) race.

The race happens in _____ (month/months) in (name of town/city).

I am (not) interested in this race because _____ .

**7** Write about another famous race, either in your country or in another country. Use the prompts in exercise 6 to help you.

### AFTER UNIT 5 YOU CAN ...

Talk about things you can and can't do.

Give your opinion about transport where you live.

Ask and answer questions about your transport and travel arrangements.

Research famous races online.

# 06

# FOOD AND DRINK

## IN THIS UNIT

- Grammar: *there is* and *there are*; *some* and *any*; *how much* and *how many*
- Vocabulary: Food: countable and uncountable nouns; Food pairs
- Task: Describe a favourite place to eat
- Language live: Describe a place to eat; Ordering food and drink

## Vocabulary

### Food: countable and uncountable nouns

**1** Work in pairs. Match the words in the box with the photos.

| | | | | |
|---|---|---|---|---|
| grapes | an apple | water | bread | chicken |
| a banana | eggs | cheese | tomatoes | a sandwich |
| olive oil | salad | biscuits | orange juice | fruit |

**2a** Work in pairs. Complete the table with the words in exercise 1. Can uncountable nouns have a plural form?

| Things you can count (countable nouns) | Things you can't count (uncountable nouns) |
|---|---|
| grapes | water |

**b** 🎧 6.1 Listen and check.

**c** Practise saying the words.

**3** Work in pairs and discuss. What other food words do you know? Add three more to each column in exercise 2a.

# Grammar focus 1

*there is* and *there are*; *some* and *any*

1 🎧 6.2 Listen to eight sentences about the things in the photos. Are the sentences true (T) or false (F)?

## GRAMMAR

*there is* and *there are*

1 Choose the correct answers.

| Countable (singular) | **There's / There are** an apple. |
| Countable (plural) | **There's / There are** five grapes. |
| Uncountable | **There's / There are** some olive oil. |

*some* and *any*

2 Choose the correct answers.

| Countable (plural) | There are **some / any** tomatoes. <br> There aren't **some / any** tomatoes. |
| Uncountable | There's **some / any** water. <br> There isn't **some / any** water. |

3 Notice that we normally use *any* in questions.
*Are there **any** tomatoes? Have you got **any** biscuits?*
*Is there **any** water? Has she got **any** fruit?*

## PRONUNCIATION

1 Look at audio script 6.2 on page 169 and listen again. Notice how the sound at the end of one word can join onto the next word.
*There's an apple.    There are a lot of bananas.*

2 Practise saying the sentences.

## PRACTICE

1 Complete the sentences with *some* or *any*.

  1 I haven't got _____ biscuits in my picnic basket.
  2 For a healthy snack, you can eat _____ fruit.
  3 Are there _____ oranges left in the fruit basket?
  4 We've got _____ rice and vegetables for dinner.
  5 Don't drink _____ coffee before you go to bed.
  6 Have you got _____ olive oil for the salad?
  7 There's _____ coffee on the table for you.

2a Write four true sentences and four false sentences about what you can see in the photos.

b Work in pairs and take turns. Student A: Say your sentences. Student B: Close your book and say if the sentences are true or false.

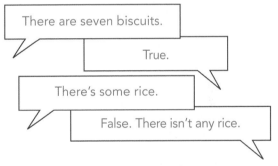

3a Heather and her friends are having a picnic. Turn to page 135 and look at the items on the picnic blanket for two minutes.

b Work in pairs and take turns. Can you remember the 12 items? Ask and answer *Yes/No* questions.

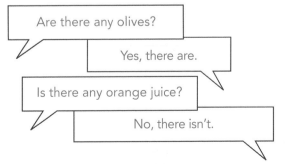

c What picnic foods do you like? Compare your ideas with other students.

Unit 6, Study & Practice 1, page 148

# Reading

### 1a Work in pairs. Look at the photos and discuss the questions.

- Which three countries / parts of the world do you think the photos show?
- What kind of food do you think people eat there?

### b Read the article and check your answers.

### 2 Read the article again. Match statements 1–8 with diets A–C.

1 They eat a lot of fish.
2 They eat a lot of olive oil.
3 They eat a lot of vegetarian food.
4 They eat vegetables as a main dish.
5 They eat vegetables for breakfast.
6 They use spices when they cook.
7 They don't eat large amounts of food.
8 They take a long time to eat their dinner.

### 3 Work in pairs and discuss.

- What are your favourite types of food?
- Which food don't you like?

# Healthy diets around the world

**Harry Chen is a fitness expert. In his new book, he describes three healthy diets from around the world and tells us what we can learn from them.**

### A The Japanese diet

People in Japan are generally very healthy and one of the main reasons is fish. The Japanese diet includes a lot of fish, which contains healthy oil. Another reason is that they also eat a lot of fruit and vegetables – for any meal, including breakfast. People in Japan eat less than in other countries. This is because: firstly, people eat small portions on separate small plates, not one big plate. Secondly, some people eat until they are about 80 percent full, then wait for ten minutes to see if they are still hungry. This is called *hara hachi bu*.

### B The Mediterranean diet

Health experts know that a lot of oil in your diet is unhealthy. The Mediterranean diet (for example, in Greece, Italy and Spain) contains a lot of oil, but it is a very healthy diet. This is because they use olive oil, which is good for your heart. Another important factor is that they eat a lot of fruit and vegetables. Vegetables in these countries are often main dishes, not just side dishes. Finally, people in this area eat with family and friends and sometimes a meal lasts several hours. This means people are relaxed and they don't eat too much.

### C The South Indian diet

There are many different regions in India with different types of food. The South Indian diet is especially healthy as it contains a lot of fruit and vegetables. There is a long tradition of vegetarian food in this area. They eat some meat, but not much. In South India, they add a lot of herbs and spices, like cinnamon and turmeric, to their cooking. The spices not only make the food delicious and attractive, but they are also good for digestion. Health experts also know that some of these spices can fight diseases, such as heart disease and cancer.

# Vocabulary
## Food pairs

**1a** Match the words in box A with the words in box B to make word pairs.

| A | fruit | herbs | knife | salt | bread |
|---|---|---|---|---|---|
| | fish | sweet | tea | food | |

| B | chips | coffee | spices | pepper | vegetables |
|---|---|---|---|---|---|
| | butter | sour | fork | drink | |

*fruit and vegetables*

*herbs and spices*

**b** 🎧 **6.3** Listen and check. For word pairs like these, we always say the words in this order and not the other way round (e.g. NOT vegetables and fruit).

> ### PRONUNCIATION
>
> **1** Listen again to the word pairs. Notice that the main stress is usually on the second word and the secondary stress is usually on the first word.
>
> fruit and vegetables
>
> **2** Practise saying the word pairs.

**2** Work in pairs and take turns. Student A: Say one word of a word pair. Student B: Say the word pair. Pay attention to word stress.

knife ...

knife and fork

pepper ...

salt and pepper

# Grammar focus 2
## *how much* and *how many*

**1a** Work in pairs and do the quiz below.

> **1** How much chocolate does the average British person eat every year?
>   **a** 1 kg  **b** 11 kg  **c** 21 kg
> **2** How much rice does the average British person eat every year?
>   **a** 4 kg  **b** 55 kg  **c** 96 kg
> **3** How many potatoes does the average British person eat every year?
>   **a** 125  **b** 500  **c** 880
> **4** How many cups of tea does the average British person drink every year?
>   **a** 730  **b** 1,095  **c** 1,460

> **IT'S A FACT!**
> In Britain, 98% of people have milk with their tea and 45% have sugar.

**b** Check your answers on page 134.

> ### GRAMMAR
>
> **1** Choose the correct answers.
>
> When we ask questions, we use:
>
> 1 *how many* with **countable** / **uncountable** nouns.
>
> 2 *how much* with **countable** / **uncountable** nouns.

## PRACTICE

**1a** Complete the questions with *how much* or *how many*.

1 _____ water do you drink every day?
2 _____ cups of tea or coffee do you drink every day?
3 _____ sugar do you have with your tea or coffee?
4 _____ oil and butter do you eat with your food?
5 _____ red meat do you eat every week?
6 _____ bread, rice and pasta do you eat every day?
7 _____ vegetables do you eat every day?
8 _____ fruit do you eat every day?
9 _____ sweets and biscuits do you eat every day?
10 _____ hours' sleep do you have every night?
11 _____ time do you spend on a computer every day?
12 _____ kilometres do you walk every day?

**b** Work in pairs and take turns. Ask and answer the questions.

> How much water do you drink every day?
>
> I drink about six glasses of water every day.

> **Unit 6, Study & Practice 2, page 149**

# Task

## Describe a favourite place to eat

## Preparation Listening

1   Work in pairs. Look at the photos and discuss.

   • When you have a special meal with your family or friends, do you usually go to a restaurant or stay at home? Why?
   • What kind of restaurant do you prefer: a cheap local restaurant or an expensive restaurant? Why?

2a   🎧 6.4 Listen to three people talking about their favourite place to eat. Write J (Jo), T (Tristan) or K (Kate) next to the sentences below.

   1   He/She loves fish and chips.
   2   He/She doesn't like expensive restaurants.
   3   He/She likes noodles with meat.
   4   He/She often goes to a restaurant for lunch.
   5   He/She always has Sunday lunch with his/her family.
   6   He/She thinks it's a great place to go with your friends.

b   Listen again and tick the phrases you hear in the Useful language box.

**a Describe the place and why you like it**
The name of my favourite restaurant is ...
I like it because (I love fish and chips).
It's my favourite place to eat because ...
It's a great place to go with (your friends).
My favourite place to eat is/isn't ...
I love eating there because ...

**b Describe the atmosphere**
You can sit outside and the view is really nice.
It's always busy.
It's got a fun, lively atmosphere.
It's very friendly.
There are a lot of young people.
It's (not) expensive.

**c Describe the food**
The speciality is (*bun cha*).
A typical dish is (*lomo saltado*).
It's made with fish and vegetables.
It's cooked with onions and tomatoes.
It's delicious!

# Task Speaking

**1a** Choose your favourite place to eat. Make notes using the ideas below.

- the name of the place
- where it is
- why you like it
- the atmosphere
- what kind of food you get there

**b** You are going to talk about your favourite place to eat. Spend some time preparing what you are going to say. Ask your teacher for any words/phrases you need.

> Useful language a–c

**2** Work in small groups and take turns. Talk about your favourite place to eat.

**3** Work in pairs. Tell your partner about the students in your group and their favourite places to eat.

Practise talking about your favourite place to eat.

Film/Record yourself talking.

Share your film/recording with other students.

## *Giuseppe's*

**GIUSEPPE'S – CARDIFF'S FAMOUS ITALIAN RESTAURANT**
15 Market Street, Cardiff

*Cardiff's oldest Italian restaurant!*
*We are famous for our delicious Italian food and lively atmosphere.*

Owner: Giuseppe Mazzini
Opening hours: 12–2, 6–10.30 (closed Sunday, Monday)

LUNCHTIME SPECIAL OFFER ANY PIZZA OR PASTA **£6.95**

Look on our website for more details:
www.giuseppesrestaurantcardiff.com Follow us on Twitter.

## *Giuseppe's*

### Menu

**Pizza Margherita**
tomato sauce, mozzarella cheese
**£8.95**

**Pizza Napoli**
tomato sauce, mozzarella cheese, anchovies
**£9.50**

**Pizza Four Seasons**
tomato sauce, mozzarella cheese, ham, mushrooms, olives
**£9.50**

**Pasta**
Spaghetti Bolognese

... the restaurant is quite small (there are only 12 tables). But it's always busy and the service is very friendly and efficient. This is a good place to go for a good cheap meal with friends ...

MORE REVIEWS (12)

## Writing
### Describe a place to eat

**1a** Work in pairs. Look at the photo and discuss.

- What kind of restaurant do you think it is?
- Are there any similar restaurants in your town or country? Do you ever eat there?

**b** Read the restaurant card, menu and review. Complete the information in the table.

| Restaurant name | |
|---|---|
| Address | |
| Type of food / Typical dishes | |
| Days/times open | |
| Words to describe food/atmosphere | |

**2** Read the description of Giuseppe's restaurant in an email from Marco to his friend Danny. Complete the gaps with information from exercise 1b.

**3a** Think of a place to eat that you know. Make notes using the ideas in exercise 1b.

**b** Write 80–100 words about the restaurant. Use the description in exercise 2 to help you.

**Re: my favourite place to eat**

Hi Danny,
You want recommendations about where to eat near here? Well, the name of my favourite place to eat is
**1**_____ . It's in **2**_____ , near the city centre.

On the menu, you can find typical **3**_____ food; there are many types of pizza and pasta. It's not very expensive: a Pizza Margherita costs only **4**_____ .
The restaurant is always **5**_____ . I often go there with some of my friends and we like it because the service is
**6**_____ and **7**_____ , and there is a very
**8**_____ atmosphere.

It's open **9**_____ days a week, from **10**_____ at lunchtime and from **11**_____ in the evening.

Try it! I hope you like it!
Marco

| Menu | Small | Medium | Large |
|---|---|---|---|
| Cappuccino | £2.10 | £2.45 | £2.70 |
| Espresso | £1.70 | £1.90 | £2.10 |
| Americano | £1.60 | £1.80 | £2.00 |

**Muffins all £1.50**
(chocolate, blueberry, banana)

# Speaking
## Ordering food and drink

**1** Look at the menu and answer the questions.

   1 How many sizes of cappuccino can you get?
   2 How many flavours of muffin can you get?

**2** ▶ Watch the video and answer the questions.

   1 What does customer A order? How much does
     it cost?
   2 What does customer B order? How much does
     it cost?

**3a** Complete the phrases with one word only.

   1 Hello, I'd _____ a coffee, please.
   2 _____ you like a cappuccino?
   3 Anything _____ ?
   4 _____ I have one of those, please?
   5 Eat _____ or takeaway?
   6 _____'s £3.95, please.
   7 What _____ you like?
   8 Small, _____ or large?
   9 _____ you.
  10 You're _____ .
  11 How much is _____ ?
  12 Keep the _____ .

**b** ▶ Watch and listen to the key phrases and check
your answers.

### PRONUNCIATION

   **1** Watch and listen again to the key phrases. Do they sound
     polite and friendly?

   **2** Practise saying them, using polite, friendly intonation.

**4** Work in pairs. Student A: You are the server in a
café. Student B: You are the customer. Use the menu
from exercise 1 and the ideas below to prepare and
practise a conversation. Remember to be friendly.

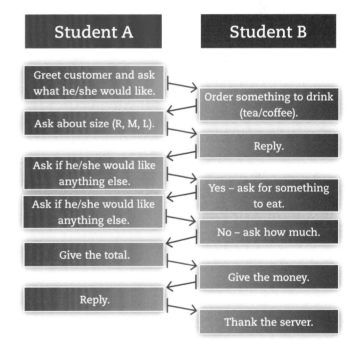

| Student A | Student B |
|---|---|
| Greet customer and ask what he/she would like. | |
| | Order something to drink (tea/coffee). |
| Ask about size (R, M, L). | |
| | Reply. |
| Ask if he/she would like anything else. | |
| | Yes – ask for something to eat. |
| Ask if he/she would like anything else. | |
| | No – ask how much. |
| Give the total. | |
| | Give the money. |
| Reply. | |
| | Thank the server. |

### AFTER UNIT 6 YOU CAN ...

Ask and answer questions about food (using *there is/
are, how much/many*).

Write a short description of a café or restaurant.

Order food and drink in a café or restaurant.

# 07
# LIFE STORIES

## IN THIS UNIT

- Grammar: Past simple: *was/were;*
  Past simple: regular and irregular
  verbs
- Vocabulary: Life events; Past time
  phrases
- Task: Tell a life story
- World culture: The Information Age

# Amazing children
### What do you know about them?

1 The composer Wolfgang Amadeus Mozart was from:
  **a** Austria      **b** Germany      **c** Russia

2 The Jackson 5 – with lead singer Michael Jackson – were
  a famous pop group in:
  **a** the 1950s     **b** the 1970s     **c** the 1990s

3 Twin actors Mary-Kate and Ashley Olsen were in their first
  TV show at the age of:
  **a** 6 months     **b** 9 months     **c** 9 years

4 Skater Tara Lipinski was an Olympic gold medallist in 1998
  when she was only:
  **a** 12           **b** 15           **c** 18

5 Footballer Pelé's first football club was in:
  **a** Santos       **b** São Paulo     **c** Rio de Janeiro

6 Actress Tatum O'Neal was an Oscar winner at the age of:
  **a** 10           **b** 14           **c** 18

# Grammar focus 1

## Past simple: *was/were*

**1** Work in pairs. Look at the photos and answer the questions.

  **1** How old do you think the people are?
  **2** Which photo shows:

- a pop group?
- a composer?
- an actress?
- an ice skater?
- a footballer?
- twins?

**2**  🎧 **7.1** Do the quiz on page 60. Then listen and check.

---

### GRAMMAR

#### *be*: past forms

**1** Notice the past forms of *be*.

*Wolfgang Amadeus Mozart **was** a famous composer.*
*Ryan O'Neal **wasn't** an Oscar winner.*
*The Jackson 5 **were** a famous pop group in the 1970s.*
*Mary-Kate and Ashley **weren't** in the show together.*
***Was she** a gold medal winner?*
***Were they** famous when they were young?*

**2** Notice that we say:

*He **was born** in Austria.*
*They **were born** in 1986.*

**3** Complete the gaps.

| | |
|---|---|
| **+** | I *was*<br>he/she/it _____<br>you/we/they _____ |
| **–** | I _____ (= was not)<br>he/she/it _____ (= was not)<br>you/we/they _____ (= were not) |
| **?** | _____ I?<br>_____ he/she/it?<br>_____ you/we/they? |

---

## PRACTICE

**1** Use the prompts to make sentences with *was/wasn't* and *were/weren't*.

Mozart / a singer ✗ / a composer ✓
*Mozart wasn't a singer. He was a composer.*

  **1** Michael Jackson and his four brothers / in a jazz group ✗ / in a pop group ✓
  **2** The Olsen twins / born in / 1976 ✗ / 1986 ✓
  **3** Tara Lipinski / a gold medal winner at the / Summer Olympics ✗ / Winter Olympics ✓
  **4** Pelé / the youngest player / in the 1962 World Cup ✗ / in the 1958 World Cup ✓
  **5** Tatum and Ryan O'Neal / in a film together in / 1983 ✗ / 1973 ✓

---

**2a** Complete the questions with *was* or *were*.

  **1** Where _____ you born?
  **2** Where _____ your parents born?
  **3** What _____ your favourite food when you _____ a child?
  **4** _____ you interested in sport when you _____ young?
  **5** Who _____ your best friend when you _____ 11 years old?
  **6** What _____ the name of your favourite teacher at school?
  **7** Who _____ three important people in your life when you _____ a child?
  **8** _____ you scared of anything when you _____ a child?

**b**  🎧 **7.2** Listen and check.

---

### PRONUNCIATION

**1** Listen again to the questions. Notice the weak form of *was* /wəz/ and *were* /wə/.

**2** Practise saying the questions.

---

**3** Work in pairs. Ask and answer the questions in exercise 2a.

> Where were you born?

> I was born in Prague. How about you?

**Unit 7, Study & Practice 1, page 150**

# Reading and vocabulary
## Life events

**1a** Put the life events in the box in a logical order. (There is more than one possible answer.)

get a job
meet someone
have children
start school
get married
leave school
start a business
go to university
move to a different town/country
study maths/history ...
graduate from university

**b** Work in pairs and compare your order of events.

*First, you start school …*

*Then, when you are 18, you leave school …*

*Next, …*

**2** Work in pairs and discuss.

- Do you like sharing information about your life on blogs and social networking sites? Why / Why not?
- Do you like reading about other people's life events / interests on these sites? Why / Why not?

**3a** Work in pairs. Look at the photos and the title of the article about Ben Silbermann. What do you think are his interests? What extraordinary business did he start?

**b** Read the article and check your ideas.

**4** Read the article again and complete the information about Ben Silbermann below.

**5** Work in groups and discuss.

- How many different websites do you look at every week? Which ones are your favourites?
- Do you post photos online? If so, how many and what kind of photos? If not, why not?
- Do you know anyone who collects things? What do they collect and why?

## Ben Silbermann

1 Year of birth: _____
2 Place of birth: _____
3 Childhood interests: _____
4 Study (what/where): _____
5 Change of US state: _____
6 First job (where/when): _____
7 First business (when): _____

# An ordinary man …
## an extraordinary business

Ben Silbermann was an ordinary boy. He was born in 1982 in Iowa in the USA and he loved collecting things: stamps, leaves and especially insects. At the time, he felt like any other child … but as a young man in his 20s, his love of collecting became big business.

He went to Yale University and studied chemistry and political science. In 2006, when he graduated from university, he moved to the state of California and got a job at Google. Silbermann met a lot of people there who were very interested in technology, and he decided two things: he wanted to start a business and he wanted to do something he loved.

He worked at Google for two years. Then, in 2008, Silbermann left his job and he started his own business with two friends: Paul Sciarra and Evan Sharp. In November 2009, they got an apartment together in Palo Alto, California and started work on Pinterest.

Silbermann and Sharp realised they both loved collecting, and they made a 'virtual pinboard' – pages online where you 'pin' pictures of things you like and things you 'collect'. Their idea was to connect everyone in the world through the things they find interesting.

And it seemed that a lot of people liked their idea. When Pinterest started in March 2010, it grew quickly and had 10 million users after the first year. This was an amazing number compared with Twitter and Facebook: Twitter took two years to reach 10 million users and Facebook took over five years. Just a year after starting, Pinterest was worth $200 million and had over 421 million page views. Silbermann's ordinary interest as a boy certainly became an extraordinary business.

# Grammar focus 2
## Past simple: regular and irregular verbs

**1** Look at sentences a–d and answer the questions.

  **1** Which sentences are about Ben Silbermann's life now?

  **2** Which sentences are about his life in the past?

  **a** He **lives** in the USA.

  **b** He **got** a job at Google in 2006.

  **c** He **started** his own business with two friends.

  **d** He **loves** collecting things.

### GRAMMAR

**Regular verbs**

**1** Find the past form of these verbs in the article.

  love  study  graduate  move  want
  work  decide  start

**2** How do we form the Past simple of regular verbs?

**Irregular verbs**

**3** Find the past form of these verbs in the article.

  feel  become  go  get  meet
  leave  make  have  take

## PRACTICE

**1a** Use the prompts below to make correct past sentences about Ben Silbermann's life.

born / the USA
*He was born in the USA.*

  **1** as a child / love / collecting things

  **2** go / Yale University

  **3** at university / study / chemistry and political science

  **4** when he was 24 / move / to California

  **5** work / for Google for two years

  **6** leave / job / 2008

  **7** get / an apartment with two friends / 2009

  **8** start / online company Pinterest / 2010

**b** Work in pairs and take turns. Close your book and tell your partner six things about Ben's life.

**2a** Write five sentences about your own life events and interests.

**b** Work in pairs and take turns. Ask and answer questions about your sentences.

> I was born in the USA.
>> Really? Where?

### PRONUNCIATION

**1** 🎧 **7.3** Look at audio script 7.3 on page 169. Listen and count the number of syllables you hear.

  worked = 1  studied = 2

**2** Notice that only verbs ending with /t/ or /d/ sounds have an 'extra' syllable in the Past simple.

  want-ed  wait-ed  need-ed  decid-ed

**3** 🎧 **7.4** Listen to eight pairs of sentences. Which sentence is Past simple (a or b)?

**4** Practise saying the Past simple sentences.

**3a** Work in pairs and look at the photos below.
Student A: Turn to page 134. Read about the life of Grace Hopper and complete the sentences.
Student B: Turn to page 136. Read about the life of Steve Jobs and complete the sentences.

**b** Tell each other about your person.

Unit 7, Study & Practice 2, page 150

# Listening
## Jackie Kennedy Onassis

**1** Look at the photos and read the book extract below. Who are the people in the photos?

**IT'S A FACT!**
When Jackie Kennedy died, she left over $43 million to her two children.

**2a** You are going to hear the first part of the story of Jackie Kennedy Onassis. Before you listen, can you guess which verb belongs in each gap?

| be | begin | fall | get | meet |
|----|-------|------|-----|------|
| joke | spend | study | travel | |

**1** Jackie _____ born on Long Island, near New York, in July 1929.

**2** She _____ a happy childhood in and around New York.

**3** She _____ in the USA and at the Sorbonne in Paris, France.

**4** In 1951, she _____ work as a journalist, and she also _____ John F. Kennedy, the future President of the United States.

**5** They _____ in love, and they _____ married two years later.

**6** The Kennedys _____ to many countries together. On one trip to France, the President _____ , 'I am the man who accompanied Jackie Kennedy to Paris ...'

**b** 🎧 7.5 Listen and complete the sentences with the correct form of the verbs in the box.

**3a** 🎧 7.6 Listen to the second part of the story. Number the events in the order you hear them.

**a** death of John F. Kennedy    *1*
**b** death of Robert Kennedy
**c** death of Jackie Kennedy    *8*
**d** Jackie Kennedy married Aristotle Onassis
**e** Jackie Onassis worked for a publishing company
**f** Jackie Kennedy left the USA
**g** death of Aristotle Onassis
**h** Jackie Onassis returned to the USA

**b** Listen again and write the date/year when each event happened.

**a** death of John F. Kennedy
*22 November 1963*

**4** Think of a person with an amazing life (a friend, a family member or a famous person). Write sentences about him/her using the ideas below.

- He/She was born in ... (place) in ... (year).
- He/She spent his/her childhood in ... (place).
- He/She studied at ...
- He/She got married to ... in ...
- He/She became ... in ...

### Jackie Kennedy Onassis: An Amazing Life

Jackie Kennedy Onassis was one of the great style icons of the 20th century. Now, around 20 years after her death, her style still influences fashions of today. She was married twice; first, to US President John F. Kennedy. Then, when she was married to Greek millionaire Aristotle Onassis, people from all over the world loved and admired her. But it wasn't all glamour – her life was also full of tragedy.

# Vocabulary
## Past time phrases

**1a** Complete the time phrases with the words in the box.

| | | | |
|---|---|---|---|
| ago | summer | morning | my last birthday |
| night | afternoon | Tuesday | 12 years old |
| a child | weekend | year | |

1 this _summer_ / _morning_ / _____ / _____ / _____ / _____

2 last _____ / _____ / _____ / _____ / _____

3 on _____ / _____

4 yesterday _____ / _____

5 when I was _____ / _____

6 20 years / ten minutes _____

**b** Complete the table with phrases from exercise 1a.

| More than a year ago | Less than a year ago but not this week | This week / Today |
|---|---|---|
| _last summer_ | _____ | _____ |
| _____ | _____ | _____ |
| _____ | _____ | _____ |
| _____ | _____ | _____ |
| | | _____ |
| | | _____ |
| | | _____ |
| | | _____ |

**2a** Read questions 1–10 of the quiz and write two more similar questions.

**b** Work in pairs and take turns. Ask and answer the questions using phrases from exercise 1. You can add more details if you like.

> When did you last go shopping for clothes?

> I last went shopping for clothes on Saturday. I bought a pair of jeans.

Unit 7, Study & Practice 3, page 151

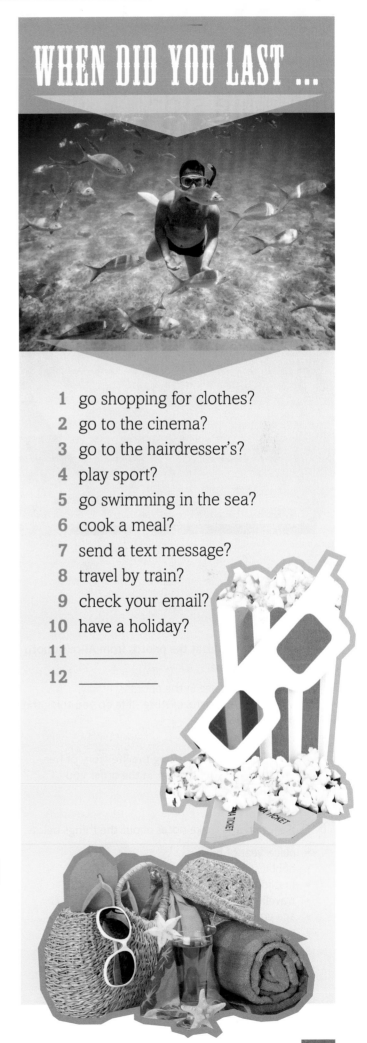

**WHEN DID YOU LAST ...**

1 go shopping for clothes?
2 go to the cinema?
3 go to the hairdresser's?
4 play sport?
5 go swimming in the sea?
6 cook a meal?
7 send a text message?
8 travel by train?
9 check your email?
10 have a holiday?
11 _____
12 _____

# Task

## Tell a life story

Fun summer job! (USA, August 199...

Todd's letter changed everything ... 14th February 2003

I loved riding my bicycle (1980, aged 8)

## Preparation Listening

1   Work in pairs. Look at the photos from Alice's photo album and discuss.

   • What can you see in the photos?
   • What different parts of Alice's life do you think the photos show?

2a   🎧 7.7 Listen to Maria telling the life story of her cousin Alice. Put photos A–F in the order you hear them.

b   Listen again and make notes about the things below.

   • place/year of birth
   • hobbies as a child
   • first job (what/where)
   • travelling (who with/how)
   • age graduated from university
   • second job (what/where)
   • when saw Todd again
   • third job (what/where)

3   Listen again and tick the phrases you hear in the Useful language box.

## Task Speaking

1   You are going to tell a life story. Decide who you're going to talk about. It could be you, someone in your family or someone you know well.

2   Spend some time preparing what you are going to say. Make notes about six important events in the life story.

> Useful language a and b

3   Work in pairs and take turns. Tell the life story, using your notes to help you.

Good times with Todd in USA ☺

**a Life events**

He/She was born in (London) in (1972).
I went to school in (London).
He/She didn't study very hard at school.
He/She studied (music technology) at university.
She didn't go to university.
I got married in (1999).
They decided to live in (Italy).

**b Past time phrases**

As a child, (Alice) loved (sports).
When he/she was 18, he/she left school.
Then, when I was 12, I became interested in (music).
He/She graduated (from university) at the age of 22.
After that, he/she got a job as a (journalist).
In the end, he/she got a job in (a hospital).

E

A fantastic class of kids to teach! (Class of 95, London)

F

I love New York – it's great to be back in the USA!

**SHARE YOUR TASK**

Practise telling the story.

Film/Record yourself telling the story.

Share your film/recording with other students.

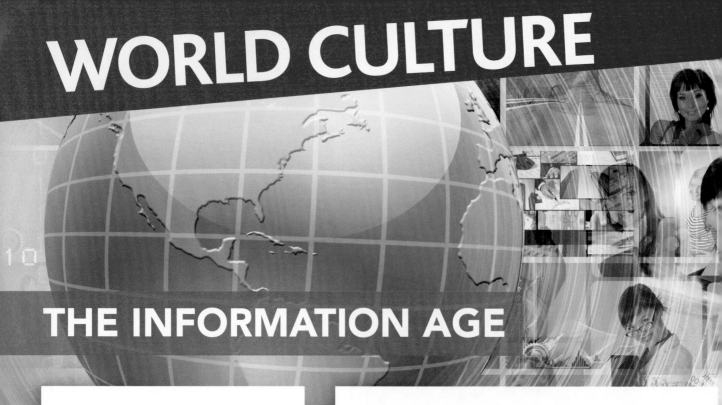

# WORLD CULTURE

## THE INFORMATION AGE

## Find out first

**1  Work in pairs and discuss.**

- What social networking websites do you use?
- How often do you use them?

**2a  Read the statements below. Do you think they are true (T) or false (F)?**

1  Flixter is a social networking site about movies.
2  Goodreads is a site for book lovers that has books in all languages.
3  Twitter has messages ('tweets') of up to 150 characters.
4  LinkedIn is a site for sharing photographs.
5  Mark Zuckerberg, the founder of Facebook, is originally from Germany.

**b  Go online to check your answers or ask your teacher.**

**Search:** Flixter / Goodreads / Twitter / LinkedIn / Mark Zuckerberg

## View

**3a ▶ Watch the video about Mark Zuckerberg and number the things (1–6) in the order you see them.**

- Harvard University
- a magazine cover
- Mark Zuckerberg with Barack Obama
- Mark Zuckerberg's first website
- the Queen of England's Facebook page
- Silicon Valley, California

**b  Watch again and complete the fact file below with the information in the box. (There is some extra information.)**

| | | |
|---|---|---|
| 1 million | 10 million | the British Prime Minister |
| Harvard | Google | philosophy |
| psychology | 800 million | 30 million |
| the Queen of England | 2004 | 2006 |
| $5 billion | $15 billion | Yahoo |

### FACT FILE

#### PERSONAL DETAILS

- Name: Mark Zuckerberg
- Born: 1984 in White Plains, New York
- Studied _____ and computer science at _____ University
- Moved to Silicon Valley in _____

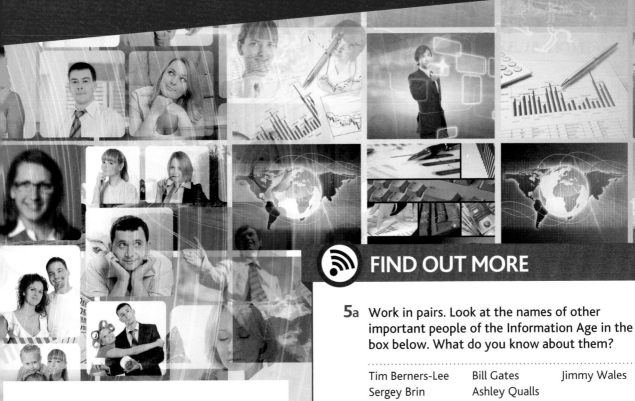

## World view

**4a** Look at the statements below. Tick the ones you agree with and cross the ones you disagree with.

> People nowadays spend too much of their time on social networking sites.

> Facebook helps us to understand people from other cultures.

> Social networking sites are only there to make money.

> Social networking is the future ... we can't live without it!

> I admire people like Mark Zuckerberg more than sportsmen or politicians.

> Social networking sites are dangerous – especially for young people.

**b** Work in pairs and compare your ideas.

## 🔊 FIND OUT MORE

**5a** Work in pairs. Look at the names of other important people of the Information Age in the box below. What do you know about them?

| | | |
| --- | --- | --- |
| Tim Berners-Lee | Bill Gates | Jimmy Wales |
| Sergey Brin | Ashley Qualls | |

**b** Go online to find out more about each person's early life (where/when born, education, etc.) and why he/she is important.

Search: [name of person] + biography

## Write up your research

**6** Complete the text about Mark Zuckerberg.

Mark Zuckerberg is one of the most important people of the Information Age. He was born in White Plains, New York and he studied ¹_____ (subject) at ²_____ (name) University.

In ³_____ (year), he started his first website, the ⁴_____ (name of first website). In ⁵_____ (year), he moved to Silicon Valley.

Now he is famous as the person behind Facebook, and he's a multibillionaire.

**7** Write about one of the people you researched. Use the example in exercise 6 to help you.

### CEBOOK FACTS

First website: thefacebook.com. It had _____ users after a few months.

Number of users worldwide: _____ million

Number of users in UK: _____

Most famous user in UK: _____

_____ tried to buy Facebook for $1 billion.

Microsoft tried to buy Facebook in 2007 for _____ .

### AFTER UNIT 7 YOU CAN ...

Ask and answer questions using *was/were*.

Talk about events in the past.

Tell your life story or the life story of someone you know.

Research important people of the Information Age online.

# FACT OR FICTION?

## IN THIS UNIT

- **Grammar:** Past simple: negative form; Past simple: question form
- **Vocabulary:** Adjectives to describe stories; Entertainment
- **Task:** Talk about an evening in or out
- **Language live:** Arranging an evening out

## Vocabulary
### Adjectives to describe stories

**1a** Look at the photos from famous films. Which type of film do you think each one is?

- a comedy
- a romance
- a science fiction (sci-fi) film
- a historical film
- an action film
- an adventure film

**b** Can you think of a film for each different category?

**2a** Find pairs of opposites in the box.

| | | | | | |
|---|---|---|---|---|---|
| sad | frightening | exciting | romantic | fast-moving | funny |
| serious | boring | happy | slow | enjoyable | |

**b** Work in pairs and discuss. What films have you seen recently? Which adjectives describe them?

> I saw *Men in Black* last week. It was fast-moving and very funny.

...ueen of Egypt more than 2,000 ...ars ago, Cleopatra is the subject ... many books, plays and films ... ...t what do we really know ...out her?

## ...eopatra: the legend

... According to many people, she was ...e greatest beauty of ancient times. ...o of the greatest men of the ancient ...rld – Julius Caesar and Mark Antony ...oth fell in love with her.
... Her favourite luxury was taking baths ...in milk! She thought this made her ...in more beautiful.
... She fought against the Romans ... and after her last battle, she killed ...rself with a snake.

## ...eopatra: the facts

... Cleopatra was Queen of Egypt ... ...t she wasn't Egyptian, she was Greek!
... No one knows what she looked like. ...e only original image is from a coin. ...e greatest beauty of the ancient ...rld? You decide ...
... Cleopatra didn't take baths in milk. ...e Romans only started doing that ...any years later.
... She didn't fight against the Romans. ...e fought with one Roman (Mark ...tony) against another (Augustus).
... Her most recent biographer says she ...n't use a snake to kill herself ... she ...ank poison instead.

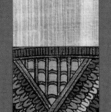

# Grammar focus 1
## Past simple: negative form

**1a** Work in pairs. Look at the picture of Queen Cleopatra of Egypt and answer the questions.

  **1** When do you think she lived?
  **2** Can you think of three adjectives to describe her?

**b** Read the text and check your answers.

### GRAMMAR

**Past simple: negative form**

**1** We make the Past simple negative form of *be* with *wasn't/weren't* (= was not / were not).
  Cleopatra *wasn't* Egyptian.

**2** We make the Past simple negative form of other verbs with *didn't* (= did not) + verb.
  She *didn't kill* herself with a snake.

## PRACTICE

**1** Work in pairs and discuss. Cleopatra lived around 2,000 years ago. Which things did/didn't people do in those days?

- make phone calls
- have baths
- listen to the radio
- wear clothes
- get married
- drive cars
- go to the cinema
- write poems and plays

> They didn't make phone calls 2,000 years ago.

> 2,000 years ago, they had baths.

**2a** Put the sentences into the correct form (positive or negative) to make them true for you.

  **1** I (go out) last night.
  **2** I (watch) a film last weekend.
  **3** I (go) to the gym yesterday.
  **4** I (see) the TV news yesterday.
  **5** I (listen) to the radio this morning.
  **6** I (read) a newspaper yesterday.
  **7** I (play) a computer game yesterday.
  **8** I (buy) a magazine yesterday.
  **9** I (drive) a car yesterday.
  **10** I (speak) English yesterday.

**b** Work in pairs and compare your sentences.

▶ Unit 8, Study & Practice 1, page 152

## Vocabulary
### Entertainment

**1** Complete the phrases below with the words in the box.

go   watch   play   cook   download   read

1 _____ dinner for friends
2 _____ to a musical
3 _____ a DVD at home
4 _____ to a party
5 _____ to a concert
6 _____ computer games
7 _____ music
8 _____ out for dinner
9 _____ a book
10 _____ to the cinema
11 _____ for a walk
12 _____ to the theatre

**2a** Look at the verb phrases in exercise 1. Which describe:

- an evening in?
- an evening out?

**b** Add two more verb phrases to each category.

**3a** Choose your five favourite activities from exercises 1 and 2. Put them in order (1–5).

**b** Work in pairs and compare your favourite activities.

What's your favourite?

My favourite is 'go to a musical', because I love singing and musicals are always really enjoyable.

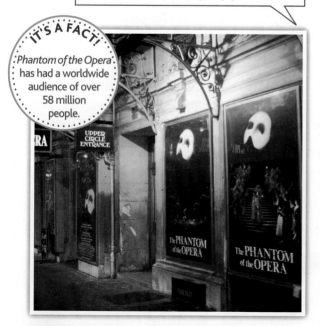

IT'S A FACT!
*Phantom of the Opera* has had a worldwide audience of over 58 million people.

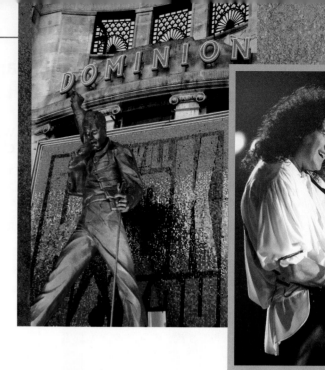

## Listening
### *We Will Rock You* – a song and a musical

**1** Look at the photos. Read the article and answer the questions.

1 Which country is the rock band Queen from?
2 Who was the lead singer?
3 Which two members still play in the band?
4 Can you name three of their hit songs?

**2a** 🎧 8.1 Listen to a radio programme about the musical *We Will Rock You*, which is based on a song by Queen. Number topics a–h in the order you hear them.

a the musical now
b when the song became a hit    1
c the story of the musical
d the early days of the musical
e who wrote the musical
f who wrote the original song
g how he got the idea for the song
h the main characters in the musical

**b** Listen again. Are the statements true (T) or false (F)?

1 The song *We Will Rock You* came out in 1970.
2 Guitarist Brian May wrote the song.
3 Sometimes people sing *We Will Rock You* at football games.
4 All the songs in the musical are by Queen.
5 The musical is set in the present time.
6 The musical came out in 2002.
7 The musical closed after only three years.
8 The musical went to Japan in 2003.

**3** Work in pairs and discuss.

- Do you know any Queen songs? Do you like them?
- Would you like to see the musical *We Will Rock You*? Why / Why not?
- What kind of music do you like? Have you got any favourite bands?

# Queen - rock legends

Queen are a British rock band. They formed in 1971 with lead singer Freddie Mercury, guitarist Brian May, bass guitarist John Deacon and drummer Roger Taylor. Freddie Mercury died in 1991 and John Deacon left the band in 1997, but Brian May and Roger Taylor continue to play together. Queen are one of the world's best-selling music artists, with 18 number one albums and 18 number one singles, including huge hits like *Bohemian Rhapsody*, *We Are The Champions* and *We Will Rock You*.

## Grammar focus 2
### Past simple: question form

**1a** Put the words in the correct order to make questions.

1 did / the song / When / come out ?
2 write / Why / he / the song / did ?
3 Brian May / the musical / Did / write ?
4 the musical / come out / did / When ?
5 good reviews / the musical / get / Did ?
6 first / did / Where / go on tour / the musical ?

b 🎧 8.2 Listen and check.

---

**GRAMMAR**

1 We form most Past simple questions with *did* + verb.
   *Did Brian May **write** the musical?* NOT *Did he wrote ... ?*
   *When **did** the musical **come** out?*

2 Notice the short answers.
   *Did the musical **get** good reviews?*
   *Yes, it **did**.*
   *No, it **didn't**.*

---

## PRACTICE

**1a** Add *did* in the correct place to make questions.

    *Did*
    ^ you play a musical instrument when you were a child?

1 where you live when you were a child?
2 you read a lot of books when you were a child?
3 your parents read books to you when you were a child?
4 when you start learning English?
5 you watch a lot of TV last weekend?
6 when you last go to a concert?
7 what music you last listen to?
8 you go for a walk last weekend?
9 when you last see a really good show?

b 🎧 8.3 Listen and check.

---

**PRONUNCIATION**

1 Listen again to the questions in exercise 1a. Notice the linking between *did* and *you/your*.

2 Practise saying the questions.

---

**2a** Work in pairs and take turns. Ask and answer the questions in exercise 1a. You can give more details if you like.

When did you last see a really good show?

I saw *We Will Rock You* last weekend.

Did you enjoy it?

Yes, it was great.

b Tell the class three things about your partner.

Unit 8, Study & Practice 2, page 152

# Task

## Talk about an evening in or out

### Preparation Listening

**1a** Work in pairs and discuss. Which of the activities in the box can you see in the photos?

| | |
|---|---|
| go to the cinema | watch a film on TV |
| go to a restaurant | go for a walk |
| go to the theatre | have a dinner party |
| stay in and read a book | go to a concert |

**b** Which of the activities in the box do you do for:

- an evening in?
- an evening out?

**c** Can you think of any more activities for an evening in or an evening out?

**2a** 🎧 8.4 Listen to Lauren, Daniel and Karl. What is each person talking about – an evening in or out?

**b** Listen again and complete the table.

| | Lauren | Daniel | Karl |
|---|---|---|---|
| **What?** | jazz concert | | cinema |
| **Who with?** | friend (Kate) | | |
| **Where?** | | | |
| **Good or bad?** | | good (fun) | |

**3a** Work in pairs. Complete the questions with one word only.

1 When did you _____ have a really good evening – in or out?
2 Who did you go _____ ?
3 How did you _____ there?
4 _____ it good?
5 What _____ you cook?
6 Who was _____ ?
7 What did you _____ of it?
8 Where _____ you see it?

**b** Check your answers in the Useful language box.

**4** Listen again and say which questions and answers you hear in each conversation. Write L (Lauren), D (Daniel) or K (Karl) next to the phrases in the Useful language box.

### Task Speaking

**1** Think about a good or bad evening you had. Look at the questions and answers in the Useful language box and make notes. Ask your teacher for any words/phrases you need.

> Useful language a and b

**2a** Work in pairs. Ask and answer questions about your evening.

> When did you last have a really good evening out?

> I had a really good evening out last weekend.

**b** Work with a new partner. Tell him/her about your evening or your first partner's evening.

## USEFUL LANGUAGE

**a Questions**

When did you last have a really good/bad evening – in or out?

What did you do/cook?

Who did you see?

Who did you go with? / Who was there?

How did you get there?

What did you think of it? / Was it good?

Where did you see it? / Where was it?

**b Answers**

I went to (a fantastic concert).

I saw a band (called the Ravens).

It was brilliant / funny / sad / exciting / good.

I had a dinner party.

I didn't really enjoy it.

It was awful/terrible/boring.

## SHARE YOUR TASK

**Practise talking about your evening or your partner's evening.**

**Film/Record yourself talking about your evening or your partner's evening.**

**Share your film/recording with other students.**

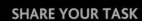

# LANGUAGE LIVE

Are you free on Friday?

## Speaking
### Arranging an evening out

1 Work in pairs and discuss.

- How often do you go out with friends?
- Where do you go?
- Do you ever go out to eat?
- Who do you usually go with?

2a ▶ Andy wants to arrange an evening out with his colleagues. Watch the video and answer the questions.

1 When is the evening out?
2 Does each person say *yes* or *no*?

b Watch again and write the reason each person gives for saying *yes* or *no*.

3a Complete the phrases with the words in the box.

| | | | | | |
|---|---|---|---|---|---|
| about | busy | can't | free | go | good |
| idea | love | sorry | time | would | |

1 Are you _____ on Friday?
2 How _____ an evening out?
3 Sounds _____ !
4 Sorry, I _____ . I'm _____ .
5 Maybe another _____ .
6 _____ you like to come?
7 Do you want to _____ for a pizza?
8 Why not? Good _____ !
9 We'd _____ to!
10 I can't come, _____ !

b ▶ Watch and listen to the key phrases and check your answers.

---

**PRONUNCIATION**

1 Watch and listen again to the key phrases.

2 Practise saying them.

---

4a Work in pairs. Prepare a conversation for two people arranging an evening out. Use the ideas below to help you.

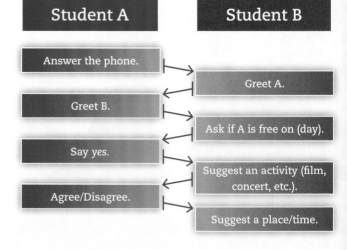

| Student A | Student B |
|---|---|
| Answer the phone. | |
| | Greet A. |
| Greet B. | |
| | Ask if A is free on (day). |
| Say yes. | |
| | Suggest an activity (film, concert, etc.). |
| Agree/Disagree. | |
| | Suggest a place/time. |

b Practise your conversation.

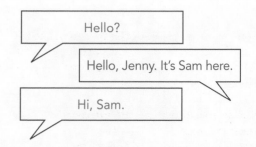

Hello?

Hello, Jenny. It's Sam here.

Hi, Sam.

# Writing
## Arranging an evening out

**1** Ahmed and Bianca are arranging an evening out for their class. Read their text messages and put them in the correct order (1–7).

**a** Annabel's Place is a bit expensive ... How about Viva Italia on Bold Street?

**b** Hi, Ahmed ... about the end-of-course meal on Friday ... any ideas for a place/time?  *1*

**c** Sure, no problem.

**d** Good idea ... let's go to Viva Italia, then. What time?

**e** Let's go to Annabel's Place ... the food's good and it's not too expensive.

**f** OK, fine. Can you tell the others?

**g** How about 7 o'clock? In front of the restaurant?

**2** Use the information from exercise 1 to complete Bianca's email to her classmates.

>
>
> Re: meeting place
> _____
>
> Hi, everyone!
> It's the last day of our course on ¹_____ ,
> so let's have a night out to celebrate!
>
> The meal is at the ²_____ restaurant on
> ³_____ Street. The meeting time is
> ⁴_____ o'clock, and the meeting place is
> ⁵_____ the restaurant.
>
> See you there!
> Bianca

**Nina's Noodle Bar**
**Fun fast food ... Snacks and tasty meals ...**
*Menu includes:* noodles, rice, vegetables, chicken, duck and much more!
Good prices – friendly service – lots of tables.
Good location in the town centre: 77 High Street.
Phone to book.
For details go to **www.ninasnoodlebar.com**

**Jerkmania –**
**Caribbean Chicken**
Hot spicy chicken from genuine Caribbean recipes
Huge menu with a range of dishes
Eat in or takeaway
No booking necessary
Central location: 24 Station Road (near the station)

**Green Leaf**
- Busy, popular vegetarian restaurant – with interesting new dishes
- Veggie burgers, Indian and Mediterranean dishes, hot and cold food

Green Leaf is at 2 Mortimer Street.
It's modern and cool! It's the place to be!
Discounts for groups of over ten people.
**Book on 07786 343990**

**3a** You want to arrange a meal out for your class. Choose a restaurant you know or one of the restaurants opposite.

**b** Write an email inviting your classmates out to the restaurant. You can invent details about the place, time, etc. Use the email in exercise 2 and the phrases in the box to help you.

| | |
|---|---|
| Let's have an evening out ... | Hi, everyone! |
| The meal is at ... on ... | It's ... |
| The meeting time/place is ... | See you there! |

**AFTER UNIT 8 YOU CAN ...**

**Talk about things you did/didn't do in the past.**

**Ask and answer questions about an evening in/out that you had.**

**Arrange an evening out with friends.**

# 09

# BUY
# AND
# SELL

## IN THIS UNIT

- **Grammar:** Comparative adjectives; Superlative adjectives
- **Vocabulary:** Describing objects; Shops and services
- **Task:** Choose souvenirs from your country
- **World culture:** Famous markets

## Vocabulary
### Describing objects

**1a** Look at the items in the photos. Choose three adjectives from the box to describe each item.

| | | | |
|---|---|---|---|
| fast | expensive | pretty | fashionable |
| easy to use | cheap | stylish | old |
| powerful | economical | uncomfortable | unusual |

*The car is fast, expensive and powerful.*

**b** Work in pairs and compare your ideas.

**2** Work in pairs and discuss.

- Which of the items in the photos do you like / not like? Say why using the adjectives in exercise 1a.

> I don't like the jewellery – it's expensive, but I don't think it's pretty.

- Have you got any of the items in the photos? Describe them using the adjectives in exercise 1a.

> I've got a watch. It's cheap, but it's also stylish.

# Grammar focus 1
## Comparative adjectives

**1** Look at the two leather jackets from an online shopping site. Which do you prefer? Why?

**A**

**ubuy** [                    ]

**NEW MEN'S FAUX LEATHER JACKET**

Item condition: **New**
Size: **LARGE**
Colour: **Black**

**BUY IT NOW** £29.99

**B**

**ubuy** [                    ]

**GENUINE VINTAGE MEN'S LEATHER JACKET … MADE IN THE USA!**

Item condition: **Pre-owned**
Size: **MEDIUM**
Colour: **Brown**

**Current bid** £250

**2** Work in pairs and answer the questions.

Which jacket (A or B) is:
1 newer?
2 bigger?
3 more stylish?
4 more expensive?

## PRACTICE

**1** Work in pairs and look at the items from an online shopping site. Make sentences comparing each pair of items using the adjectives in the box.

*Dress A is newer than dress B.*

**1**
Dress A: Designer dress – new   £89.99
Dress B: Vintage 1940s dress   £54.99

new        unusual        pretty

**2**
Car C: 1963 Triumph – top speed 106 mph   £8,500
Car D: 2003 Corvette – top speed 180 mph   £12,500

fast        expensive        stylish

**3**
Camera E: 8 cm x 5 cm – simple functions   £105
Camera F: 15 cm x 10 cm – multifunctions   £199

small        easy to use        cheap

Unit 9, Study & Practice 1, page 154

## Grammar focus 2
### Superlative adjectives

**IT'S A FACT!**
Harrods is the UK's biggest department store, with 5,000 staff from 50 countries.

**1a** Work in pairs and look at the photos of three famous department stores: Harrods, Macy's and Shinsegae. Do you know where they are?

**b** Read about the Shinsegae department store in South Korea. Why is it famous?

**2** Read the article again. What do these numbers refer to?

**a** 190,000   **b** 300,000   **c** 95,000   **d** 14

**3** Work in pairs and discuss.

- Would you like to go shopping in Shinsegae ? Why / Why not?
- Do you prefer shopping in small shops or large department stores? Why?
- Do you have a department store in your town? Do you like it? Why / Why not?

### GRAMMAR

**1** Complete the superlative sentences using the adjectives *big* and *expensive*.
1 Shinsegae in Busan is the _____ department store in the world.
2 All the _____ brands are on the ground floor.

**2** Write the superlative adjectives.
1 big → bigger → *the biggest*
2 new → newer → _____
3 busy → busier → _____
4 beautiful → more beautiful → _____
5 good → better → _____

**3** Read the article again and check your answers.

### Shinsegae: A huge shopping experience

Shinsegae in Busan, South Korea is the biggest (and some people say, the best) department store in the world. Thousands of visitors come every day – making it one of the busiest shops in the world. On the opening day in March 2009, 190,000 shoppers spent over $6 million.

*Shinsegae* means 'new world' in Korean – and the store is one of the newest and most impressive buildings in Busan, with nearly 300,000 m² of shopping space. This means that Shinsegae is bigger than Macy's, the famous store in New York City, by over 95,000 m².

Let's start at the ground floor: here are all the most expensive brands, like Prada and Louis Vuitton. Then, going up the 14 floors of this huge world, you find not only shops and restaurants but also a gym, a cinema, an art gallery and even an ice rink. And right at the top there are restaurants where you can see some of the most beautiful views of Busan.

## PRACTICE

**1a** Complete the questions in the quiz with superlative adjectives.

**b** 🎧 9.2 Listen and check.

**2a** Work in pairs and do the quiz.

**b** 🎧 9.3 Listen and check.

**3a** Write five questions with superlative adjectives using some of the ideas below.

- busy shopping street in your town
- old person in your family
- good restaurant in your town
- untidy person you know
- beautiful place in your country
- tall person in your class
- popular singer from your country
- new thing in your bag

*Which is the busiest shopping street in your town?*

**b** Work in groups and take turns. Ask and answer your questions.

> What is the newest thing in your bag?
>
> My phone is the newest thing. I bought it last week.

**Unit 9, Study & Practice 2, page 154**

# The biggest and the best!

**1** How much does _____ (expensive) handbag in the world cost?
a $3,800          b $380,000          c $3,800,000

**2** The _____ (fast) car in the world goes from 0 to 60 miles per hour in how many seconds?
a 2.4 seconds      b 4.2 seconds      c 6.4 seconds

**3** How old is Hamleys, _____ (famous) toy shop in the world?
a 50 years old     b 100 years old    c 250 years old

**4** Who were _____ (popular) pop group of the 20th century?
a The Beatles      b the Rolling Stones   c the Eagles

**5** Who is _____ (rich) person in the world?
a Bill Gates, founder   b Carlos Slim Helú,    c the Sultan
  of Microsoft            Mexican businessman     of Brunei

**6** Which is _____ (high) capital city in the world?
a La Paz, Bolivia   b Addis Ababa,      c Thimphu,
                      Ethiopia             Bhutan

**7** Where is _____ (tall) hotel in the world?
a Bangkok          b Dubai             c Hong Kong

**8** How many passengers does _____ (big) cruise ship in the world carry?
a 2,000            b 4,000             c 6,000

# Vocabulary
## Shops and services

**1a** Match the words in the box with photos A–L.

| | | |
|---|---|---|
| a clothes shop | a pharmacy | a gift shop |
| a butcher's | a shoe shop | a bookshop |
| a baker's | a hairdresser's | a post office |
| a dry-cleaner's | an estate agent's | an optician's |

**b** Work in pairs and answer the questions.

Where do you:
1 go to post letters and parcels?
2 buy sausages and other meat?
3 buy bread and cakes?
4 rent a flat or house?
5 get a present for a friend?
6 have a haircut?
7 buy shoes and boots?
8 buy jeans, jackets and T-shirts?
9 buy books?
10 get glasses and sunglasses?
11 buy toothpaste and medicine?
12 take your clothes when they're dirty?

**2** Work in pairs and take turns. Ask and answer questions about the last time you visited one of the places in exercise 1a.

When did you last go to a gift shop?

I went last Saturday.

What did you buy?

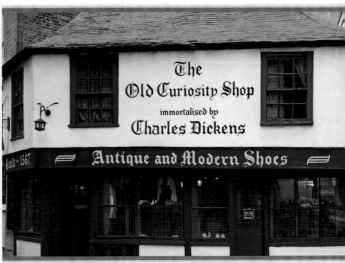

# Top five unusual shops

**Are you looking for a present for someone? Or do you want to buy something for yourself? Or perhaps you just want to enjoy the shopping experience ... in the most interesting and unusual shops in the world. Here are our top five!**

**1** If you're looking for something perfect, come to Senbikiya in Tokyo, Japan! Senbikiya is an elegant shop with beautiful things to buy. But you don't buy designer clothes and handbags here. You buy fruit – perfect and very expensive fruit. There are beautiful apples for $25 each, and 12 perfect strawberries cost $82 a box. Yes, it's expensive ... but it's very popular.

**2** Or maybe you're looking for something old ... something other people don't want any more? Then Beacon's Closet in New York, USA is the place for you. This is a clothes shop with a difference – an 'exchange' store where people bring clothes they don't want and other people buy them. The clothes are good quality – and cheap! We found a party dress for $20 and a designer coat for $60.

**3** Sometimes the building is what makes your shopping experience special; for example, The Old Curiosity Shop in London, England. It is a tiny old shop which Charles Dickens wrote about in 1841. There are lots of big modern buildings around it now, but the shop keeps its old, historical style inside. Nearly 450 years after the shop first opened, it is now a shoe shop with unusual designer shoes.

**4** From a tiny building to a huge one: the famous bookshop El Ateneo Grand Splendid in Buenos Aires, Argentina. The shop covers an area of 2,000 m² – and every year it has around a million visitors. In 1919, the building opened as a theatre, but in February 2000, it became one of the biggest – and most beautiful – bookshops in the world, keeping many of the features of the old theatre.

**5** Perhaps you want everything: the amazing building and the cool products ... then come to L'Usine in Ho Chi Minh City, Vietnam. The building is an old clothes factory with big windows and ceiling fans. Inside, there is a café, an art gallery and many interesting things to buy: designer clothes, a vintage bicycle, a colourful watch ... We think this is the coolest shop in the world!

## Reading

**1a** Work in pairs and discuss.

- What is the biggest shop you know?
- What is the smallest shop you know?
- What is your favourite shop? Why?

**b** Read the article and answer the questions.

Which shop:
- is the biggest?
- is the smallest?
- is the coolest place to be?
- has the most perfect products?
- has the cheapest designer clothes?

**2** Read the article again. Are the statements true (T) or false (F)?

1 In Senbikiya, you can buy clothes as well as fruit.
2 In Senbikiya, strawberries cost $25 each.
3 The clothes in Beacon's Closet are second-hand.
4 The Old Curiosity Shop first opened in 1841.
5 The Old Curiosity Shop is now modern inside.
6 Around 1,000,000 people go to El Ateneo Grand Splendid every year.
7 El Ateneo Grand Splendid is in an old factory building.
8 L'Usine is in an old theatre building.

**3** Work in pairs and discuss.

- Which of the shops in the article would you most like to visit? Why?
- Do you like shopping? Why / Why not?
- How often do you go shopping for clothes and shoes? Where do you usually go?
- What is your favourite shop in your town? Why?

# Task

## Choose souvenirs from your country

### Preparation Listening

1   Work in pairs. Look at the photos and discuss.

- What souvenirs can you see in photos A–E?
- Which country do you think each souvenir comes from: Canada, Ukraine, Egypt, Scotland or Thailand?
- When did you last buy a souvenir? What was it? Where did you buy it? Who was it for?

### The Taylor family

Bob and Amy Taylor and their two children (Josh, aged 11, and Lorna, aged 8) are from the UK. They often have visitors from different countries staying in their house. They love meeting people from different countries and they love collecting souvenirs from all over the world.

2   Read the information about the Taylor family. Where are they from? What do they like doing?

3a   🎧 9.4 Four people are going to stay with the Taylor family in the UK. Listen to them talking about which souvenirs from their countries they are going to buy for the family.

|        | Where does he/she live? | What souvenirs does he/she choose? | How does he/she describe the souvenir? |
|--------|-------------------------|-------------------------------------|-----------------------------------------|
| Tina   |                         |                                     |                                         |
| Lee    |                         |                                     |                                         |
| Karim  | Egypt                   |                                     |                                         |
| Oksana |                         |                                     |                                         |

b   Listen again and complete the table.

c   Listen again and tick the phrases you hear in the Useful language box.

# Task Speaking

1 Think of a souvenir from your country for each person in the Taylor family. Use some or all of the ideas below. Ask your teacher for any words/phrases you need.

- something to eat or drink
- a doll or figure of a famous person
- an item of clothing
- a model of a famous building or place
- an ornament or something useful for the house
- a music CD or DVD

2 Work in pairs. If you and your partner are from the same country, decide on the best souvenir from your country for each person in the Taylor family. If you are from different countries, tell your partner about the best souvenir from your country for each person in the family.

> Useful language a and b

3 Tell other students about the souvenirs you chose.

## USEFUL LANGUAGE

**a Asking for ideas**
What do you think?
Why don't we buy a (silk shirt)?
Have you got any ideas for (the children)?
Do you think we should choose a scarf?
How about (some jewellery)?
Everybody loves (silk) from (Thailand).
What did you choose for (the little girl / her)?

**b Giving ideas and explaining your choice**
(Thailand) is famous for (silk products) ... so ...
I think a good souvenir from (Thailand) is (a silk shirt).
(A silk shirt) is a fantastic souvenir.
What's a good souvenir from your country?
That's very typical of (Thailand).
I think jewellery is better, because ...
(Matryoshka dolls) are very typical of (Ukraine).
It's small and easy to carry.
I think it's a very nice souvenir for (a child).

B

C

E

## SHARE YOUR TASK

Practise talking about the souvenirs you chose.

Film/Record yourself talking about the souvenirs you chose.

Share your film/recording with other students.

# WORLD CULTURE

# FAMOUS MARKETS

## Find out first

**1a** Work in pairs and discuss. Which of these things do you often/ sometimes/never do?

- buy and sell things on eBay
- go to department stores
- go to second-hand shops

**b** Try to answer the questions in the quiz below.

### Shopping around the world

1   Millions of people buy and sell on eBay. Where was its founder, Pierre Omidyar, born?
2   Galeries Lafayette, Harrods, and Macy's are world-famous department stores. Where can you find them?
3   Walmart is the world's biggest supermarket chain. How did the company get its name?
4   What is the connection between buying books online and a river in South America?
5   *Bazaar* and *souk* are types of what? Where can you find them?

**c** Go online to check your answers or ask your teacher.

Search: Pierre Omidyar / Harrods / Galeries Lafayette / Macy's / Walmart history / buy books / bazaar / souk

## View

**2** You are going to watch a video about famous London markets. Before you watch, check you understand the meaning of the words/phrases in the glossary.

GLOSSARY
*antiques*       old pieces of furniture, jewellery, etc.
*second-hand*    not new
*stalls*         small shops in a market

**3** ▶ Read phrases 1–9 below. Then watch the video and match each phrase to a market in the box.

| | |
|---|---|
| Borough Market | Brick Lane Market |
| Camden Market | Portobello Market |

1   Get there early – the market is very busy!
2   … next to London Bridge station on the South Bank of the River Thames.
3   … perfect for 'foodies' – people who love eating!
4   It's full of colour and unusual fashion ideas.
5   … people come here to buy clothes, arts and crafts – everything really!
6   … in the East End of London.
7   … next to a canal near the centre of the city.
8   … a famous market in Notting Hill, West London.
9   … this is the place where Asia meets London.

**4a** Watch again and answer the questions. What time does each market open? What does each market sell?

**b** Which market(s) would you like to visit? Why?

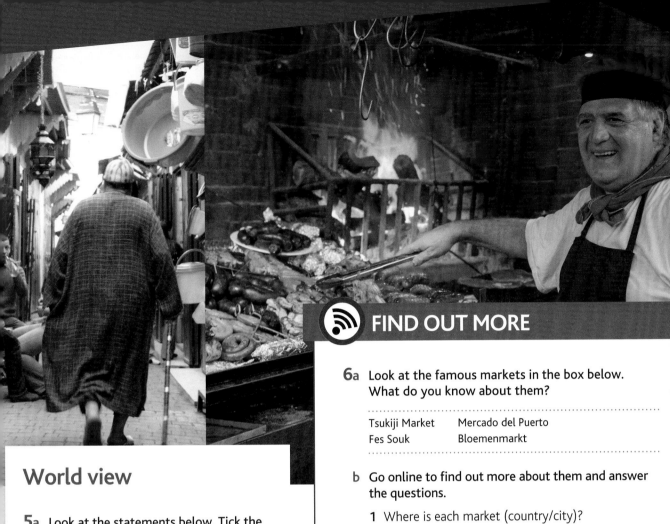

# World view

## 5a Look at the statements below. Tick the ones that are true for you.

- ❝ I often go to markets at the weekend.
- ❝ You can buy things cheaper in a market than in a shop in my country.
- ❝ I never buy clothes at markets.
- ❝ I like buying food at markets.
- ❝ I hate shopping – I buy everything online.
- ❝ We have a very famous market in my town.

**b** Work in pairs and compare your answers.

## FIND OUT MORE

**6a** Look at the famous markets in the box below. What do you know about them?

Tsukiji Market    Mercado del Puerto
Fes Souk       Bloemenmarkt

**b** Go online to find out more about them and answer the questions.

1 Where is each market (country/city)?
2 What can you buy there?

Search: Tsukiji Market / Mercado del Puerto / Fes Souk / Bloemenmarkt

## ▶ Write up your research

**7** Write a paragraph about one of the markets you researched. Use the prompts below to help you.

The _____ (name of market) is a famous market in _____ (town/country).

People come here to buy _____ and _____ (clothes, food, antiques, etc.).

It's open _____ (days of the week, time of the day).

I would/wouldn't like to go there because _____ .

# 10

# LOOK GOOD

## IN THIS UNIT

- Grammar: Present continuous; Present simple or continuous?
- Vocabulary: Clothes; Describing personality
- Task: Analyse your personality
- Language live: Asking for goods and services; Describing people

## Vocabulary
### Clothes

1a Match the items of clothing in the box with pictures A–M.

| | | | | |
|---|---|---|---|---|
| a suit | a tie | trousers | jeans | a baseball cap |
| sunglasses | a skirt | trainers | a jumper | a dress |
| a jacket | shorts | a shirt | | |

b Can you add three more items of clothing to the box?

c Which of the items of clothing in the box are usually worn by (a) men (b) women (c) men and women?

### PRONUNCIATION

1 🎧 10.1 Listen to the pronunciation of the words in exercise 1a.

2 Practise saying the words.

# Grammar focus 1
## Present continuous

**1** Read the sentences and look at the picture. Use the information to label each person in the picture.

1 Tom and Val are sitting on the grass.
2 Val is sending a text message.
3 Tom is wearing a blue shirt.
4 Mel and Kim are having lunch.
5 Mel is wearing jeans.
6 Kim is eating a sandwich.
7 Denzil is wearing a tie.
8 Pippa is looking at her watch.
9 Frank is listening to music.

### GRAMMAR

1 We use the Present continuous for actions happening now or around now. Complete the gaps below.

| | | |
|---|---|---|
| + | I'm<br>He/She _____<br>You/We/They're | reading a newspaper. |
| − | I'm not<br>He/She _____<br>You/We/They aren't | wearing a tie. |
| ? | What am I<br>_____ he/she<br>What are you/we/they | doing? |

## PRACTICE

**1a** Look at the picture again for two minutes.

**b** Turn to page 136 and answer as many questions as you can. Don't look at the picture.

**2a** Make true sentences for you.

I (sit) near the door.
*I'm not sitting near the door. I'm sitting near the window.*

1 I (wear) jeans today.
2 We (listen) to music at the moment.
3 I (work) alone on this exercise.
4 The sun (shine) today.
5 The teacher (write) on the board.
6 I (hold) my pen in my left hand.

**b** Work in pairs and compare your sentences.

**3a** Write five more sentences to describe what other people in the class are/aren't wearing or doing.

**b** Compare your sentences with other students.

Unit 10, Study & Practice 1, page 156

# Listening
## Clothes at work

**1** **Work in pairs and discuss.**

- Do you wear a uniform at school or work? If so, what do you think about it? If not, would you like to wear a uniform?
- Who wears a uniform in your country? Which uniforms do you like best? Why?

**2a** **What do you think these four people wear at work?**

- Katie, female, aged 22, shop assistant
- Marlon, male, aged 29, personal trainer
- Louisa, female, aged 37, company director
- Sam, male, aged 34, IT manager

**b** 🎧 **10.2 Listen to Katie, Marlon, Louisa and Sam talking about what they wear at work. Write K (Katie), M (Marlon), L (Louisa) or S (Sam) next to the items in the box.**

| | | |
|---|---|---|
| a uniform | trainers | tracksuit trousers |
| earrings | a tie | a skirt suit |
| a dress | a sports shirt | shorts |
| trousers | a jacket | jewellery |
| a shirt | | |

**c** **Listen again. Are these statements true (T) or false (F)?**

1 Katie wears a uniform at work.
2 She likes the clothes she wears to work.
3 Marlon likes the look of sports clothes.
4 He pays for all his work clothes.
5 Louisa wants to look confident and reliable in her work clothes.
6 She loves the clothes she wears to work.
7 Sam always wears smart clothes at work.
8 He usually wears a dark coloured tie.

**3** **Work in pairs and discuss.**

- What clothes do you usually wear at work? Why?
- Do you think the clothes people wear at work are important? Give examples of different jobs.

IT'S A FACT!
On average, women in the USA own 19 pairs of shoes and men own seven pairs.

# Grammar focus 2
## Present simple or continuous?

**1a** **Work in pairs. Look at the photos of Katie, Marlon, Louisa and Sam at a fancy-dress party and discuss.**

- What are Katie, Marlon, Louisa and Sam wearing to the party?
- What do you think is the 'theme' of the party?

**b** **Read the text below and check your ideas.**

It's Saturday evening. Normally, when Katie is at work, she wears cool, stylish clothes. Tonight, she looks like a Spanish dancer – she's wearing a red dress and black shoes. She's also got a flower in her hair. Marlon usually wears sports clothes, but this evening he is Sherlock Holmes. He's wearing a suit and the famous Sherlock Holmes hat! Louisa usually wears a smart suit at work, but tonight she looks very different. She is wearing a long white dress and looks like the Statue of Liberty. When Sam is at work, he wears a shirt and tie and he always looks smart. This evening, he's wearing a spaceman costume and is completely covered from head to toe! Why are they all wearing these clothes? They are going to a fancy-dress party to celebrate their friend Susi's birthday. Susi wants everyone to come to the party dressed as someone or something beginning with the letter 'S'.

**2** **Work in pairs and discuss.**

- Which party costume do you like best?
- What costume would you choose for a fancy-dress party beginning with the letter 'S'?

**2a** Complete the text with the Present simple or Present continuous form of the verb in brackets.

I usually ¹_____ (go) to work in an office, but on Fridays, I ²_____ (work) at home. When I go to the office, I ³_____ (wear) a smart suit and earrings. Today, I ⁴_____ (work) at home so I ⁵_____ (wear) very casual clothes – tracksuit and trainers. I ⁶_____ (not wear) any jewellery today.

At my sister's college, people usually ⁷_____ (wear) casual clothes. They normally ⁸_____ (wear) jeans and maybe a shirt or jumper. The teacher ⁹_____ (not wear) a suit – he usually wears jeans, too. Today it's really hot, so my sister ¹⁰_____ (wear) shorts and a T-shirt.

**b** 🎧 **10.3** Listen and check.

**3** Work in groups. Tell other students what you normally wear at school/work and what you wear at the weekend. Tell them what you are wearing at the moment.

> **Unit 10, Study & Practice 2, page 156**

## GRAMMAR

### Present simple

1 Look at the sentence below. Choose the correct answer.

Louisa usually <u>wears</u> a smart suit at work.

This is *generally true* / *happening now*.

2 We use these words/phrases with the Present simple.

usually   always   often   normally   every day

### Present continuous

3 Look at the sentence below. Choose the correct answer.

Tonight she<u>'s wearing</u> a long white dress.

This is *generally true* / *happening now*.

4 We use these words/phrases with the Present continuous.

now   today   at the moment

## Vocabulary
### Describing personality

**1** Look at the adjectives describing personality in the box below. Which do you think are positive? Which are negative?

| reliable | confident | friendly | sociable | shy |
|---|---|---|---|---|
| cheerful | moody | bossy | determined | kind |
| organised | easy-going | hard-working | | |

**2a** Choose three adjectives from the box in exercise 1 which you think describe:

- your personality.
- a teacher.
- a businessperson.
- a nurse.
- a shop assistant.

**b** Work in pairs and compare your ideas.

**3** Work in pairs and take turns. Imagine you are one of the people below and describe your appearance and personality.

- a good friend
- someone in your family
- someone you work or study with
- someone who lives near you

## PRACTICE

**1a** Choose the correct tense.

1 *Do you usually wear* / *Are you usually wearing* smart or casual clothes to work or college?
2 What kind of clothes *do you wear* / *are you wearing* today?
3 *Do you wear* / *Are you wearing* boots, trainers, sandals or shoes today?
4 What kind of shoes *do you normally wear* / *are you normally wearing*?
5 *Do you ever wear* / *Are you ever wearing* glasses?
6 *Do you wear* / *Are you wearing* glasses now?
7 *Do you wear* / *Are you wearing* jewellery today?
8 What kind of jewellery *do you usually wear* / *are you usually wearing*?
9 *Do you wear* / *Are you wearing* a hat at the moment?
10 How often *do you wear* / *are you wearing* a hat?

**b** Work in pairs and take turns. Ask and answer the questions.

# Task

## Analyse your personality

### What do **colours** say about you?

The colours that we choose in our lives can tell us about our personality. Your favourite colour is often your 'personality' colour. It's the colour that shows your basic character and your strengths. It isn't always the colour you wear all the time – it's the colour you like most.

Let's take a look at each colour. If you like red, you are a confident person who likes a lot of action in your life. Orange means you are a sociable person – you like being in group situations. People who like yellow are usually cheerful – they are often organised, too. If you wear a lot of green, you are probably a kind person who is also quite shy at times. Maybe you like blue – then you are probably an easy-going person; someone who likes a calm, peaceful life. Purple shows that you are reliable and hard-working. People who like black are usually reliable, too – but sometimes they can be bossy. Brown clothes show that you are a kind, friendly person who cares a lot about family and friends. People who wear a lot of white are usually very determined people who like doing things on their own.

Your least favourite colour is also important. It can show what kind of person you would like to be. For example, if you don't like red, then you would probably like to be more confident. If your least favourite colour is orange, maybe you would like to be more sociable. So take a look at the colours you're wearing and see what they say about you!

### Preparation Reading and listening

**1a** Work in pairs and write a list of all the colours you can think of.

**b** Compare your list with other students and add two more colours to your list.

**c** Work in pairs and discuss.

- Which colours do you like best?
- Which do you like least?

**2** Read the article and choose the correct answers.

1 Your 'personality' colour is:
   a the colour you're wearing now.
   b your favourite colour.
2 Your least favourite colour:
   a doesn't show much about your personality.
   b shows an aspect of your personality you would like to improve.

**3a** 🎧 10.4 Listen to two students talking about the information in the article. Answer the questions.

1 Which colours do they talk about?
2 Do they think the information about personality is correct?

**b** Listen again and tick the phrases you hear in the Useful language box.

**a Asking questions**

What's your (least) favourite colour?
What colours are you wearing now?
Do you think that's right?
What does that say about me?

**b Explaining and interpreting information**

(Red) clothes mean you are a confident person.
You like wearing (black), so you're (reliable).
You're probably a (determined) person because
    you like wearing (white).

**c Reacting to information**

I think that's absolutely right!
Yes, I'm a (very reliable) person.
I don't think that's right.
No, I'm not very (confident). In fact, I think I'm
    quite (shy).

# Task Speaking

1   Work in pairs and take turns. Find out more about your
    partner's personality using the information in the article.
    Start by asking, 'What is your favourite colour?' Look at the
    Useful language box and ask your teacher for any words/
    phrases you need.

> Useful language a–c

2a  Work in groups. Tell other students about your personality
    or your partner's personality.

b   Discuss the questions.

    • How true was the information about your personality
      and your partner's personality?
    • Do you think this is a good way of analysing someone's
      personality?

# LANGUAGE LIVE

How Much?

## Speaking
### Asking for goods and services

**1** Work in pairs. How many shops can you think of in one minute?

**2** Put the words/phrases in the box into the categories below.

| | | |
|---|---|---|
| an appointment | a haircut | hairspray |
| it suits you | a larger size | too big |
| too small | try it on | wash |
| not too short | How would you like | gel |

- at a hairdresser's
- in a clothes shop

**3a** ▶ Watch the video. Number the words/phrases in exercise 2 in the order you hear them.

**b** Watch again and answer the questions.

**At a hairdresser's**
1 Does the young man have an appointment?
2 How does he want his hair cut?
3 How much does the haircut cost?
4 Why is the young man unhappy?

**In a clothes shop**
5 How many jackets does the man try on?
6 Do the two women like the first jacket?
7 What is the problem with the second jacket and the third jacket?
8 Which jacket does the young man decide to buy in the end?

**4a** Complete the phrases.

**At a hairdresser's**
1 I'd _____ a haircut, please.
2 Do you have an _____ ?
3 How would you like your _____ cut?
4 Not _____ short, but not _____ long.
5 Do you want a _____ ?
6 No, thanks. Just a _____ .
7 _____ that? Do you like it?
8 _____ do I owe you?

**In a clothes shop**
1 What do you _____ ?
2 The colour's OK, but it's _____ small.
3 Have you got this in a larger _____ ?
4 Try it _____ .
5 It's no good. It's _____ big.
6 I like that. It _____ you.
7 We'll _____ this one.
8 How would you like _____ ?

**b** ▶ Watch and listen to the key phrases and check your answers.

**5a** Work in pairs. Prepare your own conversation at a hairdresser's or in a clothes shop. Use as many of the key phrases in exercise 4a as possible.

**b** Practise your conversation.

# Writing
## Describing people

**1** Look at the photos below and answer the questions.

Who:
1 has got grey hair?
2 has got blue eyes?
3 is slim?
4 is wearing a white T-shirt?
5 is in his forties?
6 has got curly hair?
7 is reading a newspaper?
8 is wearing casual clothes?
9 is wearing smart clothes?
10 has got long straight hair?
11 has got a pony tail?
12 is wearing a leather jacket?

**2** Complete the table below with the words/phrases in the box.

| in his early twenties | short hair |
| reading a newspaper | blonde hair |
| carrying a bag | standing up |
| in her teens | good-looking |
| medium-length hair | sitting down |
| holding a book | wearing lipstick |
| a nice person in her late thirties | |

| He/She is ... | He/She has got ... |
| --- | --- |
| in his early twenties | |

**3** Read the description below. Which person in the photos do you think it is?

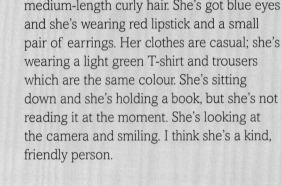

This person is good-looking. She's probably in her late thirties. She's slim and she's got medium-length curly hair. She's got blue eyes and she's wearing red lipstick and a small pair of earrings. Her clothes are casual; she's wearing a light green T-shirt and trousers which are the same colour. She's sitting down and she's holding a book, but she's not reading it at the moment. She's looking at the camera and smiling. I think she's a kind, friendly person.

**4** Write a description of one of the other people in the photos or someone in your class. Include information about:

- general impression / age.
- hair, eyes, etc.
- clothes.
- what he/she is doing at the moment.
- his/her personality.

Martha

Kamilla

Paolo

Pedro

**AFTER UNIT 10 YOU CAN ...**

Talk about present activities.

Describe people's clothes, appearance and personality.

Ask for goods and services (e.g. in shops and at the hairdresser's).

Write a description of a person.

95

# 11

# NATURE

## IN THIS UNIT

- **Grammar:** Question words;
  Quantifiers: *a lot of, a little, a few,
  not any, not much, not many*
- **Vocabulary:** Animals and natural
  features; Big numbers
- **Task:** Devise a general knowledge
  quiz
- **World culture:** Animals in danger

**IT'S A FACT!**
Dogs can't see
colours. At traffic
lights, guide dogs look
at the traffic – not
the lights.

## Vocabulary
### Animals and natural features

**1a** Work in pairs and look at the photos. Which of the things in the
box can you see?

| | | | | | |
|---|---|---|---|---|---|
| dog | camel | mountain | horse | donkey | desert |
| llama | beach | ocean | elephant | volcano | fish |
| chimpanzee | snake | forest | rat | lake | valley |
| dolphin | sea | river | whale | | |

**b** Put the words in the box into the categories below.

- animals
- natural features

**c** Add more words to each category.

**2** Work in pairs and discuss.

- Which animals in exercise 1a are common in your country?
- Which natural features in exercise 1a do you have in your
  country? Do you ever visit any of them?

# WORKING ANIMALS

There are countless animals that help us in our everyday lives. From dogs to elephants, fish to llamas, we use animals in so many different ways.

**People use animals to carry people or heavy loads – sometimes for long distances, across mountains and deserts.**

- In many countries, this is often the job of horses and donkeys.
- In South America, they often use llamas; and in North Africa, camels. Camels can carry up to 450 kg (that's the weight of an average cow!) and walk up to 65 km a day.
- In South-East Asia, people use elephants not only to carry things but also to pull trees in the forests. Elephants are extremely strong and can pull up to 1,500 kg (that's the weight of a medium-sized car!).

**Dogs are very popular as pets, but they also have a huge number of uses.**

- Dogs can help people with different disabilities. There are guide dogs to help people who can't see (e.g. to cross a road) and hearing dogs to help people who can't hear (e.g. to hear the doorbell).
- Dogs are useful in rescue situations, too. They can look for people lost under snow or collapsed buildings.
- Farmers use dogs to keep their sheep and cows under control. The police use dogs to help catch criminals.
- Sniffer dogs do another important job – using their sense of smell to help find drugs and other illegal things at airports.

**People also use animals for more surprising things.**

- 'Reading' dogs listen to children read, giving those children more confidence.
- You can relax with 'fish therapy', as the fish eat dead skin off your feet.
- In some countries, people train rats to help detect dangerous explosives on land.
- People use dolphins in a similar way to detect dangerous explosives in the sea.

# Reading

**1a** Work in pairs. Look again at the photos. What kind of work do you think these animals do?

**b** Read the article. Which animals from Vocabulary exercise 1a are mentioned?

**2** Read the article again and answer the questions.

Which animal can:
1 help people cross a road?
2 improve the skin on your feet?
3 find illegal items like drugs?
4 carry heavy loads in South America?
5 look for missing people?
6 help children learn to read?
7 look for dangerous items at sea?
8 transport trees in South-East Asia?

**3** Work in pairs and discuss.

- Which of the working animals in the article are you surprised about?
- Do you know about any other working animals? What do they do?

# Listening
## Intelligent animals

**1** Work in pairs and discuss.

- What experience of pets do you have?
- What experience of wild animals do you have?
- Which of the animals in the photos do you think is the most intelligent? In what way?

**2a**  **11.1** Listen to a radio programme about intelligent animals. Number the animals in the order you hear them.

- dogs
- parrots
- whales
- dolphins
- chimpanzees

**b** Listen again. Which things can each animal do?

- speak to each other
- speak like humans
- paint pictures
- use computers
- remember names
- remember numbers

**3** Work in pairs and answer the questions.

**1** Which animal on the radio programme impressed you the most? Why?

**2** How good are you at remembering:

- names of people you meet?
- friends' birthdays?
- phone numbers?
- PIN numbers (for bank cards, etc.)?

# Vocabulary
## Big numbers

**1** Match the numbers in A with how you say them in B.

| A | | B | |
|---|------|---|------|
| 1 | 50 | a | five thousand |
| 2 | 500 | b | five billion |
| 3 | 505 | c | five hundred |
| 4 | 5,000 | d | five million |
| 5 | 50,000 | e | five point five |
| 6 | 500,000 | f | five hundred thousand |
| 7 | 5,000,000 | g | fifty thousand |
| 8 | 5,000,000,000 | h | fifty |
| 9 | 5.5 | i | five hundred and five |

**2** **11.2** Listen and write down the nine numbers you hear.

---

### PRONUNCIATION

**1** Listen again to the numbers and notice the pronunciation.

**2** Practise saying them.

**3a** Look at sentences 1–9. Try to guess the number that belongs in each gap.

1 The approximate number of active volcanoes in the world is _____ .

2 The country with the largest number of active volcanoes is Indonesia, with over _____ .

3 The approximate top speed of a killer whale is nearly _____ kilometres per hour.

4 The average distance that killer whales swim every year is _____ kilometres.

5 The height of some giant redwood trees in California is over _____ metres.

6 Camels can survive without water in temperatures of 50°C for approximately _____ hours.

7 The average weight of a male African elephant is _____ kilograms.

8 The approximate rat population of New York City is _____ .

9 Damascus in Syria is perhaps the world's oldest city – it is _____ years old.

b 🎧 11.3 Listen and check.

# Grammar focus 1
## Question words

1 Choose the correct question words.

1 *How many / How much* active volcanoes are there in the world?

2 *Which / How many* country has got the largest number of active volcanoes?

3 *How far / How tall* are some of the giant redwood trees in California?

4 *What / How fast* can killer whales swim?

5 *How far / How old* do killer whales swim every year on average?

6 *How much / How long* can camels survive without water in temperatures of 50°C?

7 *How much / How many* does a male African elephant weigh on average?

8 *What / Which* is the approximate rat population of New York City?

9 *How much / How old* is the city of Damascus?

## GRAMMAR

### Question words with two words (*how* + another word)

1 Match the question words in A with the answers in B.

| A | B |
|---|---|
| 1 **How far** (e.g. New York to Los Angeles) | a five |
| 2 **How fast** (e.g. top speed of this car) | b 65 kg |
| 3 **How long** (e.g. this TV programme) | c 80 kph |
| 4 **How many** (e.g. my family members) | d 1 m 65 cm |
| 5 **How much** (e.g. your weight) | e 25 years |
| 6 **How old** (e.g. your brother) | f 3,900 km |
| 7 **How tall** (e.g. you) | g about an hour |

### *what* and *which*

2 We use *what* when there are many possible answers.

*What is the approximate rat population of New York City?*

3 We use *which* when there are a limited number of possible answers.

*Which country has got the largest number of active volcanoes?*

2 Work in pairs and take turns. Ask and answer the questions in exercise 1 without looking at Vocabulary exercise 3a. How many answers can you remember?

**3a** Make questions using words/phrases from columns A and B. You can also use words/phrases from columns C and D, if necessary.

*How old are you?*

*How far do you walk every week?*

| A | B | C | D |
|---|---|---|---|
| How old | are you | like | every day |
| How tall | do you | swim | every night |
| How fast | can you | study | every week |
| How far | | run | |
| How long | | walk | |
| How much water | | speak | |
| How many languages | | play | |
| What kind of food | | drink | |
| Which sports | | sleep | |

b Work in pairs and take turns. Ask and answer your questions.

> How far do you walk every week?

> I walk about ten kilometres every week.

Unit 11, Study & Practice 1, page 158

## Listening
### South Africa

**1** Work in pairs. Look at the photos and discuss. How much do you know about the Republic of South Africa? Think about the topics below.

- famous places
- wildlife (animals and plants)
- weather
- natural features (mountains, volcanoes, etc.)

**2a** 🎧 11.4 Aletta works for the South African Tourist Board. Listen to her talking about places to visit. Tick the topics you hear in exercise 1.

**b** Listen again and choose the correct answers.

**1** How many species of plant can you find on Table Mountain?
  **a** 150 **b** 1,000 **c** 2,200
**2** How high are the Tugela Falls?
  **a** 800 m **b** 850 m **c** 950 m
**3** How many species of animal can you find in the Kruger National Park?
  **a** 50–100 **b** 100–150 **c** 150–200
**4** How fast can a cheetah run?
  **a** 60 kph **b** 80 kph **c** 100 kph
**5** How many years old is the Salpeterkop volcano?
  **a** 66 million **b** 60 million **c** 6 million

**3** Work in pairs and discuss.

- Would you like to visit South Africa? Why / Why not?
- What do you think is most interesting about South Africa?
- What is similar to and different from your country?

## Grammar focus 2
### Quantifiers: *a lot of, a little, a few, not any, not much, not many*

**1a** Choose the correct answers.

**1** There **isn't / aren't** many countries in the world where you can see all these amazing things.
**2** If you only **has / have** a little time, here are four places you really must visit!
**3** Table Mountain **has / have** a lot of different varieties of plants.
**4** There **isn't / aren't** much chance of winning that race!
**5** There **isn't / aren't** any active volcanoes in South Africa.
**6** There **is / are** a few volcanoes; for example, the Salpeterkop volcano.

**b** Look at audio script 11.4 on page 173 and check your answers.

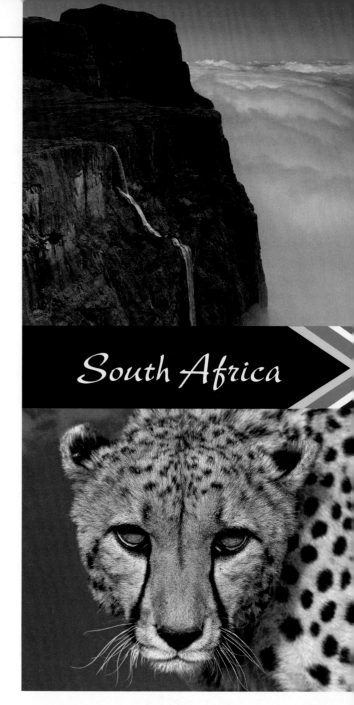

South Africa

### GRAMMAR

**1** Complete the table with the underlined phrases in audio script 11.4 on page 173. You can use the same phrase more than once.

| | with countable nouns (and plural verb) | with uncountable nouns (and singular verb) |
|---|---|---|
| Large quantity/ number | 1 a lot of | 2 _____ |
| Small quantity/ number | 3 _____<br>4 _____ | 5 _____<br>6 _____ |
| Zero quantity/ number | 7 _____ | 8 not any |

## PRACTICE

**1** Choose the correct answers.

The Kalahari Desert is a huge desert area in Botswana, Namibia and South Africa. Its name comes from the word *kgala*, which means 'place where there isn't ¹*a few / any / many* rain'. In fact, ²*a little / a few / not many* rain falls there. There is only about 76–190 mm a year, which isn't ³*much / many / any* rain. But even so, you can see ⁴*a few / a lot of / any* wildlife: there are ⁵*a lot of / a little / not much* types of tree – such as acacia trees – and the spring rain brings flamingos to the region.

There aren't ⁶*many / a few / a little* people living there, but you can still see ⁷*a few / a little / any* Bushmen. The Bushmen, or San, have lived in the area for thousands of years. Because there is only ⁸*a few / a little / a lot of* water, they get most of their liquids from gathering plants and desert fruits.

**2a** Use the ideas below to make true sentences about your country.

| In _____ (name of country) | there is there are | a lot of a little a few not any not much not many | snow rain deserts lakes dangerous wildlife high mountains active volcanoes |
|---|---|---|---|

*In Brazil, there isn't much snow. There is a little snow in the winter on the high mountains in the south.*

**b** Work in pairs and compare your sentences.

Unit 11, Study & Practice 2, page 158

# Task

## Devise a general knowledge quiz

### WHO, WHAT, WHERE, WHEN?

1 Where is the River Ganges?
2 Who became President of Russia
  on 26th March 2000?
3 How many kilometres are there in one mile?
4 How far is it from the Earth to the sun?
5 When did Spain win the World Cup?
6 What is the capital city of Peru?
7 Who sang the hit song *Crazy in Love* in 2003?
8 Which volcano destroyed the city of Pompeii
  in the year AD 79?
9 What sport do people play at Wimbledon,
  England?
10 What is the name of Bart Simpson's father
  in the TV series *The Simpsons*?

Arts

History

Sport

## Preparation Reading and listening

1a Work in pairs. Look at the photos and the five
   categories for a quiz. Discuss the questions.

   • Which is your favourite category in a quiz? Why?
   • Which is your least favourite? Why?

b Look at the quiz 'Who, What, Where, When?' and
  divide the questions into the five categories.

2 Work in pairs and look at the quiz. Match the
  questions to the answers in the box below.

| | | | |
|---|---|---|---|
| Beyoncé | India | tennis | 150 million km |
| Vladimir Putin | 2010 | Homer | Vesuvius |
| Lima | 1.6 km | | |

3a 🎧 11.5 Listen to two people doing the first part of
   the quiz. Do they have the same answers as you?

b Listen again and tick the phrases you hear in the
  Useful language box.

4 Check your answers on page 136. How many
  questions did you get right?

## Task Speaking

1a You are going to write your own general knowledge
   quiz. Work in three teams (A, B and C). Write two
   questions for each category. You can use your own
   ideas or the information on page 133 for Team A,
   page 134 for Team B and page 136 for Team C.
   Ask your teacher for any words/phrases you need.

> Useful language a

b Think of the correct answer and one incorrect
  answer for each question. Write all your answers
  in a box.

Science

Countries

## USEFUL LANGUAGE

**a Asking questions**
Where is (the River Ganges)?
Who (became President ... )?
How many (kilometres are there ... )?
How far (is it from ... )?
When (did Spain win ... )?
What (is the capital of ... )?
Who (sang the hit song ... )?
Which (volcano destroyed ... )?

**b Answering questions**
I think it's (in India).
This one's easy!
I'm not sure, but I think it's (India).
I've got no idea!
I can't remember.
I don't know (either).
I know this one ... it's definitely (2010).

**2a** Practise saying your questions clearly so the other teams can understand them.

**b** Play your quiz game in teams. Ask questions and show your box of possible answers to the other two teams.

> Useful language b

**c** Which team got the most correct answers?

**3** Work in pairs and discuss. What were the three most interesting things you learned?

### SHARE YOUR TASK

Practise talking about the interesting things in your quizzes.

Film/Record yourself talking about the quizzes.

Share your film/recording with other students.

# WORLD CULTURE

## ANIMALS IN DANGER

### Find out first

**1a** Work in pairs and discuss.

- Do you have a pet? What is its name?
- What is your favourite animal? Why?
- Is your country famous for any animal(s)? Which one(s)?

**b** Look at the animals in the box. Try to answer the questions for each animal.

| | | |
|---|---|---|
| crocodile | elephant | gazelle |
| giraffe | horse | lion |
| monkey | zebra | |

1 Where does it live (country/continent)?
2 What colour is it?
3 What does it eat?
4 Is it dangerous for humans? Why?
5 Does it live naturally in your country?

**c** Go online to check your answers or ask your teacher

Search: [name of animal] + image/eat/dangerous

### View

**2a** You are going watch a video about animals in danger. Before you watch, check you understand the meaning of the words/phrases in the glossary.

GLOSSARY

| | |
|---|---|
| *hunting* | killing wild animals for sport or food |
| *ivory* | white material from elephant tusk |
| *savannah* | dry grassland |

**b** ▶ Watch the video and make a list of the animals you see. Are there any animals you don't know?

**3** Read the text from the video below. Then watch again and complete the gaps with the words in the box.

| | | | | |
|---|---|---|---|---|
| crocodiles | lions | six metres | animal | male |
| hot | twenty | man | five | |

[1]_____ percent of the world is savannah, or grassland. The African savannah is home to many species which are now in danger because of hunting and changes in the environment. These include giraffes, the world's tallest mammal which can be up to [2]_____ tall, zebras and the African elephant, the world's largest living land [3]_____ .

Female elephants live in family groups, but [4]_____ elephants usually live alone. Breeze is a baby elephant who is just a few days old. In the [5]_____ October weather, he goes to the river every day to drink with the other elephants.

There is danger from [6]_____ in the water and there are also [7]_____ in the area. But the biggest danger to elephants is from [8]_____ . Seventy years ago, there were [9]_____ million elephants in Africa. Now there are only 300,000.

## World view

**4a** Look at the statements below. Tick the ones you agree with and cross the ones you disagree with.

> I don't like zoos ... it's wrong to keep animals like that.

> I would like to go to the savannah to see elephants.

> If you love animals, be a vegetarian!

> I would like to give money to help animals in danger

> Hunting is always a bad thing.

> Humans are more important than animals ... why do we worry about them?

**b** Work in pairs and compare your ideas.

## (((•))) FIND OUT MORE

**5a** Work in pairs. Look at the animals in the box below. What do you know about them? Why do you think they are in danger?

Siberian tiger     Iberian imperial eagle     mountain gorilla
giant panda     hammerhead shark

**b** Go online to find out more about each animal and answer the questions.

1 Where does it live?
2 How many live there?
3 Why is it in danger?

**Search:** [name of animal] + habitat / population size / interesting facts / endangered

## Write up your research

**6** Write about one of the animals you researched. Use the example below to help you.

Siberian tigers are an endangered species. They live in the mountains of East Russia. Their bodies are about 1.50 metres long and they weigh about 175 kilograms.

Siberian tigers are in danger because of environmental changes in the area and because of hunting. There are now only about 250–400 Siberian tigers in the world.

Hodori, the mascot of the 1988 Summer Olympics in Seoul, South Korea was a Siberian tiger!

**AFTER UNIT 11 YOU CAN ...**

Ask and answer questions about a variety of facts.

Say and understand big numbers to talk about a variety of facts.

Talk about your country using quantifiers (*much*, *a few*, etc.).

Research endangered animals online.

# 12 GOOD TIMES

## IN THIS UNIT

- Grammar: *going to* for future intentions; *would like to* and *want to* for future wishes
- Vocabulary: Celebrations and parties; Weather and seasons
- Task: Plan a festival
- Language live: Information to promote a festival; Suggestions and offers

## Vocabulary
### Celebrations and parties

**1a** Work in pairs and discuss. Which of the celebrations in the box can you see in the photos?

birthday party   graduation party   wedding party   coming-of-age party
leaving party   national holiday   religious holiday

**b** How many times each year do the celebrations in the box usually happen?

**2** Match the verbs in box A with two words/phrases in box B to make verb phrases about celebrations, parties and festivals.

**A**   decorate   make   hire   dress up in   take part in

**B**   party clothes        traditional food      the house
a parade             a band              a cake
traditional costumes   the table            a competition
an entertainer

*decorate the house, decorate the table*

**3a** Think of a celebration or party you went to. Look at the questions below and make notes.

1 What was the celebration or party for?
2 Where was it?
3 Who was there?
4 What did you wear/do/eat?

**b** Work in pairs and take turns. Tell each other about your celebration or party.

> I went to my cousin's wedding last year. It was really good fun. They made traditional food and they hired a band …

106

# Grammar focus 1
## *going to* for future intentions

**1a** 🎧 **12.1** Listen to three people talking about their plans for the weekend. Which celebration is each person talking about?

**b** Listen again. Which speaker (1, 2 or 3) mentions the things in the box below?

| | | |
|---|---|---|
| food | the beach | the hairdresser's |
| dance | drive | relax  *2* |

**2** 🎧 **12.2** Listen and complete the sentences.

1 I'm going to _____ my friend Monica.
2 We're going to _____ to the wedding together.
3 I'm not going to _____ on Monday.
4 I'm going to _____ on the beach!
5 We're going to _____ a lot of special food.
6 We're going to _____ a lot, too.

### GRAMMAR

1 To talk about future intentions, we often use
*be* + *going to* + verb.

| + | **I'm going to wear** my new party dress. |
|---|---|
| – | **I'm not going to do** anything. |
| ? | **Are** you **going to drive** to the wedding?<br>When **are** you **going to make** a cake? |

2 With the verb *go*, we usually use *be* + *going*.
*I'm going to a friend's wedding.*
NOT *I'm going to go to a friend's wedding.*

## PRACTICE

**1a** Complete the sentences with one word in the correct place.

My brother <sup>*is*</sup> going to cook a family meal tonight.
1 I'm going have a party this weekend.
2 My parents going to decorate the house next week.
3 I going to have a holiday abroad this summer.
4 I'm going buy some new clothes this weekend.
5 My friends and I going to have a picnic tomorrow.
6 I'm going make a cake tomorrow afternoon.
7 My best friend is to leave her job next month.

**b** 🎧 **12.3** Listen and check. Then make each sentence true for you.

*I'm not going to cook a family meal tonight.*

### PRONUNCIATION

1 Listen again to the sentences in exercise 1a. Notice the pronunciation of *to* with the weak form /tə/.

2 Practise saying the sentences.

**2a** Think about your plans for a celebration or party in the future. Write sentences about what you are going to do, wear, etc.

**b** Work in pairs and take turns. Ask and answer questions about your plans.

> What are you going to do this weekend?
>
> I'm going to have a birthday party …

Unit 12, Study & Practice 1, page 160

# Vocabulary
## Weather and seasons

**1** Work in pairs and discuss.

- How many seasons are there in your country (e.g. spring, summer, autumn, winter, wet season, dry season)?
- Which seasons are January, April, July and October in?

**2** Match the phrases in the box with pictures A–L.

| | | |
|---|---|---|
| It's cloudy. | It's snowing. | It's foggy. |
| It's warm. | It's sunny. | It's raining. |
| It's hot. | It's cool. | It's windy. |
| It's cold. | It's wet. | It's icy. |

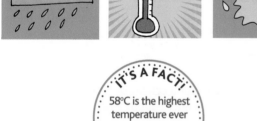

**IT'S A FACT!**
58°C is the highest temperature ever recorded – in El Azizia in Libya, in 1922.

**3** Work in pairs and answer the questions.

1 What is the weather like today?
2 Is the weather usually like this at this time of year?
3 What is your favourite season?
4 What is the weather like at that time?
5 Why do you like it?

# CELEBRATING THE SEASONS

The Sapporo Snow Festival is one of Japan's most exciting winter events – held for seven days in February. The festival started in 1950 with a group of students making sculptures with snow and ice in the park. Now, over two million people come to Sapporo to see around 400 huge sculptures. They are usually of famous people, buildings or events, and teams from different countries take part in a competition, with prizes for the best sculptures.

# Reading

**1a** Work in pairs. Look at the photos of festivals in different seasons and discuss.

- Which season do you think people are celebrating in each photo?
- Which country do you think each festival is in?

**b** Read the article and check your answers.

**2** Read the article again. Are the statements below true (T) or false (F)?

1 The Sapporo Snow Festival lasts for one week in February.
2 Two million people create amazing sculptures out of snow and ice.
3 March 22nd is the longest day of the year.
4 During the festival of Novruz Bayram, people go to the theatre to see plays.
5 In Sweden, people always celebrate Midsummer's Day on June 24th.
6 People think that bringing flowers into the house is lucky.
7 Harvest festivals are most popular along the East Coast of the USA.
8 The main focus of harvest festivals is to celebrate food produced in the area.

**3** Work in pairs and discuss.

- Which festival do you think sounds the most interesting?
- Do you have any similar festivals in your country? What are they? What do people do and wear?

In March, people in parts of Azerbaijan, Iran and Turkey celebrate the beginning of spring with the festival of Novruz Bayram. Around March 22nd, the day and the night are equal length, and people celebrate the fact that plants are starting to grow again after the winter. People light candles and share traditional food, and there are special theatre performances in the street. It is also traditional for children to go from door to door asking for sweets.

People celebrate Midsummer's Day all over the world, but it is particularly important in Sweden. Swedish people celebrate on the Friday and Saturday nearest to June 24th by dancing round a huge maypole. There is traditional music and people wear traditional costumes. They also wear crowns made of wild flowers. Special food, like the year's first strawberries, is on the menu, and people decorate their houses with flowers to bring good luck for the year ahead.

Harvest festivals in the autumn are very popular in the USA, especially in the north-east of the country, where the autumn trees are beautiful. Harvest festivals are usually held in October and they are about celebrating local food. There are always incredible displays of food, such as apples, pumpkins and garlic. Children dress up in traditional costumes and take part in parades, and there are pony rides, entertainers and plenty of traditional music.

# Grammar focus 2

*would like to* and *want to* for future wishes

**1a** 🎧 12.4 **Listen to four sentences. Which festival is each person talking about?**

**b** **Complete the sentences. Then listen again and check.**

1 I _____ see the theatre performances in the street tonight.
2 Next summer, I _____ dance round the maypole.
3 I _____ take part in the sculpture competition this winter.
4 I _____ see the pumpkin displays this afternoon.

## GRAMMAR

**1 We can use different verbs to talk about future wishes (as well as *be + going* to + verb).**

1 *want to* + verb
*I **want to wear** traditional costume for the parade this weekend.*
*I **don't want to** go to the party tonight.*
***Do** you **want to** come to the festival next weekend?*

2 *would like to* + verb
*I**'d like to make** some traditional food for the festival tonight.*
*I **wouldn't like to take part** in the parade.*
***Would** you **like to see** the pumpkin displays?*

**2 We use these common time phrases to talk about future wishes.**

next winter/year     tonight     tomorrow morning/afternoon
this weekend/month     today

# PRACTICE

**1a** **Complete the questions with *do, would* or *are*.**

1 _____ you want to watch TV this evening? What _____ you like to watch?
2 _____ you going to have a busy weekend? What _____ you like to do?
3 _____ you want to buy anything special in the next few weeks? What?
4 Are there any films you _____ like to see at the moment? Which ones?
5 _____ you going to celebrate a festival this year? Which one?
6 _____ you want to go on holiday this year? Where _____ you like to go?

**b** 🎧 12.5 **Listen and check.**

**c** **Work in pairs and take turns. Ask and answer the questions in exercise 1a.**

> **Unit 12, Study & Practice 2, page 160**

# Task

## Plan a festival

### Preparation Reading

**1** Work in pairs and discuss.

- How often do you go to local festivals or celebrations? Do you like them? Why / Why not?
- What different kinds of things can you do at local festivals in your area?

**2** Read the Auldhay Festival website and answer the questions.

1 Where and when is the festival going to happen?
2 Which music artists are going to perform there?
3 Name three special types of food you can find at the festival.
4 Are there any special activities for children? What are they?
5 What kind of accommodation is available?
6 What entertainment is there?
7 What's the name of the nearest railway station and airport?

**3a** 🎧 12.6 Listen to two people discussing the festival. Which things on the website do they talk about?

**b** Listen again. Tick the phrases you hear in the Useful language box.

### Task Speaking

**1** You are going to plan a festival celebrating your own town or region. Work in pairs and spend some time planning your festival. Use the questions in Reading exercise 2 and the headings on the website to help you. Ask your teacher for any words/phrases you need.

**2** Work in small groups and take turns. Ask and answer questions about your festivals.

> Useful language a and b

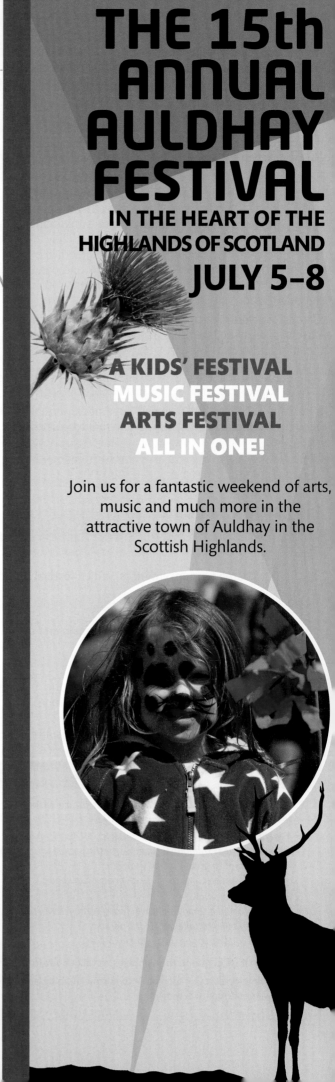

**THE 15th ANNUAL AULDHAY FESTIVAL**

IN THE HEART OF THE HIGHLANDS OF SCOTLAND

**JULY 5–8**

**A KIDS' FESTIVAL**
**MUSIC FESTIVAL**
**ARTS FESTIVAL**
**ALL IN ONE!**

Join us for a fantastic weekend of arts, music and much more in the attractive town of Auldhay in the Scottish Highlands.

## USEFUL LANGUAGE

**a Asking about the festival**
When is the festival going to happen?
What (music) are you going to have?
How about (food)?
Are there any special activities for (children)?
Are you going to have (dancing)?

**b Describing your festival**
It's going to be (at the beginning of July / at the end of November).
It's going to be in a really beautiful park.
(Salsa Fling) are going to play at the festival.
We're going to have (cookery demonstrations).
We've got a lot of (activities for children).
There are a lot of good hotels nearby.
There's going to be (traditional Scottish dancing).

**Music:** Enjoy the best of Scottish music on our main stage, including singer-songwriter Barbara McDowell, Scottish–Brazilian fusion band Salsa Fling and world-famous Scottish folk duo the Protractors ... live on stage on Saturday 7th July from 6.30 p.m.

**Food:** Visit our Highland Food Café and try one of our local specialities – Scottish haggis, Scotch broth or Scottish shortbread. And why not come along to one of the traditional Scottish cookery demonstrations?

**Children:** Kids' activities: drawing classes, face-painting, arts and crafts workshops ... and much, much more.

**Literature:** Poetry reading by local poet Andy Craig.

**Dancing:** Traditional Scottish dancing demonstrations by the Auldhay Highland Dancers ... learn Scottish Highland dancing with the experts!

---

**Camping:** Festival campsite available. Find out about local hotels at auldhayhotels.com or contact Tourist Information: +44 (0)9561 768026 (Mon–Fri, 9–5.30; Sat, 9–4).

**Getting there:** Trains run to Auldhay Station every 30 mins from Aberdeen. Journey time: 25 mins. For train times, see the Scotrail website. By car: take the A903, 18 miles north of Aberdeen. By air: Aberdeen Airport. Regular flights from London Heathrow, Amsterdam, Birmingham, Dublin, Manchester.

## SHARE YOUR TASK

**Practise talking about your festival.**

**Film/Record yourself talking about your festival.**

**Share your film/recording with other students.**

## Writing
### Information to promote a festival

**1a** Look at the photos and discuss.

- What can you see in the photos?
- Where do you think this festival takes place?
- What do you think they are celebrating?

**b** Read the text about the Boi Bumbá festival and check your answers.

**2** Read the text again and decide if the statements below are true (T) or false (F).

1 The festival happens at the end of June.
2 There is only one Boi Bumbá festival in Brazil.
3 Dressing up is a big part of the festival.
4 There are four nights of parades and shows.
5 The parades are also a competition.
6 You must buy tickets in advance for the festival.

**3** Read the text again and match paragraphs 1–3 with descriptions a–c.

a tickets / accommodation / getting there
b what the festival is / what you can do and see
c when and where the festival is going to take place

**4** Think about the festival you planned on page 110. You are going to write some information to promote your festival. First, make notes about your festival using the paragraph descriptions (a–c) in exercise 3.

**5** Write about your festival using your notes.

## BOI BUMBA FESTIVAL

This year, the Boi Bumbá festival is going to take place from 27–30th June. There are many Boi Bumbá festivals in Brazil, but the one in our town, Parintins, is the biggest and the best!

In English, the words *boi bumbá* mean 'beat the bull'. The festival is about the story of a bull which comes back to life. To celebrate this, the town divides into two teams and everyone dresses up in fantastic costumes. This year, as usual, everyone is going to get together in the town centre to watch the two teams put on spectacular shows for three nights. There are colourful parades and a lot of dancing and singing. After the parades, the city has food, drink and a big party for everyone. On the fourth day, we're going to find out who the winning team is. It's very exciting!

You don't need to buy tickets for the Boi Bumbá festival, but you need to book early to find somewhere to stay for the three nights. Phone the Tourist Office for details on: 55-41-3351-6778.

Why don't we ...?

# Speaking
## Suggestions and offers

**1** Work in pairs. Look at the photo and discuss. What things can you do to celebrate a birthday?

**2a** ▶ Watch the video. How many different ideas do you hear for the woman's birthday?

**b** Watch again and number suggestions a–f in the order you hear them.

  **a** Let's go there ...
  **b** Why don't we ... ?
  **c** Shall I ... ?
  **d** Why don't you ... ?
  **e** How about ... ?
  **f** Where shall we ... ?

**c** Where do the friends decide to go to in the end?

**3a** Put the words in the correct order to make and respond to suggestions and offers.

  **1** for a meal / Why / we / don't / go out ?
  **2** Where / go / we / shall ?
  **3** about / Thai Kitchen / How ?
  **4** bowling / go / Let's !
  **5** That / sounds like / good idea / a
  **6** phone / some tickets / and book / I'll
  **7** Shall / to come / I / ask Ben if / he wants ?
  **8** then / Yes, / OK

**b** ▶ Watch and listen to the key phrases and check your answers.

**4a** Work in pairs. Write a short conversation for one of the situations below. Include at least three different suggestions.

- You are arranging a night out at the cinema with a friend.
- An old friend is coming to visit for the weekend. Make some suggestions where to take him/her.
- You are planning a leaving party for a colleague.

> What shall we do tonight?

> How about going to the cinema?

> That's a good idea!

**b** Practise your conversation.

**AFTER UNIT 12 YOU CAN ...**

Talk about your future plans and intentions.

Talk about plans for a festival in your town or region.

Make suggestions and offers.

Write some information to promote a festival.

# 13

## LIVE AND LEARN

### IN THIS UNIT

- Grammar: *have to* and *don't have to*; *might* and *will*
- Vocabulary: School and university subjects; Education and training
- Task: Complete a careers questionnaire
- World culture: A dream come true

## Vocabulary
### School and university subjects

**1a  Work in pairs and discuss.**

- Which of the subjects in the box can you see in the photos?
- Which subjects do/did you study at school or university?

| | | | |
|---|---|---|---|
| geography | science | information technology | media studies |
| languages | medicine | design and technology | economics |
| performing arts | law | leisure and tourism | maths |
| business studies | history | literature | engineering |

**b**  Add three more subjects to the box. Compare your ideas with other students.

**2**  Work in pairs and discuss. For which of the subjects in exercise 1a do you need to be good:

- with numbers?
- with people?
- at art?
- at remembering facts?

- with your hands?
- with machines?
- at writing?
- at speaking?

**3**  Work in pairs and discuss.

- Which of the subjects in exercise 1a interest you the most? Why?
- Which of the subjects are you least interested in? Why?
- When did you start primary school? When did you start secondary school? Which did you like best? Why?
- Is it difficult to get into university in your country? Which courses are most difficult to get on? Why do you think this is?

# Grammar focus 1
## *have to* and *don't have to*

**1** Read the email below and answer the questions.

    **1** What course is Daniel going to do?
    **2** When does it start?

**2** Read the email again and choose the correct answers.

    **1** Daniel *likes / doesn't like* his job at the moment.
    **2** He wants to teach **children / adults**.
    **3** He *has / hasn't* got the right qualifications to be a teacher.
    **4** He wants to do a **part-time / full-time** course.
    **5** He *lives / doesn't live* a long way from the college.

---

**Unread Message**

From    daniel:)scott@my_mail
Subject  Hi Eva!

Hi Eva!
I told you before that my job is a bit boring and that I really want to teach geography in a secondary school. Well, I've decided to do it!

    Before I can get a job as a teacher, I have to do a training course and get the right qualifications. And the thing is, I can't afford to leave work while I do the training. But I've found a college where I can do a part-time course, so I don't have to stop work completely. It's a two-year course and I have to go to college evenings and weekends. I also have to do a lot of studying at home.

    The college is near where I live, so I don't have to travel very far, which is good. It starts next month ... I'm really excited about it all!

    How is your new course? Do you have to do a lot of homework? Write soon and tell me all about it.

Daniel

**SEND**

---

### GRAMMAR

**1** Match sentences 1–4 with meanings a and b.
    1 Before I can get a job, I **have to do** a training course.
    2 I **have to go** to college evenings and weekends.
    3 I can do a part-time course, so I **don't have to stop** work completely.
    4 The college is near where I live, so I **don't have to travel** very far.

    a It is necessary to do this.
    b It isn't necessary to do this.

### PRONUNCIATION

**1** 🎧 **13.1** Listen to the sentences in the grammar box. Notice the pronunciation of *to* with the weak form and the linking between *have* and *to* /hæf/tə/.

**2** Listen again and practise saying the sentences.

### PRACTICE

**1a** Make sentences about your country using *have to* and *don't have to*.

    **1** In most schools in my country, you:
      **a** _____ wear a uniform.
      **b** _____ study a foreign language.
      **c** _____ do sport every day.
    **2** When you have an interview for a job or course, you:
      **a** _____ show all your qualifications.
      **b** _____ talk about your experience.
      **c** _____ show you can speak a foreign language.
    **3** When you are learning to drive, you:
      **a** _____ learn with a qualified instructor.
      **b** _____ take a written test as well as a practical test.
      **c** _____ do a first-aid test.

  **b** Work in pairs and compare your ideas.

Unit 13, Study & Practice 1, page 162

115

# Vocabulary

## Education and training

**1a** Choose the correct answers.

1 *lose* / *fail* an exam
2 *go* / *get* into university
3 *get* / *make* a degree
4 *make* / *do* a course (in media studies)
5 *decide* / *choose* a career (in engineering)
6 apply *to* / *for* a job or course
7 *take* / *have* an interview
8 train *to* / *for* be (a chef)
9 *do* / *be* unemployed
10 *do* / *earn* money

**b** Read the college advert and check your answers.

**Chesterton College of Adult Education**

Did you fail your exams?

Do you need some advice about choosing a career?

Do you need to earn money?

Do you want to get a university degree?

Do you want help with applying for a job?

Are you unemployed?

**Why don't you come and talk to us about what we can offer you?**

At Chesterton College of Adult Education …
* you can do courses in geography, literature, media studies … a wide range of subjects.
* you can train to be a chef, a teacher, a plumber … all different kinds of jobs.
* you can talk to an advisor about choosing a career in engineering, medicine … whatever interests you.
* you can get help with how to get into university or how to apply for a job.

**Come and have an interview today!**

See our website: info@chesterton.com
or phone 01228 345231.

**Chesterton College of Adult Education**
**Live and learn!** It's never too late to learn something new.

**2** Work in pairs. Put the verb phrases in exercise 1a into the categories below. Some can go in more than one category.

* college/university
* work

**3a** Complete the sentences with the correct form of the verb phrases in exercise 1a.

1 I'm going to _____ to be a chef next year.
2 It's very expensive to get a _____ in my country.
3 I was very upset when I _____ my exam.
4 A lot of people _____ unemployed in my country at the moment.
5 I get very nervous when I _____ an interview for a job.
6 I started _____ money when I was 15.
7 When people apply _____ a job in my country, they usually do it online.
8 Next year, I'm going to _____ a course in something in the evenings.
9 I'd like to _____ into university to study in the USA.
10 I chose a _____ in teaching because I wanted long holidays.

**b** Which of the sentences do you agree with or are true for you?

**c** Work in pairs and compare your answers.

# Listening
## Two career paths

**1**  Work in pairs and discuss.

- Which jobs/careers pay the most money in your country?
- Is money important to you when choosing a career?
- What else do you look for when choosing a career?
- Do you have an 'ideal' job?

**2**  🎧 **13.2** Listen to two people talking about their careers. Match the people to topics 1–6 below. Write L for Lorraine and M for Martin.

1  having a lot of money
2  having time to spend with family/friends
3  having a stress-free life
4  having your own business
5  working for a large company
6  combining work and a hobby

**3**  Listen again and answer the questions.

**Lorraine**
1  Did Lorraine pass all her exams at school?
2  Were her parents unemployed?
3  At what age did she start work?
4  Did she like her job as manager of the shop?
5  How many shops did Lorraine open in ten years?
6  How much is her business worth now?

**Martin**
7  What did Martin's parents do their degrees in?
8  What did Martin do his degree in?
9  Did he like his job when he worked for a large company?
10  Did he spend a lot of time with his family?
11  Does Martin think that teaching the guitar is stressful?
12  Would he like to earn more money?

**4**  Work in pairs and discuss.

- Which person (Lorraine or Martin) do you think you are most similar to? Why?
- Which careers are more popular with men? Which are more popular with women? And which are more popular with young people? Why do you think this is?
- If you apply for a job in your country, do you normally have an interview? What happens?
- Is it easy or difficult to get a job at the moment? Are many people unemployed?

# From slates to iPads ...

## Language learning then, now and in the future

"Textbooks might be a thing of the past very soon ...

IT'S A FACT!
In Europe, 94% of students learn a foreign language. In the USA, it's only 10%.

### Then ...

It's 6 a.m. on a Monday morning 500 years ago – time for lessons to start at the local grammar school. The main aim of the lesson is to study the grammar of Latin – the international language of the time (in Europe, at least) and the language of all university courses. The pupils are all boys – if girls receive any education at all, they get it at home. The boys take out their slates – there will be no pencil and paper until the 19th century. They learn grammatical rules and translate sentences, and the boys have to speak Latin at all times. If they fail at all, their punishment is up to 50 strokes of the cane!

### Now ...

No one knows how many people are learning English today – one common estimate is one billion people, or a third of the world's population. Technology has become more and more important in how people learn: cassettes (which first became popular in the 1970s), CDs and video have brought 'real English' into the classroom. Many classrooms have internet access, video facilities and interactive whiteboards. But in most cases, one thing hasn't changed ... there's still a teacher!

### In the future ...

Who knows what the language classroom of 2050 will be like. Many people think that textbooks might be a thing of the past very soon. And many classrooms won't have cassettes or CDs in the near future. Will students use iPads or smartphones instead of pen and paper? Will computers replace teachers? Other people think that English might not be as popular as it is now. Will Chinese, perhaps, or even a completely new international language designed by computers replace English? There is one thing that is for sure: technology will be at the centre of tomorrow's language education.

## Reading

**1** Work in pairs and discuss.

- Do most people in your country learn foreign languages? Why?
- Which language(s) do people learn?
- At what age do they start?
- What technology do you use in your school? How do you think technology helps learners?

**2** Read the article about language learning. Which of these things are mentioned?

- studying grammar
- learning French
- using the internet
- using languages at work
- training to be a teacher
- learning Chinese

**3** Read the article again. Match the sentence halves.

A
1 Another language might replace English
2 People started using audio cassettes
3 Latin was the international language
4 People started using pencil and paper
5 About one billion people study English
6 Textbooks might disappear

B
a about 50 years ago.
b in the 16th century.
c in the 19th century.
d very soon.
e some time in the future.
f now.

**4** Work in pairs and discuss.

- How was language learning different in your country 500 years ago?
- What are language-learning classrooms like in your country now?

# Grammar focus 2
## *might* and *will*

**1a** Complete the sentences using *will*, *won't* (*will not*), *might* and *might not*.

  **1** Textbooks _____ be a thing of the past very soon.

  **2** Many classrooms _____ have cassettes or CDs in the near future.

  **3** English _____ be as popular as it is now.

  **4** Technology _____ be at the centre of tomorrow's education.

  **b** Read the last paragraph of the article and check your answers.

---

### GRAMMAR

**1** Look again at exercise 1a. Match the modal verbs with the definitions below.
  1 The speaker is sure something will happen.
  2 The speaker is sure something will not happen.
  3 The speaker thinks it is possible that something will happen.
  4 The speaker thinks it is possible that something will not happen.

**2** What form of verb comes after each modal verb?

**3** Change the sentences below to make them negative.
  1 Students will do all their homework on computers.
  2 English might be the most important language.

---

## PRACTICE

**1** Choose the correct answers.

  **1** In a few years' time, printed books **will disappear / will be disappear** completely.

  **2** In the future, people **not will go / won't go** to school. They **might study / might to study** at home using a computer.

  **3** Tom isn't sure what he wants to do when he leaves school. He **will go / might go** to university, or he **won't travel / might travel** abroad for a year.

  **4** Denise finds Italian quite difficult. She says she **will study / won't study** Spanish instead.

  **5** Why not do a course in Chinese? You never know – you **might need / not might need** to speak it in the future.

  **6** Some teachers are worried that computers **will to take / will take** their jobs one day.

*holidays and travel*

*career and education*

*house and city*

*hola!*
*ciao!*

*languages*

**money**

*family*

**2a** Complete the sentences to make them true for you. Use the ideas above or your own ideas.

  **1** Next winter, I might _____ .
  **2** Next summer, I'll _____ .
  **3** Next year, I'll _____ .
  **4** In ten years' time, I might _____ .
  **5** In my life, I might not _____ .
  **6** In the next two years, I won't _____ .
  **7** One day, I'll _____ .
  **8** When I'm 65, I'll _____ .

  **b** Compare your sentences with other students.

> Next winter, I might start a course in Italian.

> Oh, really? Why do you want to learn Italian?

Unit 13, Study & Practice 2, page 162

# Task

## Complete a careers questionnaire

### Preparation Reading

**1** Work in pairs and discuss.

- Which of the jobs in the photos would you like to do?
- Are there any other jobs/careers that you would like to have?

**2** Complete the careers questionnaire.

**3a** 🎧 13.3 Listen to two people discussing the questionnaire. Answer the questions below.

   **1** What answers did the man mostly get?
   **2** Did he agree with the results of the questionnaire?

**b** Listen again and tick the phrases you hear in the Useful language box.

### Task Speaking

**1a** Work in pairs and compare your answers to the questionnaire.

   **1** How many answers are the same?
   **2** How many answers are different?
   **3** Which letter did you choose the most?

**b** Look at the results on page 133 to find out what your answers mean.

**2** Work in pairs and discuss. Do you agree with the results? Why / Why not? Ask your teacher for any words/phrases you need.

> Useful language a–c

**3** Work in groups. Tell other students about your or your partner's results and reaction to the questionnaire.

# So you want to get on in life?
# Are you in the right job?

**Do our quiz to find the perfect job for you ...**

1 **What's your attitude to money?**
   a I want to work hard and earn a large salary.
   b Being happy in my job and helping people is more important than money.
   c Health is more important than money.
   d Money isn't important to me.
2 **How do you feel about stress?**
   a I like stress – it gives me energy and motivation.
   b I want a quiet, calm life!
   c I try not to worry about it!
   d I feel happy when I can work and think alone.
3 **What school subjects were you good at?**
   a mathematics and sciences
   b languages
   c sport and physical education
   d music, literature and design
4 **Where do you prefer to work?**
   a both indoors and outdoors
   b mainly indoors
   c mainly outdoors
   d not important
5 **How do you like to work?**
   a I sometimes like working alone, and sometimes I like working with other people.
   b I prefer working with other people.
   c I like working in a team.
   d I prefer working alone.
6 **Which adjectives best describe you?**
   a dynamic and original
   b sympathetic and good with people
   c sporty and healthy
   d imaginative and creative
7 **How do you feel about working hours?**
   a I'm happy to work at any time and as many hours as I can.
   b I'd like to work regular hours, with evenings and weekends free.
   c It's not important.
   d I work any time I have ideas.
8 **What kind of clothes would you like to wear at work?**
   a smart, formal clothes
   b a uniform
   c casual clothes
   d not important

## USEFUL LANGUAGE

**a  Asking for results/information**
What does that mean?
What does it say?
What else?
Anything else?

**b  Reacting to results/information**
Yes, that's true.
That's absolutely right.
I think that's partly true.
That's not right.
That's rubbish!

**c  Justifying your reaction**
I like doing things and being active.
I'll work as hard as I can.
I might be a bit bossy sometimes.
I won't be horrible to people.
I'm not good at maths or business.
I don't like working outdoors.
I don't want to work from nine to five.
I'm a journalist at the moment ...
I'd like to be a designer.

## SHARE YOUR TASK

**Practise talking about your or your partner's results and reaction to the questionnaire.**

**Film/Record yourself talking about your or your partner's results and reaction to the questionnaire.**

**Share your film/recording with other students.**

# WORLD CULTURE

# A DREAM COME TRUE

## Find out first

**1a** Work in pairs and discuss. How much do you know about Latin America? Try to answer the questions in the quiz below.

### What do you know about Latin America?

1 In which of these countries is Spanish not the official language?
   a Argentina    b Brazil    c Peru

2 Bogotá, Cali and Medellín are cities in which Latin American country?
   a Colombia    b Ecuador    c Mexico

3 Cuba is an island in which sea/ocean?
   a Atlantic    b Caribbean    c Pacific

4 With which country/countries do you associate these dances?
   a merengue    b samba    c tango

5 Carlos Acosta is a famous ballet dancer from which country?
   a Costa Rica    b Cuba    c Puerto Rico

**b** Go online to check your answers or ask your teacher.

Search: Argentina/Brazil/Peru language / Bogotá / Cali / Medellín / Cuba map / merengue / samba / tango / Carlos Acosta biography

## View

**2a** You are going to watch a video about Fernando Montaño, a Colombian dancer with the Royal Ballet in London. Before you watch, check you understand the meaning of the words/phrases in the glossary

**GLOSSARY**
*audition*            where actors/dancers try to get a role
*scholarship*         money you receive for studies
*to train / training*   exercise to make you fit

**b** ▶ Watch the video and number the topics (1–6) in the order you hear them.

- his time in Cuba
- coming to London and starting to learn English
- his early life in Cali
- his dream when he was a child
- his other interests
- how he keeps fit

**3** Watch again and answer the questions.

1 At what age did Fernando tell his mother he wanted to be a ballet dancer?
2 When did he start studying ballet in Colombia?
3 Fernando later won a scholarship to study in which country?
4 Why did the Director of the English National Ballet School invite Fernando to London?
5 Did Fernando know how to speak English when he came to the UK?
6 How often does he go to the gym?
7 What is his number one ambition?
8 What are his other hobbies?

## World view

**4a** Look at the statements below. Tick the ones you agree with and cross the ones you disagree with.

> I don't know anything about art, but I know what I like.

> Ballet is for girls. I prefer football.

> All politicians are dishonest, in my opinion.

> I prefer reading to watching TV.

> I can't stand classical music.

**b** Work in pairs and compare your ideas. Do you have a favourite artist/dancer/politician, etc.?

## 🔊 FIND OUT MORE

**5a** Look at the names of some other famous people from Latin America in the box below. Do you know who they are and why they are famous?

Carlos Acosta    Antônio Carlos Jobim    Eva Perón
Frida Kahlo    Mario Vargas Llosa

**b** Go online to find out more about them and answer the questions.

1 Where/when was he/she born?
2 When did he/she die?
3 Why is he/she famous?
4 What was his/her main achievement?

Search: [name of person] + biography/achievements

## ▶ Write up your research

**6** Write about one of the people you researched. Use the example below to help you.

Carlos Acosta is probably one of the world's most famous ballet dancers. He came from a poor family and was one of 11 children.

He studied at the Cuban National Ballet School, and then danced with the Houston Ballet in the USA and with the Royal Ballet in London.

I think his greatest achievement was writing his own ballet, *Tocororo – A Cuban Tale*. It is the story of a poor Cuban boy who travels to the big city.

I admire him because he is talented and successful, but he never forgets his early life.

---

### AFTER UNIT 13 YOU CAN ...

**Talk about your education and career.**

**Discuss things you have to and don't have to do.**

**Predict what will/might happen in the future.**

**Discuss what job you (and others) are most suited for.**

**Research famous people online.**

# 14

## KEEP IN TOUCH

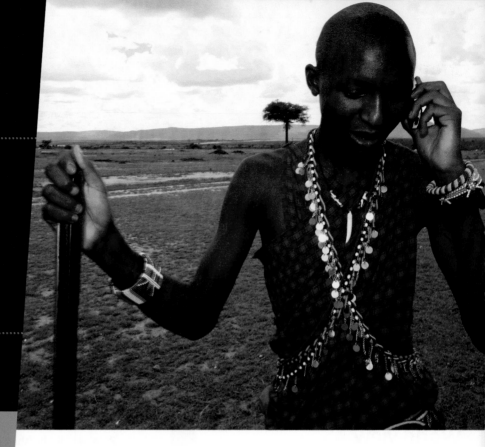

### IN THIS UNIT

- Grammar: Present perfect (unfinished time); Present perfect (with *ever*)
- Vocabulary: Ways of communicating; Technology
- Task: Keep talking
- Language live: Telephoning; A text message

## Vocabulary
### Ways of communicating

1 **Work in pairs and discuss.**

- How many phones are there in your house, including all mobile phones and landlines?
- Where do you usually keep your mobile phone during the day and during the night? Why?
- Are you interested in having the most up-to-date phone? Why / Why not?

2 **Complete the sentences with the words/phrases in the box.**

| | | |
|---|---|---|
| a smartphone | a landline | a laptop |
| a tablet computer | an internet connection | a Wi-Fi connection |

You can **make a phone call** with *a smartphone and a landline*.

1 You can **send a text message** with _____ .
2 You can **use the internet** with _____ .
3 You can **send an email** with _____ .
4 You can **send an attachment** with _____ .
5 You can **leave a voice message** with _____ .
6 You can **pick up voicemail** with _____ .
7 You can **use video chat** with _____ .
8 You can **update your status** with _____ .

3 **Work in pairs. Look again at the verb phrases in bold in exercise 2 and discuss.**

- Which do you do every day?
- Which do you do several times a week?
- Which do you do once or twice a month?
- Which do you never do? Why?

# Grammar focus 1
## Present perfect (unfinished time)

**1** Read the comments from a social networking site and answer the questions.

  **1** How many people are talking about writing something?

  **2** How many people are talking about reading something?

---

**friendsconnect**      Search

**Elaine Massey** I've had the most boring weekend ever so far! I hope it changes but nothing has happened at all ... The highlight so far: watching *Central Hospital* on TV!! ☹
*7 people like this*

**Aaron Jakes** I know how you feel! I've made five phone calls to my bank so far today ... and I've spent at least three hours on hold listening to stupid music!! Really annoying!

**Johnny Dee** *Central Hospital* ... that's rubbish! My sister has watched 12 (!!!) episodes of *Central Hospital* so far this weekend. She hasn't done anything except watch TV all weekend!

**Chrissie Leaning** Poor you! My weekend hasn't been exactly exciting either, but I'm pleased because I've written 1,000 words of my end-of-term assignment ... only another 3,000 words to go! ☺

**Leo Taylor** Why don't you get a Kindle and read a good book! I love my new Kindle! It's great ... I'm going to read lots of classic books. I've downloaded *War and Peace* ... but I haven't read any of it!

**Jayne Michaels** No sympathy! I've been at work all weekend ... and I'm still here!

*Write a comment ...*

---

**2a** Complete the sentences with *have*, *haven't*, *has* and *hasn't*.

  **1** I _____ had the most boring weekend ever so far!

  **2** My sister _____ watched 12 episodes of *Central Hospital* so far this weekend.

  **3** She _____ done anything except watch TV all weekend.

  **4** I _____ downloaded *War and Peace* ... but I _____ read any of it!

  **5** I _____ been at work all weekend ... and I'm still here!

**b** Read the comments again and check your answers.

---

## GRAMMAR

**1** Look again at the sentences in exercise 2a. Choose the correct answers to complete the rules below.

  **1** We use the Present perfect to describe actions that started in the past and are *finished* / *not finished* at the time of speaking.

  **2** With the Present perfect, we *say* / *don't say* the exact time.

**2** We often use these words/phrases to talk about the time period.

  so far     so far this weekend     this afternoon
  today     this morning

**3** We form the Present perfect with *have/has* + past participle. Look again at the sentences in exercise 2a and find two regular past participles and two irregular past participles.

**4** Look again at the comments in exercise 1 and underline more examples of the Present perfect.

---

## PRACTICE

**1a** Complete the sentences with the correct form of the verb in brackets and make them true for you.

  **1** I _____ (make) _____ phone calls so far today.

  **2** I _____ (send) _____ text messages so far this week.

  **3** I _____ (spend) _____ hours on my computer so far this week.

  **4** I _____ (write) _____ letters so far this month.

  **5** I _____ (watch) _____ DVDs this week.

  **6** I _____ (read) _____ books this year.

  **7** I _____ (receive) _____ emails today.

  **8** I _____ (take) _____ photos today.

**b** Work in pairs and compare your sentences.

> **Unit 14, Study & Practice 1, page 164**

**IT'S A FACT!**
In 2011, people around the world sent about 7 trillion text messages.

# Mind-blowing facts about modern communicatio

• The internet holds about **5 million** terabytes of data. That'
about the same as **1 million** human brains. According to expe
there are about **2 billion** internet users in the world. **70%** of
people in developed countries go online, but only **20%** of peop
in developing countries can access the internet.
• The average internet user has **25** online accounts and logs in
**8** times a day. **30%** of internet users have just **1** password for
all their online accounts, and the most common password is
'password1'. About **55%** of users choose words which have som
personal meaning, and **15%** write down both their password an
username.
• Many people use Wi-Fi hotspots in public places, such as café
airports and hotels. **46%** of them are worried about viruses and
hackers. Many people type in personal information while using
public Wi-Fi: **22%** regularly type in email passwords, **21%** log
Facebook and **8%** do online banking, but they are unaware abo
how to be totally secure.
• The first computer virus appeared in 1981. The first virus to
affect mobile phones appeared in 2005. And the first anti-virus
software came out in 1990. There are now about **6,000** new
computer viruses every month.
• **87%** of internet users go online with their smartphone at lea
once a day. About **80%** keep their smartphone switched on 24-
and **23%** use it during mealtimes.
• **500,000,000** people in the world have a Facebook account
– that's about one in every 13 people. The average user has **13**
'friends', and **48%** of adults check their Facebook page as soon
they wake up in the morning. Every **20** minutes, Facebook users
around the world upload **2,716,000** photos.

## Reading and vocabulary
### Technology

**1a** Work in pairs and try to answer the questions.

1 How many internet users are there in the world?
 a half a billion
 b one billion
 c two billion
2 How many new computer viruses are there
 every month?
 a 60
 b 600
 c 6,000
3 How many people in the world have a Facebook
 account?
 a 500,000
 b 5,000,000
 c 500,000,000

b Read the article and check your answers.

**2** Read the article again and match the sentence halves.

**A**
1 One in five people
2 About one third of people
3 22 percent of people
4 In 2005,
5 500 million people
6 Four in five people
7 23 percent of people

**B**
a have their phone on all day, every day.
b have a Facebook account.
c use their mobile phones while they're eating a meal.
d have access to the internet in developing countries.
e type in their email password on a public computer.
f the first mobile phone virus appeared.
g have only one password for all their online accounts.

## 3a Check the meaning of the words/phrases in bold. Look at the article to help you.

1 Can you **access the internet** from your school or work?
2 When did you first become an **internet user**?
3 How often do you use **Wi-Fi hotspots** in cafés?
4 Approximately how many **online accounts** have you got?
5 How many different **passwords** and **usernames** have you got?
6 Have you had a **virus** on your computer? Have you got **anti-virus software** on your computer?
7 What kind of information do most computer **hackers** want?
8 Do you ever **upload** or **download** photos, videos or music?

b Work in pairs and take turns. Ask and answer the questions.

c Which fact in the article do you think is the most surprising? Why?

# Grammar focus 2
## Present perfect (with *ever*)

1 🎧 14.1 Listen to three conversations and answer the questions.

**Conversation 1**
1 How many online accounts has the woman got?
2 Does she write down her passwords?

**Conversation 2**
3 When did the woman lose her mobile phone?
4 Where did someone steal the man's mobile phone?

**Conversation 3**
5 What is wrong with the woman's computer?
6 What important things has she got on her computer?

2 Listen again and complete the questions and answers.

**Conversation 1**
1 Have you ever _____ your password?
2 Yes, I _____ … many times. I can only remember it when I write it down!

**Conversation 2**
3 _____ you ever lost your mobile phone?
4 No, I _____ . I've never lost it, but someone stole it once.

**Conversation 3**
5 Have you _____ had a virus on your computer?
6 Yes, I have. I've _____ two or three, I think.

## GRAMMAR

We use *ever* with the Present perfect to ask about things you have done at 'some time in your life up to now'. The time period we are talking about is 'your life', which isn't finished. We don't need to say exactly when the things happened (it is not important).

1 **Look at the sentence pairs below. Which question or answer is correct (a or b)?**
1a Have you bought ever clothes online?
 b Have you ever bought clothes online?
2a Yes, I have.
 b Yes, I have bought.
3a No, I haven't.
 b No, I haven't ever.

## PRONUNCIATION

1 🎧 14.2 Listen to the questions and answers in exercise 2. Notice the pronunciation of *have*:
1 in the questions with weak forms /ə/ .
   *Have you ever …?*
2 in the answers with strong forms /æ/ .
   *Yes, I have.*
   *No, I haven't.*

2 Listen again and practise saying the questions and answers.

## PRACTICE

1a Use the prompts to make questions with the Present perfect and *ever*.

use video chat
*Have you ever used video chat?*
1 buy anything online
2 lose your mobile phone
3 make a phone call in English
4 spend more than a week without a phone/computer
5 do a dangerous sport
6 stay awake for the whole night
7 study in a foreign country

b Write three more questions of your own.

2 Work in pairs and take turns. Ask and answer the questions in exercise 1.

> Have you ever used video chat?
>
> Yes, I have … I often use video chat with my sister in the USA.

Unit 14, Study & Practice 2, page 164

# Task

Take part in a game

# Talk for a minute!

NUMBER OF PLAYERS: 2+
EQUIPMENT NEEDED: Game board, topics and questions
(page 137), a watch or timer
AIM: To 'take' as many squares as you can by talking for
a minute about the topics/questions related to the letters on
the board

## RULES OF THE GAME

1 The youngest player starts. The next player is the person on
his/her left.
2 Take turns to choose a letter on the board. When you have
chosen a letter, look at page 137 for the topic starting with
that letter. You then have a minute to talk about the questions
related to that topic.
3 The other players time one minute and say 'Stop!' when one
minute is up.
4 If you can speak for a minute about the questions, you can
'take' that square by writing your name on it. No other player
can 'take' that square.
5 If you can't speak for a minute about the topic, the square
stays blank. Other players can choose that letter to speak
about if they want.
6 Continue to take turns to choose letters on the board until all
the squares are 'taken' (when all the squares have the names
of the players on them).
7 The winner is the player who has 'taken' the most squares.

## USEFUL LANGUAGE

**a  Giving yourself time to think**
So, let me think.
Right, let's see then.
So, the question is ...
I'm going to talk about ...
I want to talk about ...

**b  Expanding your ideas**
What I mean is, ...
What else?
So, is there anything else?
Another thing I'd like to say is ...
Some other examples of this are ...
... and things like that.

## Preparation Reading and listening

1 Look at the game and read the rules. Then answer the questions.

1 How many people can play the game?
2 What do you need to play the game?
3 How do you win the game?

2a  🎧 14.3 Listen to two people playing the game and answer the questions.

1 Which letter/topic does the woman choose?
2 Does she manage to speak for a minute and 'take' the square?

b Listen again and tick the phrases you hear in the Useful language box.

## Task Speaking

1a Work in small groups. Make sure you understand the rules and have got all
the equipment you need. Decide who is going to start. Ask your teacher for
any words/phrases you need.

b Play the game.

> Useful language a and b

2 Did you find it easy or difficult to talk for a minute? Who was the winner?

### SHARE YOUR TASK

**Practise talking about one of
the topics from the game.**

**Film/Record yourself talking
about one of the topics from
the game.**

**Share your film/recording with
other students.**

# LANGUAGE LIVE

CU 2moro

## Speaking
### Telephoning

**1** Work in pairs and discuss.

- What are the people in the photo doing?
- How often do you use your phone to:
  - chat to friends?
  - send text messages?
  - check the internet?
  - listen to music?

**2a** ▶ Watch the first part of the video. Tick the things you see/hear.

- a woman putting her coat on
- a man dropping his phone on the floor
- a man giving his name and phone number

**b** Watch again and complete the form for the taxi.

> Taxi for Mr / Ms: _____
>
> From (address): _____
>
> To: _____
>
> Pick-up time: _____
>
> Number of passengers: _____

**3a** ▶ Watch the second part of the video. Tick the things you see/hear.

- a mobile phone ringing
- a woman looking for her mobile phone
- a man sending a text message
- a woman apologising

**b** Watch again and write what you think the caller says.

1 **A:** Emma Johnson speaking. Who's that?
   **B:** _____
2 **A:** Oh, hi! How nice to hear from you. How are you?
   **B:** _____
3 **A:** Oh, I'm fine. Where are you?
   **B:** _____
4 **A:** Really? Perhaps we can meet somewhere.
   **B:** _____
5 **A:** Yes, I'd love to but, listen, it's not a good moment to talk. I'm with someone ...
   **B:** _____
6 **A:** Can I call you back?
   **B:** _____

**4** ▶ Watch the third part of the video. Tick the things you see/hear.

- a man getting angry
- a woman taking a photo on her phone
- a man dialling a wrong number

**5a** Complete the key phrases with the words in the box.

| about | call | here | number | soon |
|-------|------|------|--------|------|
| speaking | that | talk | who's | |

1  Emma Johnson _____ .
2  _____ that?
3  It's not a good moment to _____ .
4  Can I _____ you back?
5  Talk _____ . Bye!
6  This is Richard Goodley _____ .
7  I'm calling _____ a taxi.
8  Is _____ A1 Taxis?
9  Wrong _____ .

**b** ▶ Watch and listen to the key phrases and check your answers.

**6a** Work in pairs. Look again at the conversation in exercise 3b. Prepare a similar conversation and add different details.

**b** Practise your conversation.

# Writing
## A text message

**1** Some people use 'text speak' when they send text messages. Others prefer 'normal' English. Work in pairs and discuss.

- Which do you use in your own language? Why?
- Would you use text speak in any other types of writing?
- Do you know any text speak in English?

**2** Match the 'text speak' in the box with the words and phrases below.

| n | 2moro | u | wd | 4 | luv | thx | ur |
|---|-------|---|----|----|-----|-----|-----|
| 2 | c u | @ | abt | gr8 | btw | r | xx |

| | |
|---|---|
| 1  about | 9  love |
| 2  and | 10  you |
| 3  are | 11  see you |
| 4  at | 12  thanks |
| 5  by the way | 13  to/two |
| 6  for | 14  tomorrow |
| 7  great | 15  would |
| 8  kisses | 16  your |

**3** Read the text messages below and put them in the correct order.

**a**  Hi, Katy! Thx 4 ur text ... Yes, wd love 2 meet 2moro. c u @ Roebuck's, abt 5?

**b**  Fantastic!!! What is it? r u engaged?

**c**  That's gr8, c u @ 5. btw ... I've got some important news 4 u ...

**d**  Hi Sue! ... Joe & I will be in town 2moro. wd u like 2 meet 4 a coffee? Luv Katy  1

**e**  Tell u 2moro Love & xxxxxx Katy

**4** Rewrite the messages in 'text speak'.

1  Hi, Alex. Are you free tomorrow? Would you like to go to see a film? Love Ed
2  OK. What would you like to see?
3  How about *The Queen and I?* It's at the Odeon Cinema at 7.30 p.m.
4  Great ... what time?
5  About 7.15?
6  See you there. By the way, I haven't got any money ... can you pay for my ticket?
7  I'll lend you the money.
8  Thanks for that! See you tomorrow. Love and kisses, Alex.

**5** Work in pairs. Prepare a short conversation arranging a night out by text. Either write the messages on paper or send them by mobile phone.

**AFTER UNIT 14 YOU CAN ...**

Ask and answer questions about things you've done (up to now) and things you've never done (in your life).

Talk about technology (e.g. using the internet, mobile phones).

Talk on the phone in different situations.

Write a text message.

# Communication activities

## Unit 1: Task, Speaking
### Exercise 1, page 12

**E**Bank Security     Sign in

Account name: Michiko Sato
Account number: 9987 4433

Security questions
Place of birth: Japan
Nationality: Japanese
Country of residence: USA
Married/Single: Married
Security number: 34221

**Family Law Associates**

Michiko Sato
Family lawyer

Telephone: 212 544 9887
Email: sato@familylaw.com

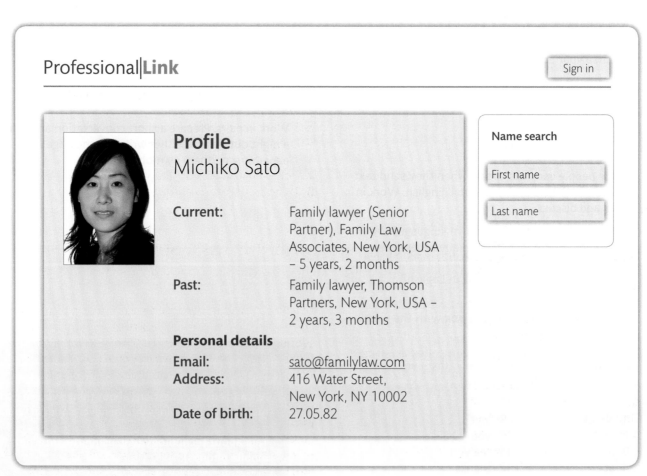

Professional|**Link**     Sign in

**Profile**
Michiko Sato

| | |
|---|---|
| **Current:** | Family lawyer (Senior Partner), Family Law Associates, New York, USA – 5 years, 2 months |
| **Past:** | Family lawyer, Thomson Partners, New York, USA – 2 years, 3 months |

**Personal details**

| | |
|---|---|
| **Email:** | sato@familylaw.com |
| **Address:** | 416 Water Street, New York, NY 10002 |
| **Date of birth:** | 27.05.82 |

Name search

First name

Last name

# Communication activities

## Unit 4: Grammar focus 2
Practice, Exercise 3, page 37
**Student A**

**Tom Daley**
Tom Daley is a champion diver. He comes from Plymouth – a town on the south coast of England. He lives there with his mother and two brothers. He spends a lot of his time training in Plymouth and in diving competitions all around the world. Tom loves diving. He says, '… in the air, you're free. It's dangerous, but I love it!' Tom doesn't have a lot of free time because he studies at the same time. He likes studying languages, especially Spanish.

## Unit 5: Grammar focus 2
Practice, Exercise 3c, page 47

**Mexico quiz**
1 Mexico has got borders with three other countries: the USA, Guatemala and **Belize**.
2 The national language is **Spanish**, but many people understand English – especially in tourist areas and near the borders.
3 The population of Mexico City, including the surrounding area, is about **18 million**.
4 There are a lot of traffic problems, so from Monday to Friday you can only drive your car into the city centre **four** times.
5 Many Mexicans travel around by taxi. The traditional colours for taxis in the city centre are **red** and **gold**.
6 Offices are usually open in Mexico City from **9.00** in the morning to 7.00 in the evening.
7 There are many famous Mexicans. For example:
 • Thalía: she's a **singer**.
 • Carlos Slim Helú: he's a **businessman**.
 • Salma Hayek: she's an **actor**.

## Unit 11: Task, Speaking
Exercise 1a, page 102
**Team A**

**Countries**
1 Riyadh is the capital city of Saudi Arabia.
2 India has around 1,600 languages.
**Science**
3 There are 100,000 centimetres in a kilometre.
4 Your heart beats approximately 100,000 times a day.
**Sport**
5 The 2012 Olympics were in London, England.
6 The most popular indoor sport in the USA is basketball.
**History**
7 Marie Curie is famous for discovering radium.
8 Walt Disney was born in 1901 and died in 1966.
**Arts**
9 Will Smith stars in the 2012 film *Men in Black 3*.
10 Adele is the first female singer to have three songs in the Top Ten at the same time.

## Unit 10: Grammar focus 1
Practice, Exercise 1b, page 89

**Answers**
1 Denzil is holding a mobile phone.
2 Mel is wearing blue jeans and a red jumper.
3 Kim is eating a sandwich.
4 Frank is sitting under a tree.
5 Pippa is wearing a green dress.
6 Tom is reading a newspaper.
7 Val is sending a text message.
8 Three people are wearing sunglasses.

## Unit 13: Task, Speaking
Exercise 1b, page 120

**Mostly a:** You are a dynamic person who is ready to do anything to be a success in life. Perhaps you will be a successful businessperson, manager or you will work in finance. But remember … money doesn't buy happiness!
**Mostly b:** Job satisfaction and 'making a difference' are more important to you than just money. Medicine, teaching or social work might be the jobs for you.
**Mostly c:** You have so much energy and you love to be outdoors. You might be a sportsperson, a fitness coach … or you might prefer to be something quiet, like a gardener.
**Mostly d:** You are a creative, person so a nine-to-five job in an office probably isn't for you. Perhaps you will be a successful musician, writer, interior designer … or even a celebrity chef!

# Communication activities

## Unit 4: Grammar focus 2
Practice, Exercise 3, page 37
**Student B**

### Victoria Pendleton
Victoria Pendleton is an Olympic cyclist. She comes from Bedford in south-east England, but now she lives in Wilmslow in the north of England. She trains in Manchester, which is nearby, and takes part in many cycling races around the world. 'I love training,' she says, 'and that's why I do it. But I hate racing.' In her free time, Victoria likes making clothes and cooking for her friends. She also works on a campaign to improve women's health and fitness.

## Unit 6: Grammar focus 2
Exercise 1b, page 55

The British love chocolate ... the average British person eats about 11 kg of chocolate every year. That's about three bars of chocolate every week on average. One of the top countries for eating chocolate is Switzerland. The average Swiss person eats about 12 kg every year.

In China, people eat more rice than almost any other country in the world ... about 96 kg every year on average. In Britain, people eat much less rice ... the average British person only eats about 4 kg of rice every year.

The average British person eats about 500 potatoes every year. That's about ten potatoes every week on average. One of the top countries for eating potatoes is Belarus. The average Belarusian person eats about 880 potatoes every year – that's about 17 potatoes every week.

Many people think Great Britain is the number one tea-drinking country in the world ... the average British person drinks about 1,095 cups of tea every year. That's about three cups of tea every day. But actually, people in Ireland drink even more tea than this ... about 1,460 cups every year – that's about four cups a day.

## Unit 7: Grammar focus 2
Practice, Exercise 3a, page 63
**Student A**

Complete the gaps with the Past simple form of the verb in brackets.

1 Grace Hopper is famous for being a mathematician and computer scientist. She helped to create the first computer and she _____ (create) the COBOL computer programming language.
2 She _____ (be) born on 9th December 1906 in New York, USA.
3 As a child, she _____ (love) taking machines apart (e.g. clocks) to see how they worked.
4 She _____ (graduate) from university with a degree in maths and physics.
5 She then _____ (become) the first woman to get a PhD in Maths from Yale University.
6 After that, she _____ (get) a job teaching maths at university.
7 She _____ (not stay) at the university. In 1941, she _____ (work) as a computer programmer and consultant in the navy.
8 In 1949, she _____ (be) part of the team which developed one of the world's first computers.
9 After that, she _____ (develop) COBOL – a computer programming language which is still in use.
10 She _____ (die) in 1992, aged 85.

## Unit 11: Task, Speaking
Exercise 1a, page 102
**Team B**

**Countries**
1 Zagreb is the capital city of Croatia.
2 The official languages in Belgium are French, German and Dutch.

**Science**
3 There are 86,400 seconds in a day.
4 Sharks have no bones and can have 30,000 teeth in their lifetime.

**Sport**
5 The 2002 football World Cup was in Japan and South Korea.
6 A marathon race is 42.195 kilometres long.

**History**
7 Madonna was born in 1958.
8 Shakespeare wrote 38 plays.

**Arts**
9 Jeremy Renner stars in the 2012 film *The Bourne Identity*.
10 The singer Emeli Sandé comes from Scotland.

# Communication activities

## Unit 6: Grammar focus 1
Practice, Exercise 3a, page 53

# Communication activities

## Unit 7: Grammar focus 2
Practice, Exercise 3a, page 63
### Student B

Complete the gaps with the Past simple form of the verb in brackets.

1 Steve Jobs is famous for being a businessman, designer and inventor. He _____ (be) co-founder and chief executive at Apple.
2 He _____ (be) born on 24th February 1955 in California, USA.
3 He was adopted because his parents _____ (be) students and couldn't look after him.
4 As a child, he _____ (love) electronics and making things with his hands.
5 When he was at school, he _____ (meet) Steve Wozniak, who also loved electronics.
6 He _____ (start) university in 1972, but he _____ (not finish) the course.
7 When he was 24, he _____ (travel) around India and _____ (become) a Buddhist.
8 After that, he _____ (get) a job at Atari as a computer technician, with Wozniak.
9 In 1976, Jobs and Wozniak _____ (start) their own company called the Apple Computer Company.
10 He _____ (die) in 2011, aged 56.

## Unit 11: Task, Speaking
Exercise 1a, page 102
### Team C

**Countries**
1 Hanoi is the capital city of Vietnam.
2 The official language of Egypt is Arabic.
**Science**
3 There are five to six litres of blood in an average human body.
4 The speed of light is approximately 300,000 kilometres per second.
**Sport**
5 There are five players in a basketball team.
6 Lionel Messi is one of the highest paid footballers ever. He's worth over $110 million.
**History**
7 Nelson Mandela was born in 1918.
8 Mozart died at the age of 35.
**Arts**
9 The musical *The Phantom of the Opera* is set in Paris.
10 Enrique Iglesias sang the hit song *Tonight* in 2011.

## Unit 10: Grammar focus 1
Practice, Exercise 1b, page 89

1 Answer as many questions as you can.
  1 What is Denzil holding in his hand?
  2 What is Mel wearing?
  3 What is Kim eating?
  4 Where is Frank sitting?
  5 What colour dress is Pippa wearing?
  6 What is Tom reading?
  7 What is Val doing?
  8 How many people are wearing sunglasses?

2 Check your answers on page 133.

## Unit 11: Task, Preparation
Exercise 4, page 102

**Countries**
1 The River Ganges is in India. The river is approximately 2,500 kilometres long, starting in the Himalayan mountains. It flows through India and Bangladesh and out into the Bay of Bengal and the Indian Ocean.
2 Lima is the capital city of Peru.
**Science**
3 There are approximately 1.6 kilometres in a mile – or 0.6 miles in a kilometre.
4 The sun is approximately 150 million kilometres from the Earth.
**Sport**
5 Spain won the football World Cup in 2010. It was in South Africa and they beat the Netherlands in the final, with a score of 1-0.
6 Wimbledon is a tennis club in England. The main championships there are in June every year.
**History**
7 Boris Yeltsin was the President of Russia from 1991 to 1999. Vladimir Putin was president from 2000 to 2008. Dmitry Medvedev became president in 2008.
8 Mount Vesuvius destroyed the city of Pompeii, near Naples in Italy, in the year AD 79. Etna is also a volcano in Italy.
**Arts**
9 Beyoncé sang the hit song *Crazy in Love* in 2003. The song also featured the rapper Jay-Z, who became her husband.
10 The name of Bart Simpson's father in the TV series *The Simpsons* is Homer. His mother is called Marge and he's got two sisters called Lisa and Maggie.

# Communication activities

## Unit 14: Task, Speaking
Exercise 1b, page 129

## Talk for a minute!

**B (Books)**
Have you read many digital versions of books? Would you rather read a digital version or a real book? Why? What are the advantages and disadvantages of each one?

**C (Computers)**
How important are computers in your life? How often do you use a computer and what for?

**D (DVDs)**
Would you rather watch a DVD at home or go to see a film at the cinema? Why?

**E (English)**
How long have you studied English? How do you feel about your progress? Which areas of English are you good at? Which areas would you like to improve?

**F (Future)**
What are you going to do when this course finishes? What are your plans for your studies, career and holidays?

**G (Games)**
How often do you play computer games? Which are your favourites? Do you play any other games? Which ones?

**J (Jobs)**
Have you ever had a really boring job or a really interesting job? What job would you most like to do? Why?

**K (Keeping in touch)**
How important is it for you to keep in touch with your friends? How do you mostly keep in touch? Why?

**L (Learning)**
How many different types of technology have you used for learning English? Which ones do you think are most useful? Why?

**M (Mobile phones)**
How do you feel if someone interrupts your conversation to use their mobile phone? How often do you use your phone when you are out with friends or at a meal with other people?

**O (Old)**
Have you ever seen an old silent black-and-white movie? Do you like that kind of film? What is your favourite type of film? Why?

**P (Photos)**
How often do you take photos? What do you usually use to take photos (phone, camera, etc.)? Do you store your photos online or in a photograph album? Why?

**R (Recycling)**
How many old phones and chargers have you recycled? Do you recycle other things? Do you think you do enough recycling?

**S (Shopping)**
Have you done much shopping online? Do you prefer shopping online or in real shops? Why? What are the advantages and disadvantages of each one?

**T (Technology)**
Have you ever spent a day without any technology? How would you feel if all technology disappeared completely? What would you miss most? Why?

**W (Writing)**
Have you ever written a letter in English? Do you often write letters or send cards to people? Why / Why not?

## STUDY 1

### *be*: positive forms

| I am = I'm | from Valencia. |
|---|---|
| You are = you're | a student. |
| He is = he's | 20 years old. |
| She is = she's | Chinese. |
| It is = it's | from Poland. |
| We are = we're | teachers. |
| They are = they're | English. |

## PRACTICE 1

**1 Complete the sentences with *am*, *is* or *are*.**

1  I _____ from Spain.
2  She _____ a student.
3  You _____ 25 years old.
4  They _____ Italian.
5  My teacher _____ from Scotland.
6  We _____ Australian.

## STUDY 2

### *be*: positive and negative short forms

| I'm (= I am) | 20 years old. |
|---|---|
| You're (= you are) | a businesswoman. |
| He's (= he is) | from Mexico. |
| She's (= she is) | Vietnamese. |
| It's (= it is) | from Australia. |
| We're (= we are) | students. |
| They're (= they are) | Polish. |

| I'm not (= I am not) | a student. |
|---|---|
| You aren't (= you are not) | married. |
| He isn't (= he is not) | Italian. |
| She isn't (= she is not) | a lawyer. |
| It isn't (= it is not) | Saturday. |
| We aren't (= we are not) | on business. |
| They aren't (= they are not) | tourists. |

**ALSO**
you aren't = (you're **not**)
he/she/it isn't = (he/she/it's **not**)
we/they aren't = (we/they're **not**)

## PRACTICE 2

**1 Rewrite the sentences using short forms.**

She is on business.
*She's on business.*
1  He is a student.
2  I am Marta.
3  You are on holiday.
4  I am not married.
5  We are not from Madrid.
6  We are from Rome.

**2 Write the short form of *be* in the correct place.**

1  I from Poland.
2  He at work.
3  You not English.
4  They Italian.
5  I not a student.
6  She 19 years old.

## STUDY 3

### Articles with jobs

We use *a/an* for jobs.
• Use *an* before vowels (*a, e, i, o, u*).
  *an **a**ctor*, *an **e**ngineer*
• Use *a* before consonants (*b, c, d, f, g, h, j, …* ).
  *a **d**octor*, *a **m**usician*

## PRACTICE 3

**1 Write the jobs in the box in the correct column in the table.**

engineer   footballer   actor   lawyer   doctor
police officer   musician   businessman

| a | an |
|---|---|
|  |  |

## STUDY 4

### *be*: personal questions

**1 Question words**

| What | 's | your job? |
| | are | your names? |
|---|---|---|
| Where | 's | Alain from? |
| | are | your friends? |
| How old | 's | Rita? |
| | are | you? |
| Who | 's | your teacher? |
| | are | they? |

## 2 Questions and short answers

| Questions | | Short answers | |
|---|---|---|---|
| **Am** I | British? | Yes, I **am**. | No, I**'m not**. |
| **Are** you | married? | Yes, you **are**. | No, you **aren't**. |
| **Is** he | Australian? | Yes, he **is**. | No, he **isn't**. |
| **Is** she | on holiday? | Yes, she **is**. | No, she **isn't**. |
| **Is** it | Friday? | Yes, it **is**. | No, it **isn't**. |
| **Are** we | friends? | Yes, we **are**. | No, we **aren't**. |
| **Are** they | in New York? | Yes, they **are**. | No, they **aren't**. |

## PRACTICE 4

**1 Complete the questions with *how*, *what* or *where*.**

_What_'s your name?

1 _____ old are you?
2 _____'s your job?
3 _____ are you from?
4 _____ do you spell your surname?
5 _____'s your work number?

## STUDY 5

### Personal pronouns and possessive adjectives

| Personal pronouns | Possessive adjectives | Example |
|---|---|---|
| I | my | **My** name's James Taylor. |
| you | your | How old is **your** car? |
| he | his | **His** address is 16 Leyton Road. |
| she | her | What's **her** telephone number? |
| it | its | The horse hurt **its** leg. |
| we | our | **Our** son is six years old. |
| they | their | What's **their** email address? |

## PRACTICE 5

**1 Choose the correct answers.**

1 A: How old are *you* / *your*?
   B: *I* / *My* am 26.
2 *His* / *He* name's Tomas. *His* / *He's* a musician and
   *his* / *he's* from Argentina.
3 Mel and I are students. *They* / *We* are in Dublin now.
   *We* / *Our* address is 24 Elm Drive.
4 Julio is from Italy. *His* / *My* children are Alessia and Silvio.
   *They* / *She* are two and four years old.
5 Selena is a doctor and *you* / *she* is from Australia.
   *She* / *Her* home town is Sydney.
6 Jenny and David are married. *Their* / *They* are on holiday
   with *their* / *they* children.

## REMEMBER THESE WORDS

**COUNTRIES AND NATIONALITIES**

| | |
|---|---|
| Australia – Australian | Japan – Japanese |
| Brazil – Brazilian | Poland – Polish |
| China – Chinese | Russia – Russian |
| Great Britain – British | Spain – Spanish |
| Ireland – Irish | the USA – American |
| Italy – Italian | Vietnam – Vietnamese |

**JOBS**

| | |
|---|---|
| an actor | a lawyer |
| a businessman | a musician |
| a businesswoman | a police officer |
| a doctor | a shop assistant |
| an engineer | a singer |
| a footballer | a waiter |

**OTHER**

| | |
|---|---|
| an address | phone/mobile number |
| a friend | really? |
| married | single |
| a name | a student |
| on business | a tourist |
| on holiday | |

## PRACTICE

**1 Write the country and nationality for each capital city.**

1 Dublin    _Ireland_    _Irish_
2 London    _____    _____
3 Moscow    _____    _____
4 Rome    _____    _____
5 Madrid    _____    _____
6 Beijing    _____    _____
7 Warsaw    _____    _____
8 Tokyo    _____    _____

**2 Add letters to complete the jobs. Then add *a* or *an*.**

_an_ a_ct_or

1 _____ b _ s _ n _ ssm _ n
2 _____ l _ _ y _ r
3 _____ d _ ct _ r
4 _____ e _ g _ n _ er
5 _____ w _ _ t _ r
6 _____ s _ _ p ass _ st _ nt
7 _____ m _ s _ c _ an
8 _____ fo _ tb _ ll _ r

## STUDY 1

### *this/that, these/those*

|  | here 👆 | there 👈 |
|---|---|---|
| **Singular** | this (book) | that (book) |
| **Plural** | these (books) | those (books) |

David, **this** is Janet Dean.
Look at **that** car over there!
Are **these** your keys?
Who are **those** people?

---

### REMEMBER!

In the answer, we usually use *it's* or *they're*.
*A: What's this/that?*
*B: It's a credit card.*
*A: What are these/those?*
*B: They're sweets.*

---

### Nouns: singular and plural

| Singular | Plural | Spelling |
|---|---|---|
| a credit card | credit cards | + -s |
| a watch | watch**es** | + -es (after -ch, -sh, -s, -x, -z) |
| a family | famil**ies** | + -ies (consonant + -y → -ies) |

### Possessive *'s*

- We use a person + -*'s* for possession.
  *Jane's brother* NOT *the brother of Jane*
  *Patrick's computer*
  *my father's name*
- We usually use *of* before things or places.
  *a picture of a car* NOT *a car's picture*
  *the Queen of England* NOT *England's Queen*
  *the Statue of Liberty* NOT *Liberty's Statue*
- If the first noun is plural, the apostrophe comes after the *s*.
  *my* **parents'** *house* (= two parents)
  *the* **teachers'** *room* (= many teachers)

### Apostrophes

We use apostrophes:
- with the short forms of *is* and *has*.
  *He's on holiday.*
  *She's got two sisters.*
- to show possession.
  *Hannah's teacher*
  *My two cousins' school*

We do not use apostrophes to show that a noun is plural.
*These are my keys.* NOT *These are my key's.*
*They've got two babies.*

## PRACTICE 1

**1 Complete the sentences with *this*, *that*, *these* or *those*.**

1 **A:** Sonia, _____ is my friend Mariko.
  **B:** Hello, Mariko.
  **C:** Hi, Sonia.
2 Is _____ man over there your father?
3 Are _____ your keys over there on the table?
4 Look at _____ photos here.
5 _____ is my phone here.
6 _____ children over there are my cousins.

**2 Put an apostrophe before the *s* where necessary.**

1 Are these your keys?
2 Thats Annas bag.
3 Shes got two sisters.
4 Whats the matter?
5 Hes Lauras cousin.
6 My fathers name is Sam.
7 Hes got three dogs.
8 Whats your brothers name?

## STUDY 2

### *have got*

**1 Positive, negative and question forms**

We use *have got* for:
- possession.
  *I've got a new mobile phone.*
  *My school's got 25 computers.*
- relationships.
  *Juan's got a new girlfriend.*
  *They've got three children.*

We can use *have* instead of *have got* in positive sentences.
*My school has 25 computers.*
*They have three children.*

| + | I/You/We/They**'ve got** (= have got)<br>He/She/It**'s got** (= has got) | a new phone.<br>a TV. |
|---|---|---|
| – | I/You/We/They **haven't got** (= have not got)<br>He/She/It **hasn't got** (= has not got) | a dog.<br>a motorbike. |
| ? | **Have** I/you/we/they **got**<br>**Has** he/she/it **got** | a dictionary?<br>a car? |

| **Short answers** | Yes, I/you/we/they **have**.<br>Yes, he/she/it **has**. |
|---|---|
|  | No, I/you/we/they **haven't**.<br>No, he/she/it **hasn't**. |

**REMEMBER!**

He's American. (= he **is**)
He's got an American car. (= he **has**)

We do not use the short form of the verb in short answers.
*Yes, I have.* NOT *Yes, I've.*
*Yes, he has.* NOT *Yes, he's.*

## 2 Question forms with question words

*How many brothers has he got?*
*What ticket number have you got?*

## PRACTICE 2

**1 Choose the correct answers.**

1 My mother **'ve got / 's got** a new car.
2 Cathy and Phil **have got / hasn't got** three children.
3 I **haven't got / hasn't got** a credit card.
4 Sam **haven't got / hasn't got** his mobile phone with him.
5 We **haven't got / has got** a pet.
6 My mobile phone **'s got / 've got** a camera.

**2 Write questions with *have you got* or *are you*.**

*Have you got* a car?

1 _____ married?
2 _____ a big family?
3 How old _____ ?
4 _____ an interesting job?
5 _____ at university?
6 _____ a pet?
7 How many brothers and sisters _____ ?
8 _____ a big garden?
9 _____ a computer at home?
10 _____ from Australia?

## REMEMBER THESE WORDS

**EVERYDAY OBJECTS**

| | |
|---|---|
| a bag | a key |
| a bottle of water | a memory stick |
| a camera | a mobile phone (a mobile) |
| a coin | a packet of chewing gum |
| a credit card | a photo |
| a dictionary | a tissue |
| glasses | a wallet |
| an identity card (an ID card) | a watch |

**FAMILY**

| | |
|---|---|
| a boyfriend/girlfriend | a husband/wife |
| a brother/sister | a mother/father |
| a cousin | a nephew/niece |
| grandchildren | parents |
| a grandmother/grandfather | a son/daughter |
| grandparents | an uncle/aunt |
| a grandson/granddaughter | |

**OTHER**

| | |
|---|---|
| beautiful | here |
| both | information |
| fantastic | interview |
| favourite person | lovely |
| fictional character | there |

## PRACTICE

**1 Complete groups 1–4 below with the words in the box.**

a camera   grandchildren   an aunt   parents   a brother
a mobile phone   a nephew   a grandfather   a niece
a mother   cousins   a DVD player

1 a father, an uncle, _____ , _____ , _____
2 a sister, a grandmother, _____ , _____ , _____
3 children, grandparents, _____ , _____ , _____
4 a TV, a computer, _____ , _____ , _____

**2 Put the words in the box into the correct category.**

a bottle of water   coins   a credit card   a dictionary
a packet of chewing gum   a wallet

| Money | Food and drink | Books |
|---|---|---|
| | | |

**3 Choose the correct answers.**

1 Maria is my aunt, so she's my father's **mother / sister / daughter**.
2 Ali is my grandfather, so he's my father's **son / husband / father**.
3 My mother is my father's **sister / daughter / wife**.
4 Liam is my uncle, so he's my grandmother's **son / husband / brother**.
5 My sister's son is my **grandson / nephew / niece**.
6 Yuko and Hiro are my son's boys, so they are my **grandson / grandchildren / grandparents**.
7 My father's grandchild is my **cousin / husband / daughter**.
8 My brother's daughter is my **nephew / niece / cousin**.
9 Mary is my mother and Tom is my father, so they are my **cousins / parents / grandparents**.
10 Lydia is my aunt's daughter, so she's my **niece / mother / cousin**.

## STUDY 1

### Present simple: positive and negative (*I, you, we, they*)

| + | I/You/We/They | **live** in a big city.<br>**have** lunch at home. |
|---|---|---|
| – | I/You/We/They | **don't go** to work by bus.<br>**don't work** in an office. |

We use the Present simple:
- for things that are generally/always true.
  *I **work** for a big company.*
  *We **live** in London.*
  *They **don't speak** Russian.*
- for habits and routines.
  *They **get up** very early.*
  *I **study** a lot at the weekend.*
  *She **goes** to work at 9.00 a.m.*

## PRACTICE 1

**1 Complete the sentences with the positive or negative form of the verb.**

We live in a house. We <u>don't live</u> in a flat.

1 I _____ to work by bus. I don't go to work by car.
2 You are from Spain. You _____ from Italy.
3 They have lunch in a café. They _____ lunch at home.
4 I _____ in a hospital. I don't work in a school.
5 We _____ students. We aren't teachers.
6 You get up very early. You _____ late.
7 I eat a lot of meat. I _____ a lot of vegetables.
8 They study at the weekend. They _____ in the evenings.
9 I _____ for a big company. I work for a small company.
10 I _____ a lot of coffee. I drink a lot of tea.

**2 Complete the sentences with the verbs in the box.**

live (x2)   study   don't live   speak   go (x2)
finish   don't go   have

My name's Ana and I [1]_____ in Budapest, the capital city of Hungary. Most people here [2]_____ in flats with their families, but we [3]_____ in a flat. We've got a small house with a garden.

I've got three brothers but no sisters. My brothers [4]_____ to school and I [5]_____ economics and English at university. English is important and most people here [6]_____ it well.

Most people here [7]_____ to work at 9 o'clock in the morning and [8]_____ at 5 o'clock. They [9]_____ home for lunch; they have lunch in the office or at a café. Then they [10]_____ a big meal at home in the evening.

## STUDY 2

### Present simple: questions and short answers (*I, you, we, they*)

| Question form | **Do** I/you/we/they | **study** at university?<br>**go** to bed late? |
|---|---|---|
| Short answers | Yes, I/you/we/they<br>No, I/you/we/they | **do**.<br>**don't**. |

**REMEMBER!**
- We do not use the full verb in the short answer.
  *Do you live with your parents?*
  *Yes, I **do**. NOT Yes, I live.*
  *No, I **don't**. NOT No, I don't live.*
- Also:
  ***Have** you got a dog?*
  *Yes, I **have**. NOT Yes, I have got.*
  *No, I **haven't**. NOT No, I haven't got.*

  ***Are** they from Chile?*
  *Yes, they **are**.*
  *No, they **aren't**.*

## PRACTICE 2

**1 Complete the questions and short answers with the correct form of the verb in brackets.**

A: <u>Do you go</u> (go) to school by car?
B: Yes, I <u>do</u> .
1 A: _____ (live) in New York?
  B: Yes, they _____ .
2 A: _____ (work) at home?
  B: No, I _____ .
3 A: _____ (get up) early?
  B: No, they _____ .
4 A: _____ (have) breakfast?
  B: Yes, I _____ .
5 A: _____ (study) Russian?
  B: No, I _____ .

**2 Complete the gaps with *do/don't*, *are/aren't* or *have/haven't*.**

A: <u>Do</u> you live in a flat?
B: No, I <u>don't</u> .
1 A: _____ Marek and Monika married?
  B: No, they _____ .
2 A: _____ your parents go out a lot?
  B: Yes, they _____ .
3 A: _____ you got a new computer?
  B: No, I _____ .
4 A: _____ you have lunch in a cafe at the weekend?
  B: Yes, I _____ .
5 A: _____ you work in the city centre?
  B: No, I _____ .
6 A: _____ they from Italy?
  B: No, they _____ .

## STUDY 3

### Telling the time

- After the hour, we use *past*. Before the hour, we use *to*.
  3.05 = five past three
  3.10 = ten past three
  3.15 = quarter past three
  3.20 = twenty past three
  3.25 = twenty-five past three
  3.30 = half past three
  3.35 = twenty-five to four
  3.40 = twenty to four
  3.45 = quarter to four
  3.50 = ten to four
  3.55 = five to four
- We can also say *three-o-five* (3.05), *three ten* (3.10), *three forty-five* (3.45), etc.

### REMEMBER!

| at | on | in |
|---|---|---|
| at 10 o'clock | on Sunday | in the morning |
| at night | on weekdays | in the afternoon |
| at the weekend | | in the evening |
| at midday | | |
| at lunchtime | | |

### PRACTICE 3

**1 Write the times.**

| quarter to four | *3.45* |
|---|---|
| 1 five past six | _____ |
| 2 twenty-five to eleven | _____ |
| 3 half past eight | _____ |
| 4 ten twenty | _____ |
| 5 twenty to twelve | _____ |
| 6 quarter past three | _____ |
| 7 nine o'clock | _____ |
| 8 quarter to ten | _____ |

**2 Write the times.**

| 1.25 | *twenty-five past one* |
|---|---|
| a 3.30 | _____ |
| b 6.15 | _____ |
| c 5.10 | _____ |
| d 11.00 | _____ |
| e 5.45 | _____ |
| f 9.35 | _____ |
| g 3.55 | _____ |
| h 7.20 | _____ |
| i 9.40 | _____ |
| j 1.05 | _____ |

## REMEMBER THESE WORDS

**COMMON VERBS**

to get up at 7.30 a.m. / early / late
to go to work / to bed early / out
  a lot
to have a bath/shower in the
  morning
to have breakfast/lunch/dinner
to have lunch at home / in a café

to live in a house/flat/city
to live with my parents/friends
to study very hard / English /
  at university
to work in an office / at home /
  for a big company

**TELLING THE TIME**

eight fifty-five / five to nine
five o'clock
one thirty / half past one

seven forty-five / quarter to eight
ten twenty / twenty past ten
two fifteen / quarter past two

**PLACES IN A TOWN**

a beach
a block of flats
a cinema
a park
a restaurant

a shopping centre
small shops
a street market
a supermarket
a swimming pool

**OTHER**

a city
(at) lunchtime
(at) midday
(at) midnight
(at the) weekend
to close
to finish
(in the) afternoon

(in the) evening
(in the) morning
(on) weekdays
to open
to start
a town
a village

## PRACTICE

**1 Complete the sentences with the words in the box.**

have   live   study   get up   go   work

1 I _____ in a big flat in Milan.
2 They _____ breakfast in a café at the weekend.
3 We _____ English after school.
4 I _____ at 6.00 in the morning.
5 You _____ to school by bus and train.
6 I _____ long hours for a big company.

**2 Choose the correct answers.**

1 I get up *at / on* half past seven.
2 They play football *in / on* Saturdays.
3 Do you have lunch *on / at* midday?
4 I don't work *at / on* the weekend.
5 Do they sleep *on / in* the afternoons?
6 I go to bed early *at / on* weekdays.
7 We watch TV *in / at* the evenings.
8 The shops close *at / on* lunchtime.

## STUDY 1

### Present simple: positive and negative (*he/she/it*)

- In the *he/she/it* positive form of the Present simple, we add *-s* to the verb.
  *He lives in London.*
  *She hates dogs.*
  *It opens at 5 o'clock.*
- These are the spelling rules for *he/she/it*.

| Verb | Rule | Example |
|---|---|---|
| most verbs | add -s | Paul wants a new car.<br>Beth comes from the USA. |
| ends in consonant + -y | change -y to -ies | This airline flies to Poland. |
| ends in: -ch, -sh, -s, -x, -z | add -es | Andy watches a lot of TV.<br>Fran finishes work at 5.30 p.m. |
| *do* and *go* | add -es | My manager goes home at 9.00 p.m.<br>Pat does all the housework. |
| have | has | He has breakfast at 7.00 a.m. |

- We form the negative with *doesn't* (= does not) + verb.
  *He **doesn't eat** meat.*
  **NOT** *He doesn't eats.*
  *She **doesn't like** coffee.*
  *It **doesn't open** on Sundays.*

| + | He/She/It | **likes** dogs.<br>**goes** to the park. |
|---|---|---|
| – | He/She/It | **doesn't like** (= does not like) Chinese food.<br>**doesn't eat** (= does not eat) fish. |

### Likes/dislikes with nouns and *-ing*

When we talk about things we like and don't like, we can use the verbs *like*, *love and hate* followed by either a noun or the *-ing* form of a verb.
*He **likes playing** football with his friends.*
*They don't **like dogs**.*
*I **hate watching** sport on TV.*
*She **loves chocolate**.*

## PRACTICE 1

**1 Write the *he/she/it* form of the verbs.**

| | | | | | |
|---|---|---|---|---|---|
| 1 | know | _____ | 6 | hate | _____ |
| 2 | study | _____ | 7 | go | _____ |
| 3 | listen | _____ | 8 | work | _____ |
| 4 | watch | _____ | 9 | have | _____ |
| 5 | do | _____ | 10 | like | _____ |

**2 Complete the sentences with the correct form of the verb in brackets.**

1 Sayed _____ (hate) cats.
2 Dominic _____ (not have) breakfast at 6 o'clock.
3 Louise _____ (not like) flying.
4 Josh _____ (love) his mobile phone.
5 Emilie _____ (not watch) TV in the evenings.
6 Jin's wife _____ (do) a lot of homework.
7 My sister _____ (wear) nice clothes.
8 Carla _____ (finish) work at 6 p.m.

**3 Find and correct the mistake with one verb in each sentence.**

1 He likes play computer games.
2 They love cook dinner for their friends.
3 She hate cats and dogs.
4 I like get up late at the weekend.
5 We love go on holiday to Spain.
6 He like coffee for breakfast.
7 I hate go to work by bus.
8 She loves watch films on TV.

## STUDY 2

### Phrases for time and frequency

We use frequency adverbs and the Present simple to say how often we do something.

0% ◄——————————————————► 100%
never    not often    sometimes    often    usually    always

- We usually put the adverb before the verb.
  *Ben **never goes** to museums.*
  *I **don't often visit** my brother's family.*
- We put the adverb after the verb *be*.
  *The winters **are sometimes** very cold.*
  *I'**m not often** home in the evenings.*
- We use different prepositions with different time phrases.
  ***in** the morning, **in** the afternoon, **in** the evening*
  ***on** weekdays, **on** Monday, **on** Saturday*
  ***at** the weekend, **at** night*

## PRACTICE 2

**1 Put the words in the correct order to make sentences.**

in the evening / usually / Ellen / studies
*Ellen usually studies in the evening.*

1 me / You / listen to / never
2 always / am / at school / I / at 9 o'clock
3 catches / He / the bus / often / to work
4 me / sometimes / on Sunday / My sister / visits
5 She / for class / often / is / late
6 on television / never / watch / I / football
7 sometimes / at home / They / English / speak /
8 never / at home / children / My / are
9 the weekend / out / often / We / don't / go / at
10 in / the / My flat / is / often / evenings / cold

## STUDY 3

### Present simple: questions and short answers (*he/she/it*)

We form *he/she/it* Present simple questions with *does* + verb.

*Does* he **live** with his parents?
*Does* she **like** London?
*Does* it **open** late?

| Question form | Does he/she/it | **live** with you? **rain** a lot in Brazil? |
|---|---|---|
| Short answers | Yes, he/she/it No, he/she/it | **does.** **doesn't.** |

### *Wh-* questions

Notice how we form *Wh-* questions with the Present simple.

| What | **does** | he/she/it | **think** of Japan? **like** eating? |
|---|---|---|---|
| Where | **does** | Juan | **come** from **live**? |
| What time | **does** | the class Anna | **start**? **get up**? |

## PRACTICE 3

**1 Complete the sentences with *do/don't* or *does/doesn't*.**

1 A: _____ you like swimming?
   B: No, I _____ .
2 What time _____ the film finish?
3 A: _____ your parents live near here?
   B: Yes, they _____ .
4 Where _____ your boyfriend work?
5 A: _____ your mother speak English?
   B: No, she _____ .
6 When _____ your class start?

**2 Match the questions with the answers.**

1 Does your brother like Vancouver?
2 Where does Elizabeth come from?
3 Where does Mr Reed live?
4 Does Maria live in Birmingham?
5 Does it rain a lot in Dubai?
6 Does she like shopping?

a No, she doesn't. She lives in Marbella.
b Yes, she does. She loves it.
c No, it doesn't.
d Yes, he does. He loves it.
e He's got a flat in San Francisco.
f She comes from Australia.

## REMEMBER THESE WORDS

**ACTIVITIES**

| | |
|---|---|
| cooking | reading |
| cycling | spending time on the internet |
| dancing | spending time with friends |
| going for walks | swimming |
| playing computer games | watching sport |

**PHRASES FOR TIME AND FREQUENCY**

| | |
|---|---|
| always | never |
| at the weekend | often |
| in the afternoon | on weekdays |
| in the evening | sometimes |
| in the morning | usually |

**OTHER**

| | |
|---|---|
| an album | in your free time |
| an artistic person | in the fresh air |
| at the beach | to learn something new |
| to check your email | to make friends |
| a concert | to make mistakes |
| a creative person | nervous |
| a friendly person | to relax with friends |
| to have fun | social networking sites |
| to have a rest | winner / to win |

## PRACTICE

**1 Add letters to complete the words in the sentences.**

1 I like g _ _ _ g for a walk with my dog.
2 She loves s _ _ _ _ _ _ g time with friends.
3 He likes p _ _ _ _ _ g computer games.
4 They like s _ _ _ _ _ _ g time on the internet.
5 I love c _ _ _ _ _ g meals for my family.
6 She likes c _ _ _ _ _ g in the park at weekends.
7 He likes w _ _ _ _ _ _ g sport on TV.
8 We love g _ _ _ g to museums at the weekend.

**2 Complete the sentences with the words in the box. You cannot use two of the words.**

always   weekend   relax   check   think   weekdays
have   fresh   free   morning

1 I get up at 7 o'clock in the _____ .
2 He loves football. He _____ plays with friends on Saturdays.
3 I _____ my email about ten times every day.
4 She loves being in the _____ air. She goes for a walk every day.
5 They _____ with friends on Friday evenings.
6 I go to the gym in my _____ time.
7 I'm tired after work, so I _____ a rest when I get home.
8 I work hard from Monday to Friday, but I don't work at the _____ .

## STUDY 1

### can/can't: possibility and ability

- We use *can* to say that it is possible to do something.
  *You can take a train from Paddington Station to Heathrow Airport.*
- We use *can't* to say that it is impossible to do something.
  *We can't take a taxi because we've only got £20.*
- We use *can* to say we are able to do something.
  *Peter can speak German very well.*
- We use *can't* to say we are not able to do something.
  *I can't play the guitar.*

**REMEMBER!**

- We always use the base form of the verb after *can*.
  *He can walk to school.*
  NOT *He can walks to school.*
  NOT *He can to walk to school.*
- We don't use *do/does* to make the question form.
  *Can you speak English?*
  NOT *Do you can speak English?*

| + | I/You/ He/She/It/ We/They | **can go** by train.<br>**can play** football very well. |
|---|---|---|
| – | I/You/ He/She/It/ We/They | **can't** (= cannot) **go** by bus.<br>**can't speak** Arabic. |
| ? | **Can** I/you/he/she/it/we/they | **buy** the tickets? |

## PRACTICE 1

**1 Use *can* and *can't* to make sentences about your school.**

buy drinks and snacks
*You can buy drinks, but you can't buy snacks.*

1 study other languages (not only English)
2 park your car
3 come to evening classes
4 study on computers
5 use the library at the weekend
6 speak to the teachers at any time
7 eat lunch in the school
8 write in the textbooks

**2 Put the words in the correct order to make sentences.**

1 drive / She / a car / can't
2 the guitar / you / Can / play ?
3 you / understand / I / can't
4 they / for us / tickets / get / Can ?
5 Indian food / cook / he / Can ?
6 Japanese / He / can / can't / but / write it / speak / he
7 can't / by bus / You / to work / go
8 English / they / Can / speak ?

**3 Complete the sentences with *can* or *can't*.**

1 I'm sorry but visitors to the hospital _____ park here.
2 You _____ use my mobile phone if you want.
3 You _____ bring your mobile phone into the exam room.
4 Students _____ borrow three books for one week.
5 You _____ leave your bicycle here. Please put it outside.
6 Please bring your ID card because you _____ enter without it.
7 You _____ pay with cash or credit card.
8 Sorry, you _____ bring food or drink into the theatre.

## STUDY 2

### Articles: *a/an*, *the* and no article

#### 1 *a/an* – indefinite article

We use *a* or *an*:
- with jobs.
  *I'm an artist.*
- with a singular noun to mean 'one'.
  *I've got a new motorbike.*
- with these phrases:
  *a lot of*
  *a long time*

#### 2 *the* – definite article

We use *the*:
- when there is one of something.
  *the capital city of France*
- with parts of the day.
  *in the morning*
  *in the afternoon*
  BUT *at night*
- with the names of some countries.
  *the USA, the UK*
- with these phrases:
  *in the city centre*
  *on the left/right*

#### 3 no article

We do **not** use *a, an* or *the*:
- with most names of people.
  *My name is Diana.*
- with towns and cities.
  *I'm from Chicago.*
- with most countries.
  *Naples is in Italy.*
  BUT *the UK, the USA, the Czech Republic ...*
- with *by* and a type of transport.
  *by bus, by train, by car*
- with times and days.
  *on Monday*
  *at 3 o'clock*
- with these phrases:
  *go to work*
  *at home*
  *most people*

## PRACTICE 2

**1 Complete the sentences with a, an, the or – (no article).**

1. My name is _____ John. I'm _____ economist and I live in _____ USA.
2. There are _____ lot of new shops in _____ city centre.
3. I usually do my homework in _____ morning, but sometimes I finish it at _____ night.
4. Most people go to _____ work by _____ bus in my town.
5. I live in _____ London, but my parents are from _____ Czech Republic.
6. He goes to school from _____ Monday to _____ Friday, and he works in _____ restaurant on _____ Saturdays.
7. I am _____ home all day today, so please phone me before _____ 2 o'clock.
8. _____ Daniel is my cousin. He is _____ architect and he lives in _____ Manchester.
9. My mum wants _____ new camera.
10. They have got _____ big house in _____ village in _____ South Africa.

**2 Cross out the extra word in each sentence.**

1. The Bangkok is in Thailand.
2. I'm a businessman and I usually work from the Monday to Friday.
3. Marie finishes school at the 3 o'clock.
4. Chris goes to the work at 4 o'clock in the afternoon.
5. The Mr William's office is on the right.
6. Sam's a teacher in the Ireland.
7. He usually travels by an underground to the city centre.
8. I usually have a breakfast at 9 o'clock at the weekend.
9. Giovanna comes from the Italy, but now she lives in the UK.
10. I've got a bicycle, but I usually go to work by the train.

**3 Choose the correct answers.**

Stephanie is Canadian but she lives in ¹*the* / – USA. She lives in ²*an* / *the* apartment in ³*the* / – city centre and she goes to work on ⁴*the* / – foot.

She's ⁵*a* / *the* businesswoman and works for ⁶*a* / – big company. She works very long hours. She usually starts work at 8 o'clock in ⁷*a* / *the* morning and finishes at 11 o'clock at ⁸*a* / – night. She sometimes works on Saturdays, too.

At ⁹*a* / *the* weekend she sometimes flies to ¹⁰*the* / – Canada to see her family. The journey to ¹¹*the* / – Toronto takes ¹²*a* / – long time. Then she has to travel by ¹³– / *the* bus to her parents' house.

## REMEMBER THESE WORDS

**TRANSPORT**

| | |
|---|---|
| a bicycle (a bike) | an underground train |
| a bus | to drive a car |
| a car | to fly to the airport |
| a ferry | to get off a bus or train |
| a motorbike | to get on a bus or train |
| a plane | to ride a bicycle |
| a scooter | to ride a scooter |
| a taxi | to take a bus or train |
| a train | to wait for a bus or train |
| a tram | to walk to work |

**TRAVELLING**

| | |
|---|---|
| to board the plane | a destination |
| a boarding pass | a flight/gate number |
| to book your ticket online | to go through immigration |
| a check-in desk | control |
| delayed | to go through security |
| Departures | luggage |
| | screens |

**OTHER**

| | |
|---|---|
| to fly | several times a week/month |
| a journey | to smoke |
| once/twice a week/month | terminal (building) |
| public transport | |

## PRACTICE

**1 Choose the correct answers.**

1. He usually **drives** / **rides** his scooter to work.
2. I get **on** / **off** the bus and then walk for five minutes to work.
3. Do you **drive** / **ride** your bicycle to work?
4. She takes a **ferry** / **tram** across the river to work.
5. She always **drives** / **rides** her car really fast.
6. They **take** / **drive** a bus to school every morning.
7. I usually **walk** / **wait** for a bus at the bus stop for about 20 minutes.
8. Sometimes I can't get **on** / **in** the bus because it's full of people.

**2 Complete the sentences with the words in the box.**

> through   pass   book   delayed   board   desk
> gate   luggage

1. It's easy to _____ your plane ticket online.
2. Can you help me carry my _____ , please? It's very heavy.
3. There is a very long queue at the check-in _____ .
4. Look! Our _____ number is A23. Let's go!
5. The flight is _____ because of bad weather.
6. I always feel excited when I _____ the plane.
7. It sometimes takes a long time to go _____ security.
8. You can print your boarding _____ at home before you go to the airport.

## STUDY 1

### *there is* and *there are*; *some* and *any*

#### 1 Countable and uncountable nouns

| Countable nouns | Uncountable nouns |
|---|---|
| eggs | milk |
| apples | butter |
| books | money |
| dogs | music |

- We can use countable nouns in the singular or plural.
  *Have you got a **cat**? Do you like **cats**?*
- Uncountable nouns do not have a plural.
  *Do you like classical music?*
  NOT *Do you like classical musics?*

**Note:** A dictionary usually says if a noun is countable or uncountable.

---

#### REMEMBER!

*Bread, toast, cake, milk, fruit juice, water, coffee* and *tea* are all uncountable nouns, but we can talk about:
- **a piece of** bread/toast/cake.
- **a glass of** milk / fruit juice / water.
- **a cup of** coffee/tea.

We can also talk about **a coffee** (= a cup of coffee) and **two teas** (= two cups of tea).

---

#### 2 *there is* and *there are*

| | Singular | Plural |
|---|---|---|
| + | There's a cup. | There are six plates. |
| – | There isn't a bottle of milk. | There aren't any cups. |
| ? | Is there a glass of orange juice? | Are there any glasses? |

| Short answers | Yes, there is. No, there isn't. | Yes, there are. No, there aren't. |
|---|---|---|

#### 3 *some* and *any*

SOME

- We use *some* in positive sentences when we don't say exactly how many or how much.
  *Have **some** grapes!*
  *There's **some** soup and bread for lunch.*
- *some* = a small number / a small amount
  Notice the difference:
  *some onions*      *a lot of onions*
  *some money*      *a lot of money*

ANY

- We usually use *any* or *no* in negatives with plural and uncountable nouns.
  *I haven't got **any** money.* (= I've got **no** money.)
  *There aren't **any** emails.* (= There are **no** emails.)
  *There isn't **any** time.* (= There's **no** time.)
- We usually use *any* in questions with plural and uncountable nouns.
  *Have you got **any** brothers or sisters?*
  *Are there **any** buses at night?*
  *Is there **any** meat in this soup?*

| | Singular countable noun | Plural countable noun | Uncountable noun |
|---|---|---|---|
| + | There's **an** apple. | There are **some** grapes. | I've got **some** soup. |
| – | I haven't got **a** bowl. | We haven't got **any** glasses. | There isn't **any** water. |
| ? | Is there **a** cinema here? | Are there **any** shops? | Have you got **any** money? |

---

#### REMEMBER!

With plural and uncountable nouns:
- we can also use *some* in these questions:
  *Would you like **some** cheese/coffee/grapes?*
  *Have you got **some** grapes / mineral water?*
- we usually use *some* in this question:
  *Can I have **some** wine/cake/oranges?*

---

## PRACTICE 1

**1 Write sentences about your town using *there is* or *there are*.**

*There are* restaurants.
1 _____ airport.
2 _____ station.
3 _____ trams.
4 _____ university.
5 _____ cinemas.
6 _____ beaches.

**2 Write questions and short answers using the prompts.**

restaurants in your town
*Are there any restaurants in your town?*
*No, there aren't.*

1 water in that bottle
  _____ ?
  Yes, _____ .
2 beaches in your town
  _____ ?
  No, _____ .
3 milk in the fridge
  _____ ?
  Yes, _____ .
4 olives in the salad
  _____ ?
  No, _____ .

**3 Complete the sentences with *some* or *any*.**

Are there <u>any</u> Mexican students in your class?

1 I'd like _____ water, please.
2 I haven't got _____ brothers or sisters.
3 I've got _____ emails from my students.
4 I'm sorry but there isn't _____ milk.
5 Are there _____ films on TV tonight?
6 There are _____ people outside.
7 We haven't got _____ oranges.
8 Is there _____ bread?

## STUDY 2

### *how much* and *how many*

• We use *how many* with countable plural nouns.
  *How many brothers/children/oranges have you got?*
  *How many cakes does Paul eat every day?*
• We use *how much* with uncountable nouns.
  *How much rice/milk/money have we got?*
  *How much coffee does Elena drink every week?*

---

**REMEMBER!**

We use *how much* to ask about prices.
*How much is it/this/that?*
*How much are they/these/those?*
A: *How much does it cost?*
B: *It's £10.*
A: *How much do they cost?*
B: *They're £50.*

## PRACTICE 2

**1 Choose the correct answers.**

1 How *many / much* brothers and sisters have you got?
2 How *many / much* students *is / are* there in your class?
3 How *many / much* money have you got with you today?
4 How *many / much* languages can you speak?
5 How *many / much* football do you watch on TV every week?
6 How *many / much* homework *is / are* there today?

**2 Complete the sentences with the words in the box.**

orange juice   are   chicken   is   plates   many
much   there

1 How _____ forks have we got?
2 How many _____ do we need?
3 How _____ soup would you like?
4 How much rice _____ there?
5 How much _____ can you eat?
6 How many people _____ here today?
7 How much _____ do you want?
8 How much sugar is _____ in this cake?

---

## PRACTICE

**1 Add letters to complete the food words.**

1 s _ _ _ _ _ _ h
2 c _ _ _ _ _ n
3 c _ _ _ _ e
4 t _ _ _ _ o
5 b _ _ _ _ _ t
6 j _ _ _ e

**2 Make food pairs using the words in the box. Make sure you write them in the correct order.**

~~vegetables~~   fish   pepper   coffee   sour   knife   bread
food   sweet   salt   fork   spices   ~~fruit~~   chips   butter
drink   tea   herbs

*fruit and vegetables*

1 _____
2 _____
3 _____
4 _____
5 _____
6 _____
7 _____
8 _____

# 07 STUDY, PRACTICE & REMEMBER

## STUDY 1

**Past simple: was/were**

| + | I/He/She/It **was**<br>You/We/They **were** | at home.<br>at school. |
|---|---|---|
| − | I/He/She/It **wasn't** (= was not)<br>You/We/They **weren't** (= were not) | here.<br>at the cinema. |
| ? | **Was** I/he/she/it<br>**Were** you/we/they | at work yesterday?<br>on holiday? |

| Short answers | Yes, I/he/she/it **was**.<br>Yes, you/we/they **were**.<br>No, I/he/she/it **wasn't**.<br>No, you/we/they **weren't**. |
|---|---|

**REMEMBER!**

*I was born in 1991.*
NOT *I born in 1991.*
NOT *I was borned in 1991.*

## PRACTICE 1

**1 Do you remember the 'Amazing children' on page 60?**
**Complete the sentences with *was*, *were*, *wasn't* or *weren't*.**

1 There _____ a young composer. What _____ his name?
2 There _____ a pop group. What _____ the name of the pop group?
3 What _____ the names of the twin actresses? Where _____ they from?
4 There _____ any Olympic runners, but there _____ an Olympic skater. What _____ her name?
5 There _____ a young footballer. What _____ his name?
6 Father and daughter Ryan O'Neal and Tatum O'Neal _____ both in a film together. One of them _____ an Oscar winner, but one of them _____ . Which one _____ the winner?

**2 Write answers to the questions in exercise 1.**

**3 Complete the sentences with *was/wasn't* or *were/weren't*.**

I ¹_____ born in Chicago on 22nd June 1977, but my parents ²_____ American. They ³_____ from Ireland. My mother's name ⁴_____ Elizabeth and my father's name ⁵_____ Ian.

My mother ⁶_____ very old when I ⁷_____ born. She ⁸_____ 17 and my father ⁹_____ 19. When I ¹⁰_____ 12 years old, we moved to Miami in Florida. It ¹¹_____ lovely and hot there. We ¹²_____ a rich family, but we ¹³_____ happy.

## STUDY 2

**Past simple: regular and irregular verbs**

• We use the Past simple to talk about:
  – a single finished action in the past.
    *My parents **met** in 1960.*
    *The film **started** at 7.30 p.m.*
  – a finished state in the past.
    *Kate **had** a happy childhood.*
    *We **lived** in a small city.*
  – a repeated action in the past.
    *She always **phoned** me on Sunday evenings.*
    *They **went** swimming every day.*
• When we use the Past simple, we often say the time of the action.
  *in 1960, at 7.30 a.m., on Sunday evenings*

**1 Regular verbs**

• We usually add *-ed* to the verb.
  *I/you/he/she/it/we/they work**ed**, want**ed**, finish**ed**, listen**ed**, watch**ed**, play**ed***
• Other spelling rules:

| Verb | Rule | Example |
|---|---|---|
| ends in *-e* (e.g. *live*) | + *-d* | She **lived** in France last year. |
| ends in consonant + vowel + consonant (e.g. *stop*) | double the final consonant | He **stopped** work at 5.30 p.m. yesterday. |
| ends in consonant + *-y* (e.g. *study*) | change *-y* to *-ied* | I **studied** economics three years ago. |

**2 Irregular verbs**

Many common verbs have an irregular past form (see the Irregular verb list on page 175).

*go → went*
*have → had*
*meet → met*
*know → knew*

## PRACTICE 2

**1 Write the past forms of the verbs.**

1 arrive _____
2 go _____
3 make _____
4 begin _____
5 have _____
6 want _____
7 become _____
8 leave _____
9 get _____
10 decide _____
11 take _____
12 die _____

**2 Complete the sentences with the Past simple form of the verb in brackets.**

1 I _____ (live) in the country when I was a child.
2 She _____ (meet) her boyfriend at a party.
3 They _____ (go) to the cinema last night.
4 I _____ (leave) work early yesterday.
5 He _____ (want) to be an actor when he was a child.
6 We _____ (have) a picnic in the park last Sunday.
7 She _____ (study) fashion at university.
8 I _____ (stop) going to the gym two months ago.

## STUDY 3

### Past time phrases

We use different prepositions with different time phrases.

**1 *in***

We use *in* with a month, a year, a decade, a century.
*in July, in 1999, in the 1980s, in the 20th century*

**2 *on***

We use *on* with particular days and parts of particular days.
*on Monday, on Friday afternoon, on my birthday, on 16th February*

**3 *from ... to ...***

*I worked for the company from 1994 to 2000.*
*The lesson was from half past six to 8 o'clock.*

**4 *yesterday*, *last* and *this***

*I saw her yesterday.* NOT *I saw her on yesterday.*
*We went shopping last weekend.*
NOT *We went shopping at last weekend.*
*He's going to university this September.*
NOT *He's going to university in this September.*

**5 *ago* (= before now)**

*They got married six months ago.*
*I phoned you about an hour ago.*

**6 *when***

*We lived in Brazil when we were children.*

## PRACTICE 3

**1 Complete the sentences with the words in the box.**

when   ago   yesterday   last   in   on

        *when*
I went to Lima ^ I was 20.

1 The concert started half an hour.
2 I phoned Jim morning.
3 We were in class together year.
4 She came to Spain 2008.
5 We took this photo we were on holiday.
6 My birthday is 20th May.

## REMEMBER THESE WORDS

**LIFE EVENTS**

| | |
|---|---|
| to get a job | to meet someone |
| to get married | to move to a different town/ |
| to go to university |   country |
| to graduate from university | to start a business |
| to have children | to start school |
| to leave school | to study maths/history ... |

**PAST TIME PHRASES**

| | |
|---|---|
| last summer/night/Tuesday/ <br>   weekend/year | 20 years / ten minutes ago |
| on Tuesday / my last birthday | when I was 12 years old / a child |
| this summer/morning/Tuesday/ <br>   afternoon/weekend/year | yesterday morning/afternoon |

**OTHER**

| | |
|---|---|
| become/became | love/loved |
| to collect things | make/made |
| a composer | meet/met |
| decide/decided | move/moved |
| feel/felt | a skater |
| get/got | start/started |
| go/went | study/studied |
| graduate/graduated | take/took |
| have/had | want/wanted |
| a hobby | work/worked |
| a journalist | |

## PRACTICE

**1 Complete the sentences with the Past simple form of the verbs in the box.**

~~move~~   leave   work   meet   study   start   get (x2)

When I was 15, my family *moved* from Edinburgh to Dublin.
1 He _____ a job in a supermarket when he was 18.
2 I _____ maths and economics at university in Leeds.
3 She _____ school at 15 with no qualifications.
4 He _____ Sonia last year and they _____ married three months ago.
5 I _____ a business in 2010 selling children's clothes.
6 I _____ for that company five years ago.

**2 Cross out the extra word in each sentence.**

1 We played football on this morning.
2 When I was ten years old ago, I cycled to school every day.
3 She had a birthday party last at weekend.
4 I went to the hairdresser's for three weeks ago.
5 They went on holiday to Spain on last summer.
6 When last she was a child, she played the piano.
7 Yesterday morning ago, I was late for work.
8 I saw a really good film on last Tuesday.

## STUDY 1

### Past simple: negative form

| I/You/He/She/It/We/They | **didn't** (= did not) | **start** at 10.00 a.m. **come** to the park. **do** the homework. **change** his phone number. |
|---|---|---|

- We use *didn't* + the base form of the verb.
- Regular and irregular verbs are the same.
  I **didn't work** at the weekend. **NOT** *I didn't worked at the weekend.*
  He **didn't play** his guitar. **NOT** *He didn't played his guitar.*
  She **didn't go** shopping. **NOT** *She didn't went shopping.*
  We **didn't drive** to the airport. **NOT** *We didn't drove to the airport.*

## PRACTICE 1

**1 Complete the sentences. Use the negative form of the verbs in the box.**

eat   play   wear   drink   go   listen   watch   drive

Two hundred years ago, people:
1 _____ computer games.
2 _____ to pop music.
3 _____ cars.
4 _____ hamburgers.
5 _____ television.
6 _____ jeans.
7 _____ fizzy drinks.
8 _____ to the cinema.

**2 Rewrite the sentences with regular Past simple verbs in the negative form.**

I watched TV last night.
*I didn't watch TV last night.*
1 He wanted to go out for dinner.
2 I walked to work yesterday morning.
3 She played the piano when she was a child.
4 I worked all day yesterday.
5 He talked to me on the phone.
6 They started the class at 6 o'clock.
7 She listened to the radio at breakfast.
8 We finished work early yesterday.

**3 Rewrite the sentences with irregular Past simple verbs in the negative form.**

He **took** the last piece of cake.
*He didn't take the last piece of cake.*
1 Tina **read** the letter this morning.
2 Jillian **left** school last year.
3 Sebastian **went** to work last night.
4 They **gave** me a present.
5 We **drove** here.
6 They **had** breakfast this morning.
7 I **wrote** that email.
8 Stacey **did** her homework last night.

## STUDY 2

### Past simple: question form

- We form most Past simple questions with *did*.

| Questions | | |
|---|---|---|
| **Did** | I/you/he/she/it/they | walk to work today? sleep well? |
| **Short answers** | | |
| Yes, I/you/he/she/it/they | | **did.** |
| No, I/you/he/she/it/they | | **didn't.** |

- We do not use the full verb in short answers.
  *Did you have a good holiday?*
  *Yes, I **did**. **NOT** Yes, I had.*
  *No, I **didn't**. **NOT** No, I didn't have.*

| What | | | **think** of South Africa? |
|---|---|---|---|
| Where | | | **live** in Spain? |
| When | | | **work** there? |
| What time | did | you he Maria they | **go** home? |
| Who | | | **speak** to? |
| Why | | | **leave** early? |
| How | | | **travel**? |

## PRACTICE 2

**1 Put the words in the correct order to make questions.**

1 this morning / Did / you / to / work / walk ?
2 their house / did / your parents / When / buy ?
3 Where / work / your father / did ?
4 did / What / you / last night / do ?
5 Did / go / John / today / swimming ?
6 have / a good / Did / you / weekend ?
7 did / go / Where / to / she / university ?
8 your sisters / to / school / go / Did / with you ?
9 you / When / did / ten / were / sport / you / like ?
10 get / the book / Did / good reviews ?

**2 Complete the questions.**

1 A: When _____ ?       B: My last holiday was in August.
2 A: Where _____ ?      B: I went to Paris.
3 A: Who _____ ?        B: I went with my sister.
4 A: How _____ ?        B: We got there by plane.
5 A: How long _____ ?   B: We stayed for a week.
6 A: What _____ ?       B: We saw the Eiffel Tower.
7 A: What _____ ?       B: I thought it was fantastic.
8 A: What _____ ?       B: I bought some postcards.

## 3 Choose the correct short answer.

1 Did your friends meet you last night?
   a Yes, they were.
   b Yes, they did.
   c Yes, they met.
2 Did Sam have any fruit for breakfast?
   a Yes, he did have.
   b Yes, he did.
   c Yes, he had.
3 Did you always want to be a doctor?
   a No, I didn't.
   b No, I wasn't.
   c No, she didn't.
4 Did you have a good day?
   a Yes, I did have.
   b Yes, we did.
   c Yes, I was.
5 Did your sisters go to school with you?
   a Yes, they were.
   b Yes, she did.
   c Yes, they did.
6 Did Annie enjoy her holiday?
   a No, she didn't.
   b No, she didn't enjoy.
   c No, she wasn't.

## REMEMBER THESE WORDS

### ADJECTIVES TO DESCRIBE STORIES

| | |
|---|---|
| boring | happy |
| enjoyable | romantic |
| exciting | sad |
| fast-moving | serious |
| frightening | slow |
| funny | |

### ENTERTAINMENT

| | |
|---|---|
| to cook dinner for friends | to go to a party |
| to download music | to go to the theatre |
| to go to the cinema | to go for a walk |
| to go to a concert | to play computer games |
| to go out for dinner | to read a book |
| to go to a musical | to watch a DVD at home |

### OTHER

| | |
|---|---|
| an action film | a historical film |
| an adventure film | a hit song |
| an audience | a lead singer |
| a band | to make phone calls |
| a (bass) guitarist | to perform/a performance |
| a comedy | a romance |
| a drummer | a sci-fi film |
| to get good reviews | to write poems and plays |

## PRACTICE

### 1 Choose the correct answers.

1 It was a very *happy / sad* film – a lot of people in the cinema cried.
2 I didn't want to stop reading this book – it was so *exciting / boring*.
3 I saw a very *frightening / enjoyable* film last night and I didn't sleep at all after that.
4 This book was very *serious / funny* – I laughed a lot.
5 There was so much action in the film – it was very *slow / fast-moving*.
6 I fell asleep during the film because it was really *boring / happy*.
7 The book was *sad / enjoyable* – I found it was very easy to read.
8 I like *romantic / frightening* films – especially when the love story has a happy ending.

### 2 Complete the sentences with the Past simple form of the verbs in the box.

cook   download   go (x4)   play   read   watch

I had a really busy weekend. On Friday evening, I ¹ *went* out for dinner with some friends. Then we ² _____ to the cinema and saw a really enjoyable film. On Saturday morning, I ³ _____ for a walk with my sister and then in the afternoon, I ⁴ _____ music and ⁵ _____ a DVD at home. In the evening, I ⁶ _____ to a party. I was tired on Sunday morning, so I got up late. In the afternoon, I ⁷ _____ computer games and ⁸ _____ a book. On Sunday evening, I ⁹ _____ dinner for some friends.

### 3 Add letters to complete the words.

1 I'm interested in reading h _ _ _ _ _ _ _ _ novels about the 18th century.
2 I went to see a good film last night. It was a c _ _ _ _ _ and I laughed a lot.
3 His ambition is to be a d _ _ _ _ _ _ in a rock band.
4 I want to see that new film – it's got very good r _ _ _ _ _ _ .
5 Everybody clapped loudly after her amazing p _ _ _ _ _ _ _ _ _ _ .
6 I don't usually like s _ _ - _ _ films – but I loved *Total Recall*.
7 A lot of people in the a _ _ _ _ _ _ were coughing during the concert.
8 He's the g _ _ _ _ _ _ _ in the band and he also sings sometimes.

## STUDY 1

### Comparative adjectives

- When we compare two things we use *than*.
  *Sarah's older* **than** *Hannah.*
  *London is more expensive* **than** *Manchester.*
- With all one-syllable adjectives, we use *-er + than*.
  *This car is* **cheaper than** *the other one.*
  *Joe is* **taller than** *his father.*
- With two-syllable adjectives that end in *-y*, we change *-y* to *-ier + than*.
  **busy:** *I am* **busier** *than I was before.*
  **pretty:** *The old part of the town is* **prettier** *than the new part.*
- With other two-syllable adjectives and adjectives of three or more syllables, we use *more + adjective + than*.
  *She is* **more famous** *than her husband.*
  *This shop is* **more expensive** *than the other one.*
  *Chinese is* **more difficult** *than Spanish for me.*
- Notice these irregular forms:
  **good:** *This road is* **better** *than it was before.*
  **bad:** *I feel* **worse** *than I did yesterday.*
- We can also compare two things using *less* instead of *more*.
  *That jacket is* **less** *expensive than this one.* (= cheaper)
  *My exam was* **less** *difficult than I expected.* (= easier)

## PRACTICE 1

**1 Complete the questions with the comparative form of the adjective in brackets.**

1 Who's _____ (tall), you or your teacher?
2 Who's _____ (young), you or your best friend?
3 Which is _____ (good), going to the cinema or watching a DVD?
4 Which is _____ (easy) for you, speaking or understanding English?
5 Which is _____ (important) for you, having a well-paid job or an interesting job?
6 Which month is _____ (hot) in your country, August or October?
7 Which is _____ (bad) for you, losing your phone or losing your wallet?
8 Which is _____ (expensive), your watch or your phone?

**2 Six of the sentences have an extra word. Find the extra words and delete them.**

1 A train is more faster than a car.
2 A taxi is more expensive than a bus.
3 A car is more easier to drive than a bus.
4 A scooter is more slower than a motorbike.
5 Riding a bicycle is more healthier than driving a car.
6 Trains are usually more bigger than buses.
7 A big car is more difficult to park than a small car.
8 Walking to work is more cheaper than driving.

## STUDY 2

### Superlative adjectives

- We form superlatives with:
  - *the* + adjective + *-est*.
    *The red dress is* **the cheapest** *in the shop.*
    *My bedroom is* **the coldest** *room in the house.*
  - *the* + *most* + adjective.
    *This is* **the most expensive** *restaurant in town.*
    *He bought* **the most comfortable** *bed in the shop.*
- We can also use *the + least + adjective*.
  *He is* **the least generous** *person I know.*
  *I found* **the least expensive** *ticket on the internet.*
- The rules are the same as for comparative forms.

| Adjective | Comparative | Superlative | Spelling rule |
|---|---|---|---|
| cheap | cheaper | the cheapest | most one-syllable adjectives: **+ -er/est** |
| nice | nicer | the nicest | adjectives ending in e: **+ -r/st** |
| big | bigger | the biggest | adjectives ending in consonant + vowel + consonant: **double the final consonant + -er/est** |
| easy | easier | the easiest | adjectives ending in *y*: **change to -ier/iest** |
| famous expensive | more famous more expensive | the most famous the most expensive | most two-syllable adjectives and adjectives of three or more syllables: **more/most + adjective** |
| good bad | better worse | the best the worst | irregular adjectives |

## PRACTICE 2

**1 Complete the sentences with the phrases in the box.**

the highest   the biggest   the shortest
the most popular   the tallest   the oldest

1. _____ waterfall in the world is Angel Falls in Venezuela. It is 979 m.
2. _____ plane flight in the world is from Westray to Papa Westray near Scotland. It takes only two minutes.
3. _____ fruit in the world is the banana.
4. _____ person ever was Jeanne Calment from France. She was 122.
5. Dutchmen are _____ in the world at 1.80 m on average.
6. _____ coin ever was from Australia. It was 100 cm x 13 cm and weighed 1,000 kg.

**2 Write the superlative form of the adjective in brackets and complete the sentences to make them true for you.**

1. The _____ (busy) month of the year for me is _____ .
2. The _____ (good) day of the week for me is _____ .
3. The _____ (bad) day of the week for me is _____ .
4. The _____ (violent) film I know is _____ .
5. The _____ (sad) film I know is _____ .
6. The _____ (exciting) holiday in my life was in _____ .
7. The _____ (boring) holiday in my life was in _____ .
8. The _____ (difficult) subject at school was _____ .

## REMEMBER THESE WORDS

**DESCRIBING OBJECTS**

| | |
|---|---|
| cheap | old |
| easy to use | powerful |
| economical | pretty |
| expensive | stylish |
| fashionable | uncomfortable |
| fast | unusual |

**SHOPS AND SERVICES**

| | |
|---|---|
| a baker's | a gift shop |
| a bookshop | a hairdresser's |
| a butcher's | an optician's |
| a clothes shop | a pharmacy |
| a dry-cleaner's | a post office |
| an estate agent's | a shoe shop |

**OTHER**

| | |
|---|---|
| busy | new |
| cool | an online shopping site |
| a department store | popular |
| famous | to post letters/parcels |
| glasses/sunglasses | to rent a flat/house |
| to have a haircut | second-hand/pre-owned |
| high | tall |
| modern | |

## PRACTICE

**1 Choose the best answers.**

1. I need to take my shoes off. They are very *stylish / uncomfortable*.
2. His car doesn't use much petrol. It's very *easy to use / economical*.
3. I'd like to buy a *cheap / pretty* bag – something not more than £10.
4. My new phone is very *fashionable / easy to use*. I didn't need the instruction booklet at all.
5. Nobody has the same clothes as her. She wears very *unusual / economical* clothes.
6. I go to work on my scooter. It's not very *powerful / stylish*, but it's quicker than a bicycle!
7. My mum got her mobile phone in 2008. She likes it but it's very *old / powerful* now.
8. I can't buy the computer I want because it's too *expensive / stylish* – it's £1,400.

**2 Complete the sentences with the words in the box. You do not need to use two of the words.**

pharmacy   shoe shop   post office   estate agent's
baker's   butcher's   dry-cleaner's   gift shop
optician's   hairdresser's   bookshop   clothes shop

1. I went to the _____ to post a letter.
2. She went to the _____ and had a haircut yesterday.
3. Can you buy some chicken at the _____ today?
4. I got some medicine at the _____ .
5. I went to the _____ because I want to rent a flat.
6. He had an eye test and got some new glasses at the _____ .
7. I took my dirty jacket to the _____ .
8. She went to the _____ to buy a present for her best friend.
9. They bought her a birthday cake from the _____ .
10. We got some new boots at the _____ .

# 10 STUDY, PRACTICE & REMEMBER

## STUDY 1

### Present continuous

- We use the Present continuous to talk about actions happening **now**.
  *I'm using the computer at the moment.*
  *Ali isn't here – he's working.*
- We also use the Present continuous to talk about actions happening **around now**.
  *We're staying in Lima this week.*
  *I'm reading a really interesting book.*

| | | |
|---|---|---|
| **+** | I'm<br>He/She/It's<br>You/We/They're | wait**ing**. |
| **–** | I'm **not**<br>He/She/It **isn't**<br>You/We/They **aren't** | play**ing**. |
| **?** | **Am** I<br>**Is** he/she/it<br>**Are** you/we/they | work**ing**? |

| | |
|---|---|
| **Short answers** | Yes, I **am**.<br>Yes, he/she/it **is**.<br>Yes, you/we/they **are**. |
| | No, I'm **not**.<br>No, he/she/it **isn't**.<br>No, you/we/they **aren't**. |

- Look at the spelling rules for the *-ing* form.

| Verb | Rule | Example |
|---|---|---|
| most verbs | add *-ing* | He's **flying** to South Africa. |
| verbs ending with *-e* | take away the *-e*, then add *-ing* | They're **living** in Beijing at the moment. |
| verbs ending with consonant + vowel + consonant | double the final consonant, then add *-ing* | She's **sitting** here now. |

- Notice how we use the Present continuous with question words.

| What | am I | doing? |
|---|---|---|
| Where | is she/he | going? |
| Why | are you/we/they | waiting? |
| Who | is/are | talking? |

## PRACTICE 1

**1 Complete the sentences with the verbs in the box.**

're waiting   'm not waiting   isn't watching   'm watching
're working   's working   're playing   's playing

1  I _____ a film on TV – it's really good.
2  He _____ football with his friends in the park.
3  We _____ for the bus at the moment.
4  You _____ very hard for your exams.
5  She _____ TV at the moment – she's asleep.
6  They _____ computer games together.
7  He _____ for a large company now.
8  I _____ for her any more – I'm going home now.

**2 Complete the sentences with the Present continuous form of the verb in brackets.**

1  I _____ (eat) an ice cream right now.
2  She _____ (not buy) a magazine.
3  He _____ (sit) on the bus now.
4  I _____ (drive) to work at the moment.
5  _____ (you / get) up now?
6  She _____ (ride) her bicycle in the park.
7  _____ (they / play) football?
8  What _____ (you / do) right now?

## STUDY 2

### Present simple or continuous?

**1 Present simple**

- We use the Present simple to talk about something that is generally true.
  *Laura comes from Rome.*
  *I don't speak Russian.*
- We also use the Present simple to talk about habits and routines, often with words like *normally, usually, sometimes*, etc. These words usually come directly before the main verb or directly after the verb *be*. They can also come at the beginning or the end of the sentence.
  *We often watch a DVD on Friday night.*
  *Do you normally wake up early?*
  *I am usually late for school.*
  *Sometimes I play football on Saturdays.*

**2 Present continuous**

- We use the Present continuous to talk about something that is happening now or around now. Compare these two pairs of sentences.
  *Jan's phoning his girlfriend.* (= now)
  *Jan phones his girlfriend about three times a day.* (= habit)

  *I'm reading a good book at the moment.* (= in the present period)
  *I read three or four books a month.* (= habit)

## PRACTICE 2

**1 Choose the correct answers.**

1  I *write* / *am writing* this email on holiday in Rome.
2  Her parents are Russian – they *come* / *are coming* from Moscow.
3  I *sit* / *am sitting* in a café with Jane right now.
4  How long *do you stay* / *are you staying* in Spain on holiday?
5  Harry *works* / *is working* in a restaurant for the summer.
6  We usually *play* / *are playing* tennis on Saturday morning.
7  Sorry, I can't come – I *study* / *am studying* today.
8  I *live* / *am living* in a flat with my parents until I go to university next year.

**2 Match the questions to the answers.**

1  Is George coming by train?
2  Does Susannah travel to work by train?
3  Are you cooking dinner?
4  Do you cook dinner every night?
5  What are you doing?
6  What do you do?

a  I'm doing my homework
b  I'm a teacher.
c  Yes, I am. I'm making spaghetti!
d  No, he isn't. He's driving.
e  No, I don't. My husband cooks dinner most days.
f  Yes, she does.

## REMEMBER THESE WORDS

### CLOTHES

| | |
|---|---|
| a baseball cap | a skirt |
| a dress | a suit |
| a jacket | sunglasses |
| jeans | a tie |
| a jumper | trainers |
| a shirt | trousers |
| shorts | |

### DESCRIBING PERSONALITY

| | |
|---|---|
| bossy | kind |
| cheerful | moody |
| confident | organised |
| determined | reliable |
| easy-going | shy |
| friendly | sociable |
| hard-working | |

### OTHER

| | |
|---|---|
| an appointment | smart clothes |
| casual clothes | to suit someone |
| a fancy-dress party | too big/small |
| jewellery | to try something on |
| a larger/smaller size | a uniform |
| a party costume | |

## PRACTICE

**1 Put the letters in brackets in the correct order to complete the sentences.**

1  She bought an expensive new _____ (rsdes) for the party.
2  Don't forget your _____ (gansessuls) when you go on holiday.
3  I wore a grey _____ (tisu) and a blue _____ (eti) at my interview.
4  I need to buy some new _____ (netairrs) for my run on Saturday.
5  Take a _____ (pemjur) with you – it will probably be cold.
6  You can't get into the Timepiece nightclub if you wear _____ (nesaj).
7  There isn't a uniform at work, but most people wear a black _____ (katcej).
8  I've got some new _____ (rotshs) for my beach holiday.

**2 Put the clothes in the box into the correct category.**

sunglasses   a baseball cap   trousers   skirt
shirt   a tie   trainers   tracksuit

| Things you wear on your head and neck | Things you wear on your feet | Things you wear on your body |
|---|---|---|
| | | |

**3 Choose the correct answers.**

1  He likes talking to people. He is *moody* / *sociable*.
2  She is always smiling. She is *cheerful* / *organised*.
3  He always tells people what to do. He is *easy-going* / *bossy*.
4  She doesn't like talking to new people. She is *kind* / *shy*.
5  He works all the time. He is *hard-working* / *sociable*.
6  She wants to succeed very much. She is *reliable* / *determined*.
7  He is someone you can trust. He is *reliable* / *bossy*.
8  She plans things well. She is *friendly* / *organised*.

## STUDY 1

### Question words

We use **what**, **which**, **where**, **when**, **why** and **how** to ask one-word questions.

#### 1 One word

A: **What's** your name? B: Irena.
A: **Which** do you prefer, London or Moscow? B: Moscow!
A: **Where** do you come from? B: Russia.
A: **When** did you come to England? B: Two weeks ago.
A: **Why** do you like it better? B: Because it's my home city.
A: **How** did you come here? B: By plane.

- We use **what** if there are many possible answers.
  A: **What's** your favourite colour? B: Blue.
- We use **which** if there are only a few possible answers.
  A: **Which** is easier: Japanese, Chinese or English? B: English, I think!

#### 2 Two words

We can make compound questions with **how** + another word.
A: **How far** is your home from here? B: About six kilometres.
A: **How long** are your lessons? B: One and a half hours.
A: **How fast** is your computer? B: Very fast!
A: **How much** bread have we got? B: Not much.
A: **How many** pets have you got? B: Five.
A: **How old** is your daughter? B: She was seven last week.
A: **How tall** are you? B: I'm two metres.

---

**REMEMBER!**
- We use **how many** for countable nouns.
  A: **How many** people are there here? B: About 200.
- We use **how much** for uncountable nouns.
  A: **How much** time have we got? B: Only five minutes.

---

#### 3 Question words and verb forms

We can use different verb forms with question words.
A: **How was** your journey? B: Very good, thanks.
A: **Which** newspaper **are** you **reading**? B: The Times.
A: **How many** names **can** you remember? B: Annie, Sally, Tom and ...
A: **How far do** you **travel** every day? B: About 100 km.

## PRACTICE 1

**1 Complete the questions with the correct question words in the box.**

....................................................................
What   How tall   When   How much   Which   How long
....................................................................

1 A: _____ are you? B: One metre 70 centimetres.
2 A: _____ does it weigh? B: Five kilograms.
3 A: _____ did you get home? B: At 8 p.m.
4 A: _____ was your holiday? B: Three weeks.
5 A: _____ team won? B: Real Madrid.
6 A: _____ is her mother's name? B: Agnes.

**2 Complete the questions.**

1 A: _____ were you born? B: In Rome.
2 A: _____ do you like best, coffee or tea? B: Coffee.
3 A: _____ cousins have you got? B: Five.
4 A: _____ do you usually drive in a town?
   B: At about 50 kph.
5 A: _____ is the station from here? B: Two kilometres.
6 A: _____ does it take you to get to school?
   B: Half an hour.
7 A: _____ are you going to go on holiday? B: In July.
8 A: _____ sugar do you take in your coffee?
   B: One spoon.
9 A: _____ is the station?
   B: About ten minutes' walk from here.
10 A: _____ is your baby? B: She's six weeks old.

## STUDY 2

### Quantifiers: *a lot of*, *a little*, *a few*, *not any*, *not much*, *not many*

#### 1 *a lot of*

We use *a lot of* to talk about a large quantity or number of things. We can use *a lot of* with both countable and uncountable nouns.
There are **a lot of cakes** on the table.
You've got **a lot of time**, so don't rush.
There was **a lot of traffic** on the road.

#### 2 *not any*

We use *not any* to talk about a zero quantity. We can use *not any* with both countable and uncountable nouns.
There are**n't any biscuits** left. Who ate them all?
We have**n't** got **any space** for another table in here.
There isn't **any chicken** on the menu.

#### 3 *a few* and *not many*

We use *a few* and *not many* to talk about a small number of things. We use *a few* and *not many* with countable nouns (not uncountable nouns). We usually use *a few* in positive statements, *not many* in negative statements and *how many* in questions.
There are **a few people** outside the cinema.
I have**n't** got **many books** I want to read.
There aren't **many chocolates** left in the box.
**How many children** have you got?

#### 4 *a little* and *not much*

We use *a little* and *not much* to talk about a small quantity of something. We use *a little* and *not much* with uncountable nouns (not countable nouns). We usually use *a little* in positive statements, *not much* in negative statements and *how much* in questions.
There is **a little water** left in that bottle.
There's **not much milk** left in the fridge.
She has**n't** got **much money** at the moment.
**How much rice** would you like?

## PRACTICE 2

**1 Choose the correct answers.**

1 There are a lot of *butter / olives* in the fridge.
2 There isn't any *tickets / time* left.
3 I've got a few *biscuits / bread* in my bag.
4 She hasn't got many *coins / money*.
5 How many *time / minutes* have you got?
6 He's got a little *food / grapes*.
7 There aren't many *cups / coffee* in the cupboard.
8 How much *space / chairs* is there in the classroom?

**2 Change the word *rice* to *potatoes* and make changes where necessary.**

I've got a little rice.
*I've got a few potatoes.*

1 There isn't much rice in the cupboard.
2 She hasn't got any rice on her plate.
3 There is a lot of rice left in the bowl.

**3 Change the word *potatoes* to *rice* and make changes where necessary.**

1 There aren't any potatoes on the shelf.
2 He's got a few potatoes in his bag.
3 I haven't got many potatoes on my plate.
4 There are a lot of potatoes in the cupboard.

## REMEMBER THESE WORDS

**ANIMALS**

| | |
|---|---|
| a camel | a fish |
| a chimpanzee | a horse |
| a dog | a llama |
| a dolphin | a rat |
| a donkey | a snake |
| an elephant | a whale |

**NATURAL FEATURES**

| | |
|---|---|
| a beach | an ocean |
| a desert | a river |
| a forest | a sea |
| a lake | a valley |
| a mountain | a volcano |

**BIG NUMBERS**

| | |
|---|---|
| five point five | fifty thousand |
| fifty | five hundred thousand |
| five hundred | five million |
| five hundred and five | five billion |
| five thousand | |

**OTHER**

| | |
|---|---|
| an active volcano | population |
| grams/kilograms | varieties of plants |
| kilometres per hour / kph | wild animals |
| metres/kilometres | wildlife |
| pets | working animals |

## PRACTICE

**1 Read the clues and complete the gaps with the words in the box**

dogs  camels  horses  donkeys  llamas  elephants
fish  chimpanzees  snakes  rats  dolphins  whales

1 live in water          _____
2 have four legs         _____
3 have no legs           _____
4 are often pets         _____
5 people use to carry things  _____
6 live in jungles        _____
7 live in cities         _____
8 have fur or hair       _____

**2 Choose the two correct answers in each sentence.**

1 We went swimming in the *river / desert / lake* near our house yesterday.
2 They spent four hours climbing up the *mountain / volcano / beach*.
3 The trees in the *valley / volcano / forest* are really beautiful.
4 These fish live in the deep water of many *oceans / seas / beaches*.
5 I live near part of a long *volcano / river / valley* going on for several kilometres.
6 The *beach / sea / desert* has very red sand.

**3 Write the numbers in words.**

1 5.4          _____
2 6,000        _____
3 70           _____
4 800          _____
5 20,000       _____
6 302          _____
7 4,000,000    _____
8 200,000      _____

## STUDY 1

### *going to* for future intentions

- We use *be + going to + verb* when we are talking about our future plans or intentions.
  *We're going to get married next summer.*
  *Jane isn't going to have a party this year.*
- We don't usually say '*going to go*' – we just use the Present continuous.
  *I'm going to the beach tomorrow.*
  **NOT** *I'm going to go to the beach tomorrow.*
  *We're going shopping.* **NOT** *We're going to go shopping.*

| + | I'm | | going to | have a party next week. |
| | He/She/It's | | | |
| | You/We/They're | | | |
| – | I'm not | | going to | study tonight. |
| | He/She/It isn't | | | |
| | You/We/They aren't | | | |
| ? | Am I | | going to | see Karen later? |
| | Is he/she/it | | | |
| | Are you/we/they | | | |

| Short answers | Yes, I am. Yes, he/she/it is. Yes, you/we/they are. |
| | No, I'm not. No, he/she/it isn't. No, you/we/they aren't. |

## STUDY 2

### *would like to* and *want to* for future wishes

- We use *want to* and *would like to* to talk to about our future wishes. *Would like to* is usually more polite.
  *I want to travel this summer.*
  *I'd like to book a room, please.*
- In the negative, we don't often use *wouldn't like to*. We prefer *don't want to*.
  *I don't want to go out tonight.*
  **NOT** *I wouldn't like to go out tonight.*

| + | I/You/We/They | want to | go out tonight. |
| | He/She/It | wants to | |
| – | I/You/We/They | don't want to | have a party. |
| | He/She/It | doesn't want to | |
| ? | Do I/you/we/they | want to | buy a new car? |
| | Does he/she/it | want to | |

| Short answers | Yes, I/you/we/they do. Yes, he/she/it does. |
| | No, I/you/we/they don't. No, he/she/it doesn't. |

| + | I/You/He/She/It/ We/They | 'd like to (= would like to) | book a table. |
| – | I/You/He/She/ It/We/They | wouldn't like to | eat that. |
| ? | Would I/you/he/ she/it/we/they | like to | watch a film? |

| Short answers | Yes, I/you/he/she/it/we/they would. |
| | No, I/you/he/she/it/we/they wouldn't. |

- We often use these common time phrases to talk about future intentions and wishes (with *going to*, *would like to* and *want to*):
  *today*
  *tonight*
  *tomorrow*
  *tomorrow morning/afternoon/evening/night*
  *this afternoon/weekend/month/summer*
  *next week/month/winter/year*

## PRACTICE 1

**1 Put the words in the correct order to make sentences.**

1 a / to / this / see / going / I / film / evening / am
2 going / not / play / weekend / He / to / tennis / is / this
3 you / Are / us / week / to / next / visit / going ?
4 book / am / to / going / the / today / tickets / I
5 have / going / She / to / a / tomorrow / is / haircut
6 not / I / get / to / early / am / going / up / tomorrow
7 they / arrive / Are / going / tonight / to ?
8 going / Is / evening / to / his / do / this / he / homework ?

**2 Complete the sentences with *going to* and the correct form of the verb in brackets.**

1 We _____ (have) lunch at 1 o'clock. Don't be late!
2 I _____ (not drive) today.
3 When _____ (you / start) your new job, Dave?
4 He _____ (meet) Christine for lunch.
5 I _____ (clean) the house.
6 They _____ (not study) this evening.

## PRACTICE 2

**1 Put the words in the correct order.**

1  want / Do / sandwich / to / you / have / a ?
2  like / please / to / tickets / I'd / two / buy
3  early / to / up / I / want / tomorrow / don't / get
4  me / a / share / like / taxi / you / to / with / Would ?
5  doesn't / cook / to / She / dinner / want
6  my / Do / to / want / you / pen / use ?
7  cake / Would / have / to / some / you / like ?
8  football / want / this / They / to / weekend / play

**2 Choose the best answers.**

1  *Would / Do* you want to go to the cinema?
2  He *would / want* like to go to a restaurant tonight.
3  I'd *want / like* to make a cake for your birthday.
4  She *doesn't / wouldn't* want to stay out late tonight.
5  *Would / Do* you like to come to a party next weekend?
6  My parents would *like / want* to meet you.
7  I *don't / wouldn't* want to play football this afternoon.
8  *Would / Do* they want to take a taxi?

**3 Complete the sentences with the words in the box.**

speak   would   want   'd   don't   do   wants   like

1  _____ you want to go to the beach?
2  What _____ you like to do tonight?
3  Does he _____ to work for a big company?
4  They'd _____ to live in the city centre.
5  She _____ to go home now. She's tired.
6  I _____ like to buy this shirt, please.
7  I _____ want to see that film. It doesn't look very good.
8  Do you want to _____ to Dad?

## REMEMBER THESE WORDS

**CELEBRATIONS AND PARTIES**

| | |
|---|---|
| a birthday party | a leaving party |
| a coming-of-age party | to make a cake |
| to decorate the house | to make traditional food |
| to decorate the table | a national holiday |
| to dress up in party clothes | a religious holiday |
| to dress up in traditional costumes | to take part in a competition |
| a graduation party | to take part in a parade |
| to hire a band | a wedding party |
| to hire an entertainer | |

**WEATHER AND SEASONS**

| | |
|---|---|
| autumn | It's snowing. |
| dry season | It's sunny. |
| It's cloudy. | It's warm. |
| It's cold. | It's wet. |
| It's cool. | It's windy. |
| It's foggy. | spring |
| It's hot. | summer |
| It's icy. | wet season |
| It's raining. | winter |

**OTHER**

| | |
|---|---|
| accommodation | live on stage |
| arts and crafts workshops | local specialities |
| a campsite | |

## PRACTICE

**1 Complete the sentences with the words in the box.**

decorate (x2)   dress up   hire (x2)   make   take part (x2)

1  I'm going to _____ a cake and some other traditional food for the festival.
2  She wants to _____ the table with pink and white flowers.
3  He's going to _____ a jazz band to play at his birthday party.
4  We're going to _____ in the parade which goes down the main street.
5  She wants to _____ in traditional costume for her 16th birthday party.
6  They always _____ an entertainer for the children at their parties.
7  They're going to _____ the house for Halloween.
8  I'd like to _____ in the competition for best music performance.

**2 Look at the pairs of sentences. Tick the pairs which make sense. Cross the pairs which don't make sense.**

It's hot.
I need a warm coat and gloves.  ✗
1a  It's cold.
  b  I can't see where I'm driving.
2a  It's windy.
  b  My hat blew away.
3a  It's raining.
  b  I need an umbrella.
4a  It's foggy.
  b  I'm going to sunbathe on the beach.
5a  It's icy.
  b  I slipped over on the pavement.
6a  It's cloudy.
  b  I need my sunglasses.
7a  It's snowing.
  b  Typical summer weather!
8a  It's warm.
  b  I'd like a cold drink.

## STUDY 1

### *have to* and *don't have to*

- We use *have to* when it is necessary or obligatory to do something.
  *You **have to drive** on the left in Britain.*
- We use *don't have to* when it is not necessary to do something, but you can do it if you want to.
  *You **don't have to go** to the party if you don't want to.*

---

**REMEMBER!**

When it is **not** OK or it is prohibited to do something, we use *can't*.
*You **can't smoke** in the classroom.*
**NOT** *You don't have to smoke in the classroom.*

---

| + | I/You/We/They | **have to** | leave. |
| | He/She/It | **has to** | |
| − | I/You/We/They | **don't have to** | leave. |
| | He/She/It | **doesn't have to** | |
| ? | **Do** | I/you/we/they | **have to go?** |
| | **Does** | he/she/it | |

| Short answers | Yes, | I/you/we/they he/she/it | **do.** **does.** |
| | No, | I/you/we/they he/she/it | **don't.** **doesn't.** |

## PRACTICE 1

**1 Choose the correct answers.**

1 I get up late on Saturdays because I **have to / don't have to** go to work.
2 Jo **has to / doesn't have to** pay. It's free for children under 12.
3 I **have to / don't have to** pass my final exams before I go to university.
4 Mike **has to / doesn't have to** wear a uniform. He can't wear his own clothes.
5 It isn't raining so we **have to / don't have to** take umbrellas.
6 We **have to / don't have to** get the bus to college. It's too far to walk.
7 You **have to / don't have to** book tickets by credit card. They don't take cash.
8 My brother **has to / doesn't have to** take his exam again. He failed the first time.

**2 Find and correct the wrong word in each sentence.**

*doesn't*
He ~~don't~~ have to get up early tomorrow.
1 I don't has to wear a suit at work. I wear anything I like.
2 You don't smoke anywhere in this building.
3 Does we have to get to school by 9.00 a.m.?
4 He doesn't has to study during the summer holidays.
5 Do you have to paying to get in?
6 You has to wear a helmet when you ride a motorbike.
7 Does they have to take off their shoes in the house?
8 You don't talk to anyone during the exam.

**3 Use the prompts to make sentences with the correct form of *have to* and *don't have to*.**

1 You / wear a seatbelt / when you drive in Britain.
2 you / do military service / in your country?
3 My brother / not wear a uniform / at his school.
4 I / not have / a visa to visit Italy.
5 your friend / take an exam this week?
6 My parents / not work any more.
7 You / go outside if you want to smoke.
8 they / book tickets for the film?

## STUDY 2

### *might* and *will*

We use *might* (*not*) and *will* (*not*) to say that something is possible or probable in the future.
- *might* = the speaker thinks it is possible that something will happen
- *might not* = the speaker thinks it is possible that something will not happen
- *will* = the speaker thinks it is probable or is sure that something will happen
- *won't* (= will not) = the speaker thinks it is probable or is sure that something will not happen

| I/You/He/She/We/They | 'll (= will) might | go to university. |
| | might not won't (= will not) | |

---

**REMEMBER!**

- We don't use *to* after *might* and *will*.
  *It **might rain** tomorrow.*
  **NOT** *It might to rain.*
- We can contract *might* and *not* (= *mightn't*) but we don't usually do this.
  *I **might not go** to the party on Saturday.*
  **NOT USUALLY** *I mightn't go to the party on Saturday.*

## PRACTICE 2

**1 Complete the sentences with *will* (*not*) and *might* (*not*) to make them true in your opinion.**

1  In ten years' time, people _____ live on other planets.
2  One day, people _____ go on holiday on the moon.
3  Flying _____ become cheaper in the future.
4  People in the future _____ live in cities under the sea.
5  There _____ be more wars in the future.
6  In 20 years' time, there _____ be more traffic than now.
7  Most of our grandchildren _____ live until they are over 100 years old.
8  In five years' time, people _____ get more diseases than now.

**2 Match the sentence halves.**

1  It's cloudy tonight so
2  Rita doesn't like Ian so
3  We need some vegetarian pizzas for the party because
4  Buy your camera on the internet because
5  Linda is good with computers –
6  It's warmer today –
7  The children can't play computer games because
8  The bus is really late so

a  it'll be cheaper online.
b  we might miss our flight.
c  it might rain tomorrow.
d  she'll mend it for you.
e  it might be frightening.
f  it'll be spring soon.
g  some people might not eat meat.
h  I'm sure she won't go to his party.

## REMEMBER THESE WORDS

**SCHOOL AND UNIVERSITY SUBJECTS**

| | |
|---|---|
| business studies | law |
| design and technology | leisure and tourism |
| economics | literature |
| engineering | maths |
| geography | media studies |
| history | medicine |
| information technology | performing arts |
| languages | science |

**EDUCATION AND TRAINING**

| | |
|---|---|
| to apply for a job/course | to get a degree |
| to be unemployed | to get into university |
| to choose a career | to have an interview |
|   (in engineering … ) | to take/pass/fail an exam |
| to do a course (in media studies … ) | to train to be (a chef … ) |
| to earn money | |

**OTHER**

| | |
|---|---|
| a foreign language | internet access |
| interactive whiteboards | video facilities |

## PRACTICE

**1 Complete the sentences using the words in the box. You do not need to use two of the words.**

media studies   geography   design and technology
maths   information technology   engineering
medicine   business studies   economics
leisure and tourism   history   performing arts

1  I'd like to do a course in _____ , especially dance and drama.
2  My brother wants to study _____ and work in a hospital.
3  I want to study _____ because I'd like to open my own hotel.
4  My friend is doing a course in _____ . She wants to be a TV producer.
5  I'm interested in _____ , especially building roads and bridges.
6  I might study _____ at university, as I'm interested in lakes and rivers.
7  I know a lot about computers now because I did a course in _____ .
8  My sister loves studying _____ , especially how people lived in the 19th century.
9  Tom is so good with numbers that he did a degree in _____ when he was 16!
10  Before Alan started his company, he did a course in _____ .

**2 Choose the correct answers.**

1  I might do a course *of* / *in* business studies next year.
2  She applied *to* / *for* a job as a nurse in the local hospital.
3  I *got* / *made* a degree in engineering after studying for five years.
4  My brother studied very hard to get *into* / *onto* university.
5  I *did* / *was* unemployed for six months last year.
6  I chose a career *in* / *of* medicine because I want to help people.
7  I might *make* / *take* my English exam next month.
8  He trained *to* / *for* be a chef and now has his own restaurant.
9  Anna was so disappointed that she *passed* / *failed* the exam.
10  He got a job in a shop while he was at university to *earn* / *take* money.

# 14 STUDY, PRACTICE & REMEMBER

## STUDY 1

### Present perfect (unfinished time)

- We form the Present perfect with *has/have* + past participle.
- Regular verbs have regular past participles. These are the same as the Past simple form (verb + *-ed*).
  *I've **finished** my homework.*
  *She **phoned** the hospital.*
- Irregular verbs have irregular past participles (see the Irregular verb list on page 175).
  *I've **spoken** to her today.*
  *He's **written** three books.*
  *We've **lost** our keys.*

| + | I/You/We/They He/She/It | **'ve** (= have) **'s** (= has) | **met** her before. |
|---|---|---|---|
| − | I/You/We/They He/She/It | **haven't** (= have not) **hasn't** (= has not) | **been** there before. |
| ? | **Have** **Has** | I/you/we/they he/she/it | **seen** him today? |

| Short answers | Yes, | I/you/we/they he/she/it | **have.** **has.** |
|---|---|---|---|
| | No, | I/you/we/they he/she/it | **haven't.** **hasn't.** |

- We use the Present perfect to talk about something that happened in the past but is **connected to the present**.
  - It happened in a present time period.
    *I've **been** very busy **today**.*
  - It happened 'some time in my life up to now' (my life is not finished).
    *She's **done** a lot of different jobs.*
    *I've **broken** my arm three times.*
- We do not say exactly when these actions happened with the Present perfect.
  *She's been to the hairdresser's.*
  NOT *She's been to the hairdresser's last week.*
- We often use these words/phrases to talk about the time period:
  *so far, so far this weekend, today, this morning, this afternoon*

## PRACTICE 1

**1 Complete the sentences with the past participle of the verb in brackets.**

1 Have you ever _____ (forget) someone's name?
2 Mark's _____ (send) about 15 text messages so far today!
3 I've _____ (buy) two new mobile phones this year.
4 We've _____ (walk) six kilometres so far.
5 Oh no, I've _____ (leave) the tickets at home!
6 Have you _____ (check) your voicemail today?
7 I've _____ (watch) five films so far this week.
8 Chantal hasn't _____ (read) any books by J.K. Rowling.

**2 Complete the sentences with the correct form of the Present perfect using the verb in brackets.**

1 He _____ (break) two plates this morning.
2 I _____ (eat) a lot of pasta this weekend.
3 They _____ (not do) any exercise this week.
4 She _____ (phone) me five times so far today.
5 _____ (you / check) your email today?
6 I _____ (not see) James this week.
7 _____ (he / fix) the computer today?
8 We _____ (take) about 25 photos so far.

**3 Complete the answers with one word only.**

1 A: Have you given him the present?
   B: Yes, I _____ .
2 A: Has she been to Scotland before?
   B: Yes, she _____ .
3 A: Have they finished the presentation?
   B: No, they _____ .
4 A: Has Joshua done his homework?
   B: No, he _____ .
5 A: Have you read this book?
   B: No, I _____ .
6 A: Has Sarah eaten her dinner?
   B: No, she _____ .
7 A: Has he spoken to the manager?
   B: Yes, he _____ .
8 A: Have you bought a new laptop?
   B: No, I _____ .

## STUDY 2

### Present perfect (with *ever*)

We can use *ever* with the Present perfect to ask about things you have done at 'some time in your life up to now'. We are interested in the action – not when it happened. With the Present perfect, we do not say exactly when the action happened.

A: **Have** you **ever been** to Australia?
B: Yes, I have. I've been three times.
A: **Have** you **ever tried** windsurfing?
B: No I haven't – but I'd love to.

### REMEMBER!

The verb *go* has two past participles: *gone* and *been*.

- *gone* = gone but not returned
  *Anna's gone shopping this morning.*
  (= she's at the shops now; she hasn't returned)
- *been* = gone and returned again
  *Anna's been shopping this morning.*
  (= she went to the shops, but now she is back)

## PRACTICE 2

**1 Complete the questions with the correct form of the verbs in the box.**

eat   sing   tell   own   meet   leave   stay   fail

1  Have you ever _____ a famous person?
2  Have you ever _____ an exam?
3  Have you ever _____ a song in public?
4  Have you ever _____ a lie?
5  Have you ever _____ up all night?
6  Have you ever _____ a pet?
7  Have you ever _____ Indian food?
8  Have you ever _____ the cinema before the end of a film?

**2 Write questions and short answers using *ever* and the prompts.**

you / break / your leg ✓
*Have you ever broken your leg? Yes, I have.*

1  you / play / basketball ✓
2  you / go / to New Zealand ✗
3  he / have / a job interview ✗
4  she / eat / Chinese food ✓
5  you / try / horse-riding ✗
6  they / see / a camel ✓
7  she / write / letter in English ✗
8  you / take / a driving test ✓

## REMEMBER THESE WORDS

**WAYS OF COMMUNICATING**

| | |
|---|---|
| an internet connection | to send a text message |
| a landline | a smartphone |
| a laptop | a tablet computer |
| to leave a voice message | to update your status |
| to make a phone call | to use the internet |
| to pick up voicemail | to use video chat |
| to send an attachment | a Wi-Fi connection |
| to send an email | |

**TECHNOLOGY**

| | |
|---|---|
| to access the internet | an online account |
| anti-virus software | a password |
| to download (photos, videos, music ... ) | to upload (photos, videos, ... ) |
| | a username |
| a hacker | a virus |
| an internet user | a Wi-Fi hotspot |
| PIN | |

**OTHER**

| | |
|---|---|
| to apologise | to get angry |
| to be on hold | so far today / this week / this |
| to dial a (phone) number | month |
| to dial a wrong number | text speak |

## PRACTICE

**1 Complete the sentences with the words in the box.**

connection   make   send   leave   pick up
attachment   update   use

1  If I'm not here, please _____ me a voice message.
2  I _____ my status on Facebook every day.
3  He finds it difficult to _____ phone calls in English.
4  I haven't got any signal on my phone so I can't _____ my voicemail.
5  She's going to _____ me a text message when she arrives.
6  You can _____ the internet for free at that café.
7  He sent an _____ with the email.
8  I wanted to write some emails but the internet _____ wasn't very good.

**2 Add letters to complete the words.**

1  I've got an o _ _ _ _ _ account for several shops.
2  Please enter your u _ _ _ _ _ _ _ or your email address.
3  My computer crashed and I lost everything when I had a v _ _ _ _ .
4  I'm going to u _ _ _ _ _ all my holiday photos onto the internet today.
5  You should never tell anyone the P _ _ for your bank card.
6  There is a Wi-Fi h _ _ _ _ _ _ in the café in the train station.
7  It's important you get some anti-virus s _ _ _ _ _ _ _ to protect your computer.
8  I usually d _ _ _ _ _ _ _ films from the internet instead of going to the cinema.
9  He hates using his mobile phone to a _ _ _ _ _ the internet.
10 I can't remember my u _ _ _ _ _ _ _ for my online bank account.

# Audio script

## UNIT 1 RECORDING 1

**A:** Hello, my name's Adam. What's your name?
**B:** Hi, I'm Teresa.
**A:** Nice to meet you, Teresa.
**B:** And you!

## UNIT 1 RECORDING 2

1 **A:** Hi! How are you?
  **B:** I'm fine, thanks. How are you?
2 **A:** This is May. She's from Hong Kong.
  **B:** Nice to meet you, May.
  **C:** Nice to meet you, too.
3 **A:** Are you from the USA?
  **B:** No, no ...
  **A:** Where are you from?
  **B:** I'm from Sydney ... in Australia.
  **A:** Oh, really?

## UNIT 1 RECORDING 5

British, American, Japanese, Chinese, Polish, Italian, Vietnamese, Russian, Irish, Spanish, Brazilian, Australian

## UNIT 1 RECORDING 6

1 Stamp *a* is from Brazil, stamp *b* is from China, stamp *c* is from Poland and stamp *d* is from Egypt.
2 The rupee is the currency of India. The rouble is the currency of Russia. The lira is the currency of Turkey. The peso is the currency of Argentina.
3 All of these words mean 'hello': *a* is in Chinese, *b* is in Italian, *c* is in Russian, *d* is in Spanish and *e* is in Arabic.
4 Samsung is a Korean company – a famous Korean electrical company. Google is an American company. Honda is a Japanese car company. Marks & Spencer is a British company.
5 Andrea Bocelli is Italian. He's from Tuscany in Italy. Delta Goodrem is from Sydney in Australia – she's Australian. Luis Miguel is from Mexico, but his parents are from Spain and Italy.

## UNIT 1 RECORDING 7

**A** Hi, my name's Lucas Kenny and this is my friend Amy. We're 26 and we're from Sydney in Australia. We aren't married – we're friends – and we're on holiday in Europe.
**B** Hello, my name's Gustavo Fonseca. I'm 19 years old and I'm from São Paulo in Brazil. I'm a student – a law student – at university in São Paulo, and I'm not married.
**C** Hello. My name's Hanna Zlotnik and I'm from Kraków in Poland. Today I'm in New York, but I'm not here on holiday. I'm here on business. I'm 33 and I'm married with two children.

## UNIT 1 RECORDING 8

I'm on holiday.
You're here.
He's from Italy.
She's single.
It's here.
We're students.
They're from Japan.
I'm not married.
You aren't on holiday.
He isn't American.
She isn't here.
It isn't German.
We aren't married.
They aren't here on business.

## UNIT 1 RECORDING 11

1 **A:** Are you a student?
  **B:** Yes, I am.
2 **A:** Is your teacher English?
  **B:** No, she isn't.
3 **A:** Are you from Brazil?
  **B:** No, I'm not.
4 **A:** Are you 21 years old?
  **B:** Yes, I am.
5 **A:** Is your name Julian Mendez?
  **B:** Yes, it is.
6 **A:** Are you on holiday?
  **B:** No, I'm not.

## UNIT 1 RECORDING 12

**A:** OK ... what's her surname?
**B:** Her surname's 'Zaman'.
**A:** How do you spell that?
**B:** Zaman ... Z–A–M–A–N.
**A:** Thank you. And what's her home number?
**B:** Er, her home number is: oh, two, oh ...
**A:** Oh, two, oh ...
**B:** ... eight ... three ... four ... eight ...
**A:** Hmm ... yes ...
**B:** ... nine ... eight ... four ... one.
**A:** OK, thanks. What's her job?
**B:** Her job? Er, I don't know.
**A:** OK ... Is she married or single?
**B:** She's married. Her husband is Yamin ... Yamin Zaman.
**A:** Thank you.

## UNIT 2 RECORDING 2

Hi, my name's Ed Turner. This is my wife Thelma ... and these are my beautiful children, Ike and Tina, and Tina's cat, Buddy. And that's our dog Bono over there. That's his little house and those are Bono's friends!

## UNIT 2 RECORDING 4

1 What's this in English?
2 Is this your wallet?
3 Is that your bag?
4 This is my friend Ben.
5 These are my parents.
6 That's my teacher over there.
7 Who are those children?
8 Are these your glasses?

## UNIT 2 RECORDING 5

**A:** Look, that's beautiful! I haven't got my camera with me. Have you got one?
**B:** No, but I've got my mobile phone. Here you are.
**A:** Oh, thanks!

## UNIT 2 RECORDING 6

I've got my mobile phone with me.
He's got his credit card.
We've got the bag.
I haven't got my watch with me.
She hasn't got her glasses.
They haven't got the keys.
Have you got a dictionary?
Has he got a camera?
Have they got a bottle of water?

## UNIT 2 RECORDING 7

1  My sister's son is my nephew.
2  My aunt's son is my cousin.
3  My brother's daughter is my niece.
4  My mother's brother is my uncle.
5  My father's mother is my grandmother.
6  My mother and father are my parents.

## UNIT 2 RECORDING 8

My name's Liz. I'm from Leeds in the north of England. I'm 27 years old and these are my five favourite people. Number 1: this is my brother, Anthony. He's, er, 25? No, 26 ... yes, he's 26 ... and he's married. He's got two children – a son and a daughter. And this is Anthony's daughter, Emily ... my niece. She's three years old. Look at her! Ah, she's lovely ... And this is my friend Elaine. She's a really good friend. She's a teacher. She's got a new job in a school in Leeds ... This is my favourite actor, George Clooney. He's fantastic. He's from the USA ... How old is he? I don't know. Fifty-something, I think ... Yeah, he's not a real person, but ... Sherlock Holmes. He's a famous British detective. He's my favourite fictional character.

## UNIT 3 RECORDING 1

1  Amrita and Geeta live in a flat in Bangalore.
2  They study at university in Bangalore.
3  They go to university by bus.
4  They have dinner in a restaurant.
5  Jairam and Sanjula live in a small village.
6  Jairam and his friends get up very early.
7  They work for a small company.
8  They have dinner at home with their families.

## UNIT 3 RECORDING 2

R = Rita    N = Niall

R:  Do you live with your family or friends?
N:  I live with my family. We live in a flat in the town centre. What about you?
R:  I live with my family, too, but not in the town centre. I get up early and go to university by bus. Do you get up early?
N:  No, I don't! I get up at nine o'clock, or sometimes ten.
R:  And do you have breakfast at home?
N:  Yes, I do. I have a cup of coffee and some bread. And you?
R:  I don't have breakfast. I have a big lunch instead ... in a café, usually. Do you have lunch in a café?
N:  Yes, I do. I have lunch in this café ... but just a small lunch, like a sandwich or something. I have lunch early ... usually at about 12.30.
R:  What about in the evening? Do you have dinner early?
N:  I have dinner at different times ... sometimes at home and sometimes I go out.
R:  And do you go to bed early?
N:  No, I don't. I go to bed about twelve o'clock ... or sometimes one or two o'clock in the morning. I study a lot in the evening ... and I go out a lot, too!

## UNIT 3 RECORDING 3

1  A: Do you live in a house?
   B: No, I don't. I live in a flat.
2  A: Do you go to English classes?
   B: Yes, I do. I study very hard.
3  A: Do you go out a lot in the evening?
   B: Yes, I do. I have dinner in restaurants a lot.
4  A: Do you have a shower in the evening?
   B: No, I don't. I have a shower in the morning.
5  A: Do you work in an office?
   B: No, I don't. I work in a hospital.
6  A: Do you get up early?
   B: No, I don't. I get up at about 8.30 a.m.

## UNIT 3 RECORDING 4

1  Do you live in a house?
2  Do you go to English classes?
3  Do you go out a lot in the evening?
4  Do you have a shower in the evening?
5  Do you work in an office?
6  Do you get up early?

## UNIT 3 RECORDING 5

**Example**
A:  What's the time?
B:  It's nine fifty-five.
C:  It's five to ten.
1  A: What's the time?
   B: It's seven fifteen.
   C: It's quarter past seven.
2  A: What's the time?
   B: It's nine thirty.
   C: It's half past nine.
3  A: What's the time?
   B: It's eight forty.
   C: It's twenty to nine.
4  A: What's the time?
   B: It's six forty-five.
   C: It's quarter to seven.
5  A: What's the time?
   B: It's twelve o-five.
   C: It's five past twelve.
6  A: What's the time?
   B: It's two twenty.
   C: It's twenty past two.
7  A: What's the time?
   B: It's four o'clock.

## UNIT 3 RECORDING 6

I live on the Isle of Lewis in the Outer Hebrides ... in a town called Stornoway. It's a very special place. The first thing is, it's a long way from everywhere else. You can take a ferry from Ullapool on the Scottish mainland. That takes two hours forty minutes.

We've got lots of shops in Stornoway. We've even got a little supermarket which is open till midnight, although most shops close at five o'clock. And one thing to remember is that everything is very busy on Saturday, especially on Saturday night, but everything is closed on Sunday. Everything!

Stornoway is very far north, so in summer the days are very long. At 10.30 in the evening, it's not dark ... you can still see the sun ... it's beautiful. We actually have a different language, called Gaelic ... but people speak English as well. Stornoway is really a fantastic place ... so come and visit us!

## UNIT 3 RECORDING 7

I = Interviewer    M = Mike

I:  So, in Melbourne do most people live in houses or flats?
M:  I'd say ... er ... most people live in houses. Most people don't live in the city centre, they live outside.
I:  OK, and what time do children start school?
M:  Usually at nine ... nine o'clock ... Yeah, my children start at nine, certainly.
I:  And what time do they finish?
M:  Three thirty. Half past three.
I:  So ... a question about people in offices ... Where do most people have lunch?
M:  Gosh ... well nowadays, people don't have time to go home ... or go to a restaurant ... so they have a sandwich outside in the park or something to eat in the office.
I:  What time do shops close in Melbourne?
M:  Well, in Melbourne, shops close about six or seven ... they're open late Thursday and Friday ... and there are 24-hour shops nowadays.
I:  Do shops close at lunchtime?
M:  No, they don't.
I:  And do shops open on Sunday?
M:  I think everything's open on Sunday nowadays.
I:  How about dinner? What time do people have dinner?
M:  At home?
I:  Yeah.
M:  Well, at home, I think most Australians eat quite early ... about six o'clock. And some restaurants are open late, but most restaurants close at around 9.30 or ten. Um... some restaurants are open late, especially Chinese restaurants.

# Audio script

## UNIT 3 RECORDING 8

I = Interviewer   M = Mike

I: OK, so let me check ... in Melbourne, most people live in houses.
M: Yeah, I think so.
I: Children start school at nine o'clock ...
M: Yeah ...
I: ... and finish at three.
M: 3.30 ... They finish at 3.30.
I: Oh sorry, yes ... they finish school at half past three, not three o'clock.
M: That's right.
I: And at lunchtime, most people don't go home or go to a restaurant – they have lunch in their office or outside.
M: OK, yeah ...
I: Most shops are open late on Thursday and Friday ...
M: Uh huh ...
I: ... and they don't close at lunchtime ... And the shops open on Sunday.
M: Yeah ...
I: And most people have dinner at about six o'clock, if they're at home ... And restaurants close at about 9.30, ten.
M: *Most* restaurants ...
I: Most restaurants ... OK, that's it! Thanks very much.
M: You're welcome!

## UNIT 4 RECORDING 1

P = Presenter

P: Adele comes from London, but she is famous throughout the world thanks to albums such as *19* and *21*. But Adele is different from many other pop stars. Emma May tells us why.

## UNIT 4 RECORDING 2

E = Emma   P = Presenter

E: Adele lives in a £6 million house in England, but she likes the simple things in life. She loves her dog, Louis Armstrong, and likes going for walks with him. She also loves spending time with her mother, Penny. She has some close friends and likes going to restaurants and spending time with them.
P: Adele loves singing, of course, but she doesn't like doing big concerts ... she says she's very nervous. She doesn't like flying ... she hates the food on aeroplanes!
E: She wears simple black clothes for concerts, but at other times she likes comfortable clothes. She doesn't have lots of crazy clothes like some pop stars. She says, 'I don't make music for eyes. I make music for ears!'

## UNIT 4 RECORDING 4

1 She likes London.
2 He watches TV.
3 He loves football.
4 She hates cats.
5 It opens early.
6 It closes late.
7 It starts at two o'clock.
8 It finishes today.
9 She understands English.
10 He goes to bed late.
11 He does the housework.
12 She studies economics.

## UNIT 4 RECORDING 5

1 Does Denise Lewis come from England?
2 Does she appear on TV?
3 Who does she work for?
4 Does she live in Birmingham now?
5 Does she like dancing?
6 What other sports does she do?
7 Where does she live now?
8 How many children does she have?

## UNIT 4 RECORDING 6

L = Lucy   C = Cassia   J = Juan   T = Tom

L: My name's Lucy, I'm from Australia ... and I love being in the fresh air; I don't like being inside. I live in Sydney, so I'm always at the beach ... and I love swimming and being near water generally. I like scenery, too, but the sea's my favourite.
C: My name is Cassia. I am from Brazil. I think I'm a very creative person. I love working with other people to create something wonderful ... a work of art, maybe, or some beautiful music. I don't play an instrument, but I sing and I love dancing, too.
J: I am Juan. I am Spanish ... I am a student at university. My subject is art history. I love music, I love painting, but I want to do something quiet, something artistic. I don't like being with a lot of other people all the time ... I like being alone sometimes, so I can think and look at beautiful scenery, or something like that.
T: I'm Tom ... I'm a professional musician, a very friendly person. I like meeting people ... and I like learning new things. I enjoy going out with friends, maybe to a bar or to a restaurant for something to eat. I like good food, but I don't like cooking.

## UNIT 4 RECORDING 7

A: OK ... Lucy ... she likes being outside ...
B: Yeah, she loves being in the fresh air ... she doesn't like being inside.
A: Yes, so maybe the painting course is good for her, because she likes being outside.
B: Mmm ... I'm not sure ... I think she wants something active.
A: Or ... the sailing course? That's outside *and* active. What do you think?
B: I think the sailing course is good for her, because she likes being near the water.
A: Yes, you're right. It's perfect for her.
B: Yes, I agree. So ... 'Sailing' for Lucy.

## UNIT 5 RECORDING 1

1 In the USA, 74% of people drive a car. In Japan, it's 59%; and in Germany, it's 53%. The average American family owns 1.9 cars.
2 More than 100 million people in the world ride a bicycle. About a third of these people are in China. In the Netherlands, about 30% of people choose to ride a bicycle. But in the USA, it's only about 2%.
3 In Italy, a country of 60 million people, 9 million people have scooters. In Rome, 500,000 people ride scooters, so they can get about easily in the city traffic.
4 In Italy, the average journey to work is about 25 minutes; and in the USA, it's about 32 minutes. In Great Britain, it's about 45 minutes – that's nearly 200 hours a year travelling to and from work.
5 Every day, more than 1 million people travel into the centre of London: 77% take a bus or train, about 20% drive and only 3% walk to work.
6 There are over 160 underground train systems in the world, including those in Paris, Shanghai, Mexico City, Seoul, Moscow, Madrid and Tokyo.
7 The London Underground, or the 'Tube', has 270 stations. Over 1,000 million passengers use the Tube every year.
8 The underground train system in Tokyo is very efficient: people usually wait no more than five minutes for a train. The only problem is that it's sometimes difficult to get on or off a train because they're often very crowded.
9 The two busiest international airports are Hartsfield–Jackson Airport in Atlanta, USA, with 71 million passengers every year, and Beijing Capital International Airport, with 60 million. That means about 160 people fly to Atlanta every minute.

## UNIT 5 RECORDING 3

1 You decide to fly somewhere for the weekend.
2 You book your ticket online.
3 You go to the airport and look for 'Departures'.
4 You go to the check-in desk with your luggage.
5 They take your luggage and give you a boarding pass.
6 You go through security.
7 You look at the screens for your flight and gate number.
8 Your flight is delayed so you wait in the departure lounge.
9 Finally, you board the plane.
10 You arrive at your destination and go through immigration control.

## UNIT 5 RECORDING 4

1  You can eat at all times of the day and night.
2  You can't sleep in Terminal 1.
3   You can play golf near the airport.
4  You can't smoke in Terminal 1.
5  **A:** Can you smoke in Terminal 2?
   **B:** Yes, you can.
6  **A:** Can you sleep in Terminal 1?
   **B:** No, you can't.

## UNIT 5 RECORDING 5

The public transport system in Hong Kong is mostly very modern, but for something different you can always take a tram. The trams are actually more than a hundred years old, but they are an interesting tourist attraction – they're not fast, but they are cheap! The underground train system is very, very clean ... and one reason for this is that you can't eat or drink on the trains. The trains are very good – you can always find a seat and the trains come every two or three minutes. Taxis are a really good way to get around Hong Kong. We have lots and lots of taxis. At busy times, you can't always find an empty taxi very quickly ... but you get one in the end.

One thing that you really need is a special travel card, called an 'Octopus' card. You pay for it and then you can use it on the whole public transport system. You can even use it to buy food and drink! So you can buy yourself a burger and a drink with your Octopus card!

## UNIT 5 RECORDING 7

I = Interviewer    F = female interviewee
I:  OK, thanks for doing the survey.
F:  That's all right.
I:  So, first question ... How do you travel to school or work every day?
F:  Well, I don't go to school and I don't go to work ... I go to university.
I:  So how do you travel to university?
F:  I go by bike.
I:  Bike, OK ... and how long does your journey take?
F:  Um, let me see ...
I:  One to ten minutes? Ten to 20 minutes? More ... ?
F:  Er, I'd say about 15 minutes.
I:  Fifteen ... so it's 'b' – ten to 20 minutes?
F:  Yeah.
I:  Question 3 ... How far do you walk every week?
F:  Hmm ... how far do I walk?
I:  Nought to five kilometres? Six to ten ...
F:  I'd say nought to five ... I go everywhere by bike, usually.
I:  Nought to five, OK ... And which of these things can you do ... Can you drive a car?
F:  Yes, I can.
I:  Can you ride a bike?
F:  Yes, of course!
I:  Can you ride a scooter?
F:  Um ... yeah ...
I:  And can you drive a van?
F:  A van? Well, I never ... no, I can't.
I:  OK, thank you ... Question 5 ... How often do you travel by car?
F:  That's interesting, because I can drive but I haven't got a car ... so I don't drive very often.
I:  Once a week? Several times a week?
F:  I'd say several times. My friend's got a car and she sometimes drives me.
I:  That's fine ... several times. OK ... Question 6 ... How often do you use public transport?
F:  Well, as I say, I usually go by bike so I don't use public transport much. Maybe once a week?
I:  Once a week, OK. What do you think of public transport in your town?
F:  What do I think?
I:  Yeah, is it a) excellent b) good c) OK or d) not good?
F:  Well, I don't know really ... I don't use public transport very much.
I:  Ah, so 'e' ... 'don't know' ... that's good. And last question ... Which is your favourite method of transport?
F:  Ah, that's an easy one!
I:  I think I know this answer ...
F:  Bicycle, of course ... I love my bicycle!

## UNIT 6 RECORDING 1

**Countable nouns:**  grapes, an apple, a banana, eggs, tomatoes, a sandwich, biscuits
**Uncountable nouns:**  water, bread, chicken, cheese, olive oil, salad, orange juice, fruit

## UNIT 6 RECORDING 2

1  There's an apple.
2  There are five grapes.
3  There are some tomatoes.
4  There are a lot of bananas.
5  There's some olive oil.
6  There's a lot of apple juice.
7  There aren't any eggs.
8  There isn't any cheese.

## UNIT 6 RECORDING 4

**Jo**
The name of my favourite restaurant is Fish Kitchen ... it's got a great location, by the river ... and when the weather's good, you can sit outside and the view is really nice. As for the food, well, the name of the restaurant is Fish Kitchen, so obviously people go for fish and chips. It's always busy, and it's very friendly ... there are always lots of families. I like it because I love fish and chips, it's not expensive and it's a great place to go with your friends.

**Tristan**
One of the fantastic things about living in London is that you can get food from all around the world. One of my favourite kinds of food is from Vietnam. Near where I work, there is a really good Vietnamese restaurant ... I often go there for lunch. The cooks are all Vietnamese and they do all the cooking in front of you. The speciality is *bun cha*, which is noodles with meat and chilli and sauce. The sauce is delicious – it's made with fish and vegetables. Mmm ... I love it!

**Kate**
I don't like expensive restaurants. My favourite place to eat isn't an expensive restaurant ... it's my grandmother's house. She lives in a small town near where I live. I have lunch there every week. My grandmother always cooks a big lunch on Sunday for the whole family. A typical dish for Sunday lunch is roast meat ... we usually have roast beef with potatoes and vegetables. I love eating there because I'm with my family. The important thing is that my grandma always cooks with love ... so I feel happy there.

## UNIT 7 RECORDING 1

1  The composer Wolfgang Amadeus Mozart is perhaps the most famous composer of all time. He was born in 1756 in the town of Salzburg, in Austria.
2  Michael Jackson began his life in the music industry with his four brothers in a group called The Jackson 5. Their first record was *I Want You Back* – in 1970 – and the group were famous throughout the 1970s.
3  Mary-Kate and Ashley Olsen are twins. They were born in 1986 in the USA and they were in their first TV show when they were just nine months old. They weren't in the show together – only one at a time – playing the same part until they were eight years old.
4  Skater Tara Lipinski won a gold medal at the 1998 Winter Olympics in Nagano, Japan. At the time, she was just 15 years old.
5  Brazilian footballer Pelé was 16 years old when he began his professional career at Santos Football Club. In 1958, he was the youngest footballer to play in a World Cup final, aged just 17, scoring two goals in the final against Sweden.
6  American actress Tatum O'Neal was only ten years old when she won an Oscar for her role in the 1973 movie *Paper Moon*. Her father, Ryan O'Neal, was also in the movie – but he wasn't an Oscar winner!

## UNIT 7 RECORDING 3

worked, studied, arrived, loved, needed, waited, believed, lived, wanted, liked, decided, invented, walked, started, died

# Audio script

## UNIT 7 RECORDING 4

1 a We wanted the bill.
  b We want the bill.
2 a I need some money.
  b I needed some money.
3 a They live in Spain.
  b They lived in Spain.
4 a I liked her.
  b I like her.
5 a They arrive at eight o'clock.
  b They arrived at eight o'clock.
6 a We worked hard.
  b We work hard.
7 a I love chocolate.
  b I loved chocolate.
8 a I believed you.
  b I believe you.

## UNIT 7 RECORDING 5

Jacqueline Lee Bouvier was born on Long Island, near New York, in July 1929. She was the daughter of wealthy parents and spent a happy childhood in and around New York. She studied at university in the USA and at the Sorbonne in Paris, France. She completed her degree in French Literature in 1951. In that same year, she began work as a journalist, and she also met the man who changed her life: the future President of the United States, John F. Kennedy.

The couple fell in love and in 1953 they got married. There were 700 guests at the wedding. They then spent their honeymoon in Acapulco, Mexico. Seven years later, in November 1960, John Kennedy won the presidential election and Jacqueline – or Jackie – Kennedy was the First Lady of the United States.

As a couple, the Kennedys travelled to many countries, including France, India and Germany. Jackie Kennedy soon became more than a president's wife: she became a style icon for women all over the world. On one trip, JFK joked, 'I am the man who accompanied Jackie Kennedy to Paris … '

## UNIT 7 RECORDING 6

In November 1963, the Kennedys left the White House for their last trip together – to Dallas, Texas. On 22nd November, a gunman shot John F. Kennedy dead. After the murder of Kennedy's brother, Robert, or Bobby, in 1968, Jackie Kennedy left America and married Greek millionaire businessman Aristotle Onassis. When Onassis died suddenly in 1975, she returned to the USA and worked for a publishing company. In 1994, she died. Among the tributes were flowers from the famous singer Frank Sinatra. The note read simply 'You are America's Queen'.

## UNIT 7 RECORDING 7

1 My cousin is called Alice. She was born in London in 1972. As a child, Alice loved sports and being outdoors. She didn't study very hard at school because she wanted to play sports all the time.
2 When she was 18, she left school, but she didn't go to university. She got a job in America – the job was teaching sports to children at a summer camp.
3 When Alice was in America, she met her boyfriend, Todd. They travelled around America together on his motorbike, but after six months she came back to the UK because she didn't have a visa.
4 After that, Alice decided to go to university. She graduated at the age of 22 and got a job in the UK as a teacher in a large secondary school.
5 She lost touch with Todd and they didn't see each other for a long time. But after 13 years, she got a letter from Todd and they decided to meet again.
6 Then Alice made some big decisions. She went back to America, got married to Todd and had two children. She went back to college and retrained as a nurse. In the end, she got a job in a hospital in New York – and she is very happy with her life.

## UNIT 8 RECORDING 1

P = Presenter   R = Reporter

P: So, today we are talking about a song … a song which is famous all over the world … which also became an incredibly successful musical. Tony Jenkins is here to talk to us about the song and musical We Will Rock You … Hello, Tony.
R: Hello.
P: First, tell me about the original song. When did the song come out?
R: Well, the British rock band Queen started writing songs and performing in the 1970s and We Will Rock You became a number one hit for them in 1977. Queen's lead singer was Freddie Mercury, but the guitarist, Brian May, wrote the song.
P: Brian May … mmm … Why did he write the song?
R: Well, he wrote it after a concert. When the concert finished, the audience didn't want to go home. They started singing a football song … a kind of chant … because they wanted Queen to come back on stage. That chanting by the audience inspired May to write We Will Rock You.
P: The song sounds a bit like a football chant, doesn't it? With the background beat of stamping and clapping …
R: That's right. In fact, people often sing We Will Rock You at football matches and other sporting events. It's a very inspirational song – an anthem really – that inspires people.
P: Yes … and what about the musical? Did Brian May write the musical?
R: Well, no, he didn't write it. British comedian Ben Elton wrote the musical, but he worked very closely with Brian May and Queen's drummer, Roger Taylor. Ben Elton wrote the story, and Brian May and Roger Taylor worked with him, fitting the songs around the story … they are all Queen songs.
P: And … what is the story?
R: Well, the story is set in the future – 300 years from now. It is a world where you can't write your own music. People watch the same films, listen to the same music, wear the same clothes and have the same opinions.
P: Who is the main character?
R: The main character is called Galileo … and he doesn't want to be the same as everyone else. He wants to be different.
P: And when did the musical come out?
R: The first performance was in May 2002 at the Dominion Theatre in London.
P: Did the musical get good reviews?
R: Well, actually no … the critics didn't like it at all.
P: Really?
R: Mmm … but the audiences loved it … and they still do. Over ten years later, it's still playing in the same theatre in London … and in many other countries in the world.
P: Where did the musical first go on tour?
R: It first went to Australia in 2003, and then to Japan in 2005. Since then, it's been to many other countries, including Spain, the USA, Russia, South Africa, Italy, Sweden, Singapore, South Korea … many countries around the world!
P: And where is it showing at the moment?
R: Well, it's …

## UNIT 8 RECORDING 3

**Example**
Did you play a musical instrument when you were a child?
1 Where did you live when you were a child?
2 Did you read a lot of books when you were a child?
3 Did your parents read books to you when you were a child?
4 When did you start learning English?
5 Did you watch a lot of TV last weekend?
6 When did you last go to a concert?
7 What music did you last listen to?
8 Did you go for a walk last weekend?
9 When did you last see a really good show?

# UNIT 8 RECORDING 4

I = Interviewer    L = Lauren    D = Daniel    K = Karl

**Lauren**

I: When did you last have a really good evening – in or out?
L: Well, last week I had a really good evening out.
I: What did you do?
L: I went to a fantastic concert.
I: Oh really. Who did you see?
L: I saw a band called the Ravens ... they're a jazz band ... traditional jazz.
I: Who did you go with?
L: I went with a friend of mine, Kate. She really likes jazz, too. We often go together.
I: Where was it? And how did you get there?
L: Oh, it was in a small café in the centre of town ... and we went by bus.
I: Was it good?
L: Yes, it was really good ... they're great. I love their music and I really like going to see live music. It was really good fun.

**Daniel**

I: When did you last have a really good evening – in or out?
D: Last weekend ... on Saturday evening ... I had a good evening in ... at home, with friends.
I: What did you do?
D: I had a dinner party ... well, not a big party; I cooked dinner for four friends.
I: What did you cook?
D: I made a delicious dish with chicken and vegetables, and then we had a dessert – chocolate, strawberries and cream. It was great.
I: Who was there?
D: Four friends of mine. I met them at work and we are all really good friends. It was fun. We often have dinner parties together.

**Karl**

I: When did you last have a really good evening – in or out?
K: Well, actually, I had a really bad evening out a couple of weeks ago.
I: Oh! What did you do?
K: I went to the cinema ... and saw a film ...
I: And ... well, what did you think of it?
K: Well, I didn't really enjoy it. Actually, it was awful. I expected it to be really good ... all the reviews I read were great. But it was really boring!
I: Where did you see it?
K: At my local cinema – five minutes' walk away.
I: And, who did you go with?
K: I went with my girlfriend ... it was her birthday. She didn't enjoy it either. It was really expensive as well! As you can imagine, she wasn't happy at all. It was a terrible evening!

# UNIT 9 RECORDING 2

1  How much does the most expensive handbag in the world cost?
2  The fastest car in the world goes from 0 to 60 miles per hour in how many seconds?
3  How old is Hamleys, the most famous toy shop in the world?
4  Who were the most popular pop group of the 20th century?
5  Who is the richest person in the world?
6  Which is the highest capital city in the world?
7  Where is the tallest hotel in the world?
8  How many passengers does the biggest cruise ship in the world carry?

# UNIT 9 RECORDING 3

1  The most expensive handbag in the world is called the Mouawad 1001 Nights Diamond Purse. It has 4,517 diamonds on it and costs $3.8 million.
2  The fastest car in the world goes from 0 to 60 miles per hour in 2.4 seconds. The Bugatti Veyron Super Sport has a top speed of 267 miles per hour and costs around £1.45 million.
3  The most famous toy shop in the world is Hamleys. The main store is in Regent Street in London and it is over 250 years old.
4  The most popular pop group of the twentieth century was the Beatles. They sold 107 million albums in the USA alone.

5  The richest man in the world is Carlos Slim Helú – a Mexican businessman. He has a personal fortune of $69 billion. Bill Gates has a fortune of $61 billion.
6  The highest capital city in the world is La Paz, in Bolivia, at about 3,600 metres above sea level. Addis Ababa, the capital city of Ethiopia, is about 2,500 metres above sea level and Thimphu, in Bhutan, is about 2,300.
7  The tallest hotel in the world is the JW Marriott Marquis Hotel Dubai, in Dubai. It's 355 metres high.
8  The biggest cruise ship in the world is called the *Allure of the Seas*. It is 360 metres long and carries over 6,000 passengers.

# UNIT 9 RECORDING 4

T = Tina    L = Lee    O = Oksana    K = Karim

**Tina and Lee**

T: Hi, Lee. You live in Thailand, don't you ... the same as me?
L: Yes.
T: So, let's decide what souvenirs we could take from Thailand ... I mean, let's see ... Thailand is famous for silk products, isn't it? Shirts, scarves ... silk scarves and things ...
L: Yes, true.
T: So, I think a good souvenir from Thailand is a silk shirt ... I think that for the father, for Bob ... a silk shirt is a fantastic souvenir. What do you think?
L: Mmm ... yes, that's a good idea. Why don't we buy a silk shirt with something like an elephant on it? That's very typical of Thailand ... they are really beautiful and colourful.
T: Yes, lovely. I think he will be very happy with that. And what about Amy, the mother?
L: Well, you can get beautiful silk scarves for women ... a colourful silk scarf, maybe.
T: Yes, you can. But I think jewellery is better, because it's difficult to buy a dress for a woman you don't know. What do you think?
L: OK, that's true. Yes, jewellery ... good idea. That's great ... And for the children ... Have you got any ideas for the children?

**Oksana and Karim**

O: Well, I'm Oksana and I'm from Ukraine. Karim, where are you from?
K: I'm from Egypt. I have no idea about souvenirs from Ukraine. What's a good souvenir from your country?
O: Well, matryoshka dolls are very typical of Ukraine and also other countries near Ukraine. They are very good souvenirs.
K: Matryoshka dolls?
O: Yes ... you know ... you have a big doll and inside the doll there's a smaller one, and inside that one, another smaller one ... four or five dolls, or maybe more.
K: Oh yes, I know.
O: In Ukraine, the matryoshka dolls are a family. The big doll on the outside, that's the dad. Then, inside, there is a smaller one – that's the mum. Then a son, a daughter, a pet, maybe a dog or cat, and the smallest is a little baby. They are fun – and pretty – I think it's a very nice souvenir for a child.
K: Yes.
O: So I chose that for the little girl in the family ... for Lorna. I think she'll like it. What about you? What did you choose for her?
K: Well, I chose a toy camel.
O: Oh, that's a good idea ... a camel ... yes ... there are lots of camels in Egypt, aren't there?
K: Yes, people use them for transporting things in the desert areas. They are interesting animals ... and children usually like them. Yes, I think a toy camel is a good souvenir.
O: Can you buy them easily?
K: Yes, you can buy them in lots of places. Lots of souvenir shops have them. You can get different sizes and they're not usually too expensive.

# UNIT 10 RECORDING 1

a suit, a tie, trousers, jeans, a baseball cap, sunglasses, a skirt, trainers, a jumper, a dress, a jacket, shorts, a shirt

# Audio script

## UNIT 10 RECORDING 2

**Katie**

I'm a shop assistant in a large fashion store. I don't have a uniform, but all the shop assistants wear the clothes from the store. I need to look stylish and friendly when I'm at work, and it's good that customers can see shop assistants wearing the clothes that they can buy. Luckily, I really like the clothes in the shop, and I wear different things every day: a dress, trousers, shorts … there's lots of variety. I love deciding what to wear in the mornings!

**Marlon**

I'm a personal trainer. I work in a gym and I teach exercise classes and help people to get fit. I love my job and I like the fact that I can wear sports clothes. My work clothes are comfortable and I think they look good, too. I usually wear a sports shirt and shorts … and trainers, of course. On colder days, if I'm outside, I wear long tracksuit trousers and a jacket. The gym provides me with all my clothes for work, so I don't have to pay for them, which is great, too!

**Louisa**

I work for a large bank in the city centre. The way I dress at work is important – I need to give the right impression. I have a lot of meetings with clients and it's important for me to look confident and reliable. I usually wear a skirt suit – a smart skirt and jacket – in a dark colour, like blue or black. I sometimes wear small earrings, but generally I don't wear much jewellery at work. Sometimes I think my work clothes are boring, but I don't mind them really.

**Sam**

I'm an IT manager – I give advice to companies on their information technology and computer systems. I like my job because I work with computers but also with people. It's important for me to look smart in my job, so that I look professional and people feel they can trust me. I always wear a shirt and tie, but I try not to look very formal … so my tie is usually a bright colour, like red … or sometimes pink.

## UNIT 10 RECORDING 3

I usually go to work in an office, but on Fridays, I work at home. When I go to the office, I wear a smart suit and earrings. Today, I'm working at home so I'm wearing very casual clothes – tracksuit and trainers. I'm not wearing any jewellery today.

At my sister's college, people usually wear casual clothes. They normally wear jeans and maybe a shirt or jumper. The teacher doesn't wear a suit – he usually wears jeans, too. Today it's really hot, so my sister's wearing shorts and a T-shirt.

## UNIT 10 RECORDING 4

A: OK. So I can analyse your personality using colours. Let's see what kind of person you really are!

B: OK, fine.

A: Well, first, what's your favourite colour?

B: Um … well, red, I think … and black. Can I say two colours?

A: Two colours … OK … maybe … but which of those is your favourite?

B: I suppose it's red. Red is my favourite, but I like black, too.

A: OK … and what is your least favourite colour?

B: My least favourite colour is brown. I don't like brown.

A: Good, OK … brown. Thanks. So let's see … what colours are you wearing now?

B: Well, I'm wearing mostly black, and a bit of white.

A: That's fine.

B: So, what does that say about me?

A: Let's see … well, red clothes mean you are a confident person. You like a lot of action in your life, too.

B: I think that's absolutely right!

A: And you like wearing black, so you're reliable.

B: Yes, I'm a very reliable person.

A: Black also means you can be bossy.

B: Yes, I think that's true, too!

A: OK … so that's all true so far. Now let's look at your least favourite colour.

B: OK …

## UNIT 11 RECORDING 1

P = Presenter    C = Charlotte

P: Hello … in our programme today we're talking about intelligent animals. Charlotte Golding is an animal expert and she studies animals, especially different kinds of extremely intelligent animals. Good morning, Charlotte.

C: Good morning.

P: So, tell us about some of the animals you study. What kinds of things can they do?

C: Well, most people know that whales and dolphins are very intelligent … they really can do some amazing things. They often work together in large groups to catch their food … They speak to each other by making noises …

P: Yes, that shows great intelligence.

C: And other animals that can speak are African grey parrots. They can learn to copy humans and to speak like them.

P: That's incredible!

C: Yes, and some of them can answer questions about things.

P: Wow!

C: Dogs, too, are very good at communicating generally … and some of them are very good at remembering things as well. One dog I studied can remember the names of thousands of things … and he can go and get whichever thing his owner asks. It's really amazing … Thousands of them!

P: Wow! I find it difficult to remember names!

C: Yes, well, talking of remembering things … One animal – one of my personal favourites – is a chimpanzee.

P: A chimpanzee?

C: Yes, he can remember sequences of numbers. He looks at a computer screen showing a sequence of numbers, from 1 to 10, for example, in different places on the screen. And when numbers disappear, he can remember exactly where each number was.

P: That's amazing!

C: Yes, and what's really amazing is that he only looks at the numbers for 60 milliseconds. When I tried it, I didn't have time to even see all the numbers. There was no chance to remember them at all!

P: No, I'm sure I couldn't do that either.

## UNIT 11 RECORDING 2

50
100
120
240
1,500
8,500
10,000
20,000
32,000,000

## UNIT 11 RECORDING 3

1   The approximate number of active volcanoes in the world is 1,500.

2   The country with the largest number of active volcanoes is Indonesia, with over 120.

3   The approximate top speed of a killer whale is nearly 50 kilometres per hour.

4   The average distance that killer whales swim every year is 20,000 kilometres.

5   The height of some giant redwood trees in California is over 100 metres.

6   Camels can survive without water in temperatures of 50 degrees Celsius for approximately 240 hours.

7   The average weight of a male African elephant is 8,500 kilograms.

8   The approximate rat population of New York City is 32,000,000.

9   Damascus in Syria is perhaps the world's oldest city – it is 10,000 years old.

## UNIT 11 RECORDING 4

South Africa is really a fantastic country to visit. It's one of the most beautiful and diverse countries in the world. We have deserts, grassland, mountains, tropical forests … There aren't many countries in the world where you can see all these amazing things! But if you only have a little time, here are four places you really must visit. One city that a lot of people want to visit is Cape Town. It's a beautiful, beautiful city … by the sea. And you can see the famous Table Mountain, where you will find a lot of different varieties of plants. In fact, there are about 2,200 species of plants … that's more than the whole of the UK!

The Tugela Falls are in the Royal Natal National Park in the east part of the country. The Tugela Falls is the second highest waterfall in the world, and the highest in Africa. The water falls 850 metres – it's incredible to see!

Of course, in South Africa we have a lot of amazing wildlife, and the Kruger National Park is the place to see it. We have a huge number of bird species – more than 500, in fact – and nearly 150 animal species. And you can find elephants, rhinoceros, zebra. My favourite is the cheetah, the fastest animal in the world. Did you know a cheetah can run at 100 kilometres per hour? There isn't much chance of winning that race! That's fast!

There aren't any active volcanoes in South Africa, but there are a few dormant volcanoes; for example, the Salpeterkop volcano. It's 66 million years old, and it's not officially extinct!

These are just a few of the fantastic places you can visit in South Africa. There are many more that I don't have time to tell you about. The best thing is to come and see us here in South Africa. You're very welcome!

## UNIT 11 RECORDING 5

**A:** OK … so, number 1 … the category is 'Countries' … Question number 1: Where is the River Ganges?

**B:** Um, let's look at the possible answers. India – or China? Er, what do you think?

**A:** I think it's in India.

**B:** I'm not sure, but I think it's India, yes.

**A:** OK … number 2 … the category is 'History' … and the question is: Who became President of Russia on 26th March 2000?

**B:** I've got no idea!

**A:** I don't know either. Let's look at the possible answers … OK, it says … umm … Boris Yeltsin … or Vladimir Putin?

**B:** Well, I think it's Boris Yeltsin … yes … Boris Yeltsin.

**A:** OK. Let's say that … Yeltsin. Now, number 3 … 'Science' … How many kilometres are there in one mile?

**B:** I know this one. It's definitely 1.6. There are 1.6 kilometres in a mile.

**A:** Yes, that sounds right and 1.6 is one of the possible answers. Number 4 … this one is also 'Science' … How far is it from the Earth to the sun?

**B:** Oh … umm … what are the possible answers?

**A:** Well, 50 million kilometres … or 150 million kilometres? What do you think?

**B:** Er, I don't know … maybe 50 million kilometres?

**A:** I've got no idea … so … OK … let's say 50 million.

**A:** Great. OK … Number 5 … 'Sport' … When did Spain win the World Cup? Do you know this one?

**B:** Yes! They won it in 2010. It was in South Africa, and they beat the Netherlands 1–0 … yes, I know this one … it's definitely 2010.

**A:** Next one … number 6 … 'Countries' … What is the capital of Peru? Umm … Bogotá? Or Lima?

## UNIT 12 RECORDING 1

1  I've got a really busy weekend because I'm going to a friend's wedding on Saturday. On Saturday morning, I'm going to the hairdresser's and then I'm going to meet my friend Monica, and we're going to drive to the wedding together. I'm really excited!

2  Next Monday is Independence Day. I'm not going to work on Monday because it's a national holiday, so I've got a three-day weekend. I'm going to the beach for three days with my family. When we're there, I'm not going to do anything – I'm going to relax on the beach!

3  On Sunday, I'm going to a big family party. It's a special day because my cousin, Gabriela, is 15 and it's her coming-of-age party. I'm going to wear my new party dress. We're going to have a lot of special food and we're going to dance a lot, too! I can't wait!

## UNIT 12 RECORDING 3

**Example**

My brother is going to cook a family meal tonight.

1  I'm going to have a party this weekend.

2  My parents are going to decorate the house next week.

3  I am going to have a holiday abroad this summer.

4  I'm going to buy some new clothes this weekend.

5  My friends and I are going to have a picnic tomorrow.

6  I'm going to make a cake tomorrow afternoon.

7  My best friend is going to leave her job next month.

## UNIT 12 RECORDING 6

**A:** OK, so when is the festival going to happen?

**B:** It's going to be at the beginning of July, the 5th to the 8th of July … that's the best time, I think. Let's hope the weather's OK.

**A:** So, music … what music are you going to have?

**B:** Well, the big attraction is the Protractors.

**A:** Oh wow, the Protractors. I've heard of them; they're good.

**B:** And we've also got Barbara McDowell, and a band called Salsa Fling are going to play at the festival.

**A:** Sounds good. And how about food? What food are you going to sell?

**B:** A lot of traditional Scottish food. Things like Scotch broth, haggis … traditional Scottish things. And we're going to have cookery demonstrations as well.

**A:** And what about activities for children?

**B:** Yes, we've got a lot of activities for children. We've got face-painting, arts and crafts workshops … And there's going to be traditional Scottish dancing.

**A:** How about accommodation?

**B:** Well, most people go to the campsite, but there are a few hotels in Auldhay. You can go to the Tourist Information office for more details.

**A:** Oh right … and how about tickets? Where can people get tickets?

**B:** Well, you can buy tickets online, or you can get them at the …

## UNIT 13 RECORDING 2

**Lorraine**

When I was young, I didn't see the point of school at all! I hated it and I failed most of my exams. I found everything boring … I just wanted to leave school and start work. My parents worked hard but didn't have much money – my father was a train driver and my mother worked in a supermarket. I think that from an early age, I knew that I wanted to earn money, and have a better life than them. So, I left school when I was 16 and started work in the local baker's shop – just a small place selling bread and cakes and things. I didn't get paid much, but it was a start! I was determined to do well, and after two years there, I became the manager of the shop. I loved it, but I realised that I wanted more. So after another three years there, I decided to start my own business. I opened a small baker's shop and, well, in the first ten years of my business, I opened 60 more shops. I worked really hard … really long hours … and my business continued to grow fast, and it is still growing. It's worth over £30 million now – I'm very proud of that!!

**Martin**

My parents both got into top universities – my father got a degree in Engineering and my mother got a degree in Maths. I passed all my exams at school with top grades, and I also got into a very good university. I got a degree in Maths and chose a career in banking. When I was in my 20s, I worked for a large company and earned a lot of money. My parents were very proud of me, of course. But after a few years, I realised I wasn't happy at all. I didn't like my job; it was stressful and boring. I had a wife and two small children, but I didn't have any time to spend with them … I was stressed all the time and I didn't have time to do the things I liked doing. What I really liked was music – playing the guitar, mostly. So I left my job and now I do small concerts and I teach the guitar to earn some money. I have a stress-free life … I can spend time with my family and friends … and I can combine my hobby – the thing I love doing – with work. I don't earn much money, but I don't mind because now I enjoy every day!

# Audio script

## UNIT 13 RECORDING 3

**A:** So, shall we look at the results?

**B:** Yes, OK.

**A:** Well, what did you get? How many a's, b's, c's and d's?

**B:** Umm … OK, let's see. Well, I got one … , two … , three … , four a's …

**A:** Four a's!

**M:** Yes, and one b, two d's and one c.

**A:** So, that's definitely mostly a's!

**B:** Yes … what does that mean, then?

**A:** Well, let's have a look at the information. Your results …

**B:** What does it say?

**A:** OK … mostly a's … It says here, 'You are a dynamic person …'

**B:** Yes, that's true. I think I am. I like doing things and being active … And … ?

**A:** … and '… you are ready to do anything to be a success in life.'

**B:** Well, I think that's partly true. I mean, I'll work as hard as I can and I might be a bit bossy sometimes, but I won't do 'anything' to be a success. I won't be horrible to people … and I won't work all the time … 24-7.

**A:** No …

**B:** What else?

**A:** OK, it says, 'Perhaps you will be a successful businessperson, manager or you will work in finance.'

**B:** Oh well, that's not right! Er … that's rubbish! I'm not good at maths or business or anything like that!

**A:** No, you're more creative, aren't you? What's your job now?

**B:** Well, I'm a journalist at the moment, but I'd like to be a designer … an interior designer. I might do a training course next year … and change my career, I think. I'd really like to do that.

**A:** So, are you 'ready to do anything to be a success in life'?!

## UNIT 14 RECORDING 1

**1** **A:** It says here that the average internet user has 25 online accounts!

**B:** Really? 25? That's a lot! How many have you got?

**A:** Oh, I don't know … two bank accounts, various shop accounts … umm … probably about ten or 12 in all.

**B:** And do you have the same password for them all?

**A:** Well, I've got nearly the same password, but it's not exactly the same for every account.

**B:** Have you ever forgotten your password?

**A:** Yes, I have … many times. I can only remember it when I write it down!

**B:** I know what you mean. I always write my passwords down, too. It's probably not very good to write them down, I suppose, but I'm sure most people do.

**2** **A:** So, why don't you send Sonia a text message and ask her about the party?

**B:** Yes, good idea … er … er … where's my phone?

**A:** Erm … I don't know … it was in your bag, wasn't it?

**B:** Oh, here it is … it's terrible not knowing where your phone is! I really lost it last summer, when I was on holiday. It was awful. Have you ever lost your mobile phone?

**A:** No, I haven't. I've never lost it, but someone stole it once.

**B:** Oh no! Really? Where? What happened?

**A:** Oh, I was at a concert … an open-air concert in a park … you know, there were thousands of people there … and after about an hour, I realised my phone wasn't in my pocket. I'm sure someone stole it.

**B:** Maybe it just fell out of your pocket.

**3** **A:** Oh, this computer is so slow. It keeps stopping and I can't do anything! It's really annoying!

**B:** Oh dear. You might have a virus. Have you ever had a virus on your computer?

**A:** Yes, I have. I've had two or three, I think.

**B:** Really? Two or three … you should do something about it or you might lose everything on your computer …

**A:** Oh, that's never happened … it just goes really slowly sometimes.

**B:** Seriously, some viruses are very dangerous – your computer might crash completely. Have you got anything important on your computer?

**A:** Oh, yes. All my homework assignments, and loads of photos and things.

**B:** You should get Daniel to look at it for you … quickly …

**A:** Really? Do you think so …

## UNIT 14 RECORDING 2

**1** **A:** Have you ever forgotten your password?

**B:** Yes, I have.

**2** **A:** Have you ever lost your mobile phone?

**B:** No, I haven't.

**3** **A:** Have you ever had a virus on your computer?

**B:** Yes, I have.

## UNIT 14 RECORDING 3

**A:** OK, well, I'm going to choose the letter 'M'.

**B:** 'M' … 'M' is … 'Mobile phones'.

**A:** OK … 'Mobile phones' … that's good. What are the questions?

**B:** 'How do you feel if someone interrupts your conversation to use their mobile phone?' And … 'How often do you use your phone when out with friends or at a meal with other people?'

**A:** Hmmm … OK …

**B:** You've got one minute to talk about those questions.

**A:** One minute – that's a long time.

**B:** OK … one minute … starting now!

**A:** OK, so, let me think … Mobile phones … I'm going to talk about mobile phones … I'm going to talk about how I feel if someone interrupts me to use their mobile phone. Well, I don't like it when people use their mobile phones all the time. What I mean is, mobile phones are good for keeping in touch with people … and for making arrangements with friends. What else? They are good for getting information if you have a smartphone … and things like that. I use my phone a lot, you know … especially to text people to say when to meet … and if I'm going to be late. It's very useful for that. But some people use their phones all the time … they are addicted … Can I say that? … Addicted to their phone. Yes, they are addicted to their mobile phone … and when you speak to them, they always look at their phone and they don't listen to what I'm saying. In my opinion, that is not polite. It is very rude and I think it is annoying. Umm … I suppose that sometimes I look at my texts when I am out with friends or at a meal, but not usually. I try to put my phone away … when I'm eating a meal, and …

**B:** OK … time's up! That's one minute! Well done.

**A:** OK, great. I can take that square!

**B:** Now, it's my turn. Um … I'm going to choose 'B' … What are the questions for the letter 'B'?

**A:** 'B' is … 'Books'.

**B:** Books? OK …

# Verb list

| VERB | PAST SIMPLE | PAST PARTICIPLE |
| --- | --- | --- |
| be | was / were | been |
| become | became | become |
| begin | began | begun |
| bite | bit | bitten |
| break | broke | broken |
| bring | brought | brought |
| build | built | built |
| buy | bought | bought |
| catch | caught | caught |
| choose | chose | chosen |
| come | came | come |
| cost | cost | cost |
| cut | cut | cut |
| do | did | done |
| draw | drew | drawn |
| drink | drank | drunk |
| drive | drove | driven |
| eat | ate | eaten |
| fall | fell | fallen |
| feel | felt | felt |
| find | found | found |
| fly | flew | flown |
| forget | forgot | forgotten |
| get | got | got |
| give | gave | given |
| go | went | gone / been |
| grow | grew | grown |
| have | had | had |
| hear | heard | heard |
| hit | hit | hit |
| hold | held | held |
| hurt | hurt | hurt |
| keep | kept | kept |
| know | knew | known |

| VERB | PAST SIMPLE | PAST PARTICIPLE |
| --- | --- | --- |
| learn | learned / learnt | learned / learnt |
| leave | left | left |
| lend | lent | lent |
| let | let | let |
| lose | lost | lost |
| make | made | made |
| meet | met | met |
| pay | paid | paid |
| put | put | put |
| read | read | read |
| run | ran | run |
| say | said | said |
| see | saw | seen |
| sell | sold | sold |
| send | sent | sent |
| show | showed | shown |
| sing | sang | sung |
| sit | sat | sat |
| sleep | slept | slept |
| smell | smelled / smelt | smelled / smelt |
| speak | spoke | spoken |
| spend | spent | spent |
| stand | stood | stood |
| swim | swam | swum |
| take | took | taken |
| teach | taught | taught |
| tell | told | told |
| think | thought | thought |
| throw | threw | thrown |
| understand | understood | understood |
| wake | woke | woken |
| wear | wore | worn |
| win | won | won |
| write | wrote | written |

**Pearson Education Limited**
Edinburgh Gate
Harlow
Essex CM20 2JE
England
and Associated Companies throughout the world.

www.pearsonelt.com

First published 2013
Tenth impression 2018
ISBN: 978-1-4479-3683-1

Set in Bliss Light 10.5pt/12pt
Printed in Slovakia by Neografia

**Acknowledgements**
*The Publisher and authors would like to thank the following people and
institutions for their feedback and comments during the development of
the material:*

Elizabeth Beck, British Council, Milan, Italy; Emily Bell, International
House, Santander, Spain; Kirsten Colquhoun, EC Cape Town, South
Africa; Tim Goodier, Eurocentres, London, UK; Stephen Greene,
Tailor-Made English, Rio de Janeiro, Brazil; Jonathan Herbert,
Birmingham, UK; Nick Kiley, International House, Tbilisi, Georgia;
Steve Longworth, Sheffield, UK; Nicola Perry, Egham, UK; Lisa
Phillips, Buenos Aires, Argentina; Chris Rogers, Trebinshun House,
Brecon, Wales; Agnieszka Tyszkiewicz-Zora, Foreign Languages
Centre, University of Łódź, Poland

**Photo acknowledgements**
*The Publisher would like to thank the following for their kind
permission to reproduce their photographs:*

(Key: b-bottom; c-centre; l-left; r-right; t-top)

**Alamy Images:** Olga A. Kolos 96t, AC Images 111cr, Peter Barritt
82/G, Andy Bishop 95t, Blend Images 66l, Mike Booth 80tr,
BrazilPhotos.com 112cr, Judith Collins 79c (Silver camera), Corbis
Super RF 82/L, dbimages 44tr, Mark Dunn 81bl, Tim E White 48tr, 57,
Oscar Elias 24tr, Gallo Images 100tr, David Gee 33bl, GoGo Images
Corporation 56tl, GooglePhotographer 86tl, graficart.net 82/H, Horizons
WWP 124tr, Peter Horree 56tr, Imagestate Media Partners Limited -
Impact Photos 107tr, incamerastock 56cl, Jeff Morgan 09 111cl, JoeFox
110cr, Michael Kemp 48cr (Bicycles), Tom Kidd 96c, Andy Lim 106t,
robert linale 83r, Matthew Mirabelli 30tl, moodboard 82/J, Valentin
Mosichev 91tl, nagelestock.com 106bl, 111tl, OJO Images Ltd 107tc,
pbpgalleries 79cr (White car), 79cr (Yellow car), Peter Adams
Photography Ltd 101cl, Picture It Photos by Leslie 130, Robert Harding
Picture Library Ltd 84tr, Pep Roig 32-33t, Maurice Savage 50t,
SERDAR 67t, studiomode 16tr (Tissues), Top-Pics TBK 100cr, A
Traverler 101bl, Wim Wiskerke 83l, WoodyStock 109cc; **Bananastock:**
28tr (Inset); **BBC Motion Gallery:** 50br (James), 50br (Jeremy), 50br
(Richard), 50br (the Stig); **Brand X Pictures:** Burke Triolo Productions
52bl; **Comstock Images:** 52c (Sandwich); **Corbis:** 27cr (Rio de
Janeiro), Bettmann 63t, 64t, D / Erik Kabik / Retna Ltd. 8b (Luis
Miguel), Dan Bannister / Tetra Images 58, Sean Davey 30bl, Everett
Kennedy Brown / epa 54tl, Franck Robishon / epa 87bl, Erik Freeland
109tr, Rick Friedman 68br, Tom Grill 40, Ian Lishman / Juice Images
115tl, 117tl, Ian Lishman / Juice Images 115tl, 117tl, Image Source 34c
(Man cheering), 59, Robbie Jack 123b, James Hardy / PhotoAlto 7tl,
Holger Leue 87tr, Lui Siu Wai / Xinhua Press 45tl, Michael Ochs
Archives 60c, Ocean 91tc, Radius Images 94, Sigrid Olsson / PhotoAlto
113, Pauline St. Denis 66tr, The Gallery Collection 60cr (Mozart), Tim
Hall / cultura 34br; **Digital Vision:** 97cl, 105bl, Rob van Petten 9tc;
**FLPA Images of Nature:** Konrad Wothe / Minden Pictures 98tl;
**Fotolia.com:** 21tl, Africa Studio 55tr, 65c, 119tl, Aaron Amat 17tl
(Glasses), Yuri Arcurs 7br (Al and Joe), 120c (Chef), Andrey Armyagov
65t, asplosh 8c (Rupee), atoss 52tc (Banana), auremar 7br (Luca), 20tr,
114bl, AVAVA 117bl, Andrey Bandurenko 78c (Bag), Galina Barskaya
7br (Alicia), bbbar 8t/b, bloomua 16c (Credit card), Sylvie Bouchard
82/A, bramgino 78c (Scooter), bridge 119br (Flowers), Lorenzo Buttitta
52c, Jacek Chabraszewski 54cr, chiyacat 47t, chrisdorney 119bl, Arkady
Chubykin 7br (Adrian), cienpiesnf 124bl, 126tl, clickit 96bl, 105tl,
crimson 79c (Pink dress), Yves Damin 53tc, determined 17tl (Photos),
DM7 119br (Rings), dontree 8c (Rouble), EastWest Imaging 39tl,
EcoView 101tr, Elnur 16tr (Water), 52c (Water), 79cl, 102tl, 102br, Jan
Engel 90-91 (Balloons), Eric Fahrner 7br (Abed), Faraways 8c (Lira),
forcdan 104-105t, Fotolibrary 80tl, full image 16c (Chewing gum), Gary
78cr (Car), gemenacom 82/K, goodluz 74, Irochka 97br, JJAVA 82/I,
Paulo Jorge cruz 110tr, 111br, karnizz 42tr, kavring 16cr (Memory

stick), Kirill Kedrinski 39tr, Kzenon 77, lenets_tan 119cl, lightpoet
116b, Vera Lubimova 53cl, lunamarina 47cl, mangostock 34bl, 39cr,
manyakotic 53tl, Mark Markau 8t/a, metlion 42tc, mezzotint 102cr,
michaeljung 67c, micromonkey 7br (Anderson family), 34bc, millaf
52tr (Grapes), Daria Minaeva 78tr, Monkey Business 24tc, 75c (Meal),
Oleksandr Moroz 78cr (Watch), Sergey Nivens 68-69t, NizArt 48cr
(School party), nyul 75cl (Cinema), okinawakasawa 16tc (Bag), Oktava
119cr, Sergey Peterman 17tl (Wallet), Picture Partners 53c, Giuseppe
Porzani 72-73t (Background), Gennadiy Poznyakov 120c (Surgeon),
Profotokris 52cr (Cheese), QQ7 51t, rabbit75_fot 67b, rook76 8t/d,
Gina Sanders 55bl, Gino Santa Maria 114cr, sashahaltam 39cl, scaliger
103tr, Schlierner 118t, sdecoret 119tr, Shock 34tc, 82/B, Silkstock 17tl
(Keys), Comugnero Silvana 8c (Peso), stocksolutions 110br, Aleksandr
Ugorenkov 78bl, 85b, Unclesam 79cr (Black camera), Serghei
Velusceac 52tc (Apple), victorpr 103tl, Videowokart 103cr, Viktor 82/C,
vladkost 84br, wajan 75t, WITTY 54br, xalanx 52cr (Chicken), yanlev
34c (Cyclist), Alexander Zam 8t/c; **Getty Images:** 2011 Blomberg 63b,
102tc, 108r, AFP 45cr, 112tl, 112tr, Bnsdeo 97tl, Joselito Briones 22,
Scott E Barbour 103br, Joshua Ets-Hokin 90tc, 90tr, Luiz Felipe Castro
46t, Tim Graham 106-107t, Jeff Greenberg 115tr, Brian Hagiwara 56cr,
Himanshu Khagta 33tl (Inset), Till Jacket 29tl (Main), James Hardy.
PhotoAlto. 76, Juan Madrigal Photo 122, Ghislain & Marie David de
Lossy 38c, Michael Ochs Archives 60bl, 64b, Redferns 8b (Andrea
Bocelli), 72tr, Clive Rose 133, SuperStock 97c, Hiroki Watanabe 11cl,
Adrian Weinbrecht 38tc, WireImage 62cr, 64c; **Glow Images:** Image
100. Corbis 117tr; **Photo courtesy Google UK:** 8c (Google);
**Honda(UK):** 8c (Honda); **Imagemore Co., Ltd:** 7br ( Argentinian
flag), 7br (Australian flag), 7br (Mexican flag), 7br (Polish flag), 7br
(USA flag), 8b (Goodrem flag), 8b (Miguel flag), 62cl (Butterfly left),
62cl (Butterfly right), 62cl (Cicada), 102tr, 103bl; **John Foxx Images:**
29tl (Inset), Imagestate 27tr (Berlin); **Marks and Spencer plc
(company):** 8c (M&S); **Mary Evans Picture Library:** Chris Coupland
21c; **Pearson Education Ltd:** 52c (Tomatoes), Debbie Rowe 41b, Jules
Selmes 42cr, 43tl, Steve Shott 34tr, Sozaijiten 43cl, 54tr, Coleman Yuen
16cr (Dictionary), 45tr; **PhotoDisc:** 52tc (Baguette), Adam Crowley
102c, Emma Lee. Life File. 61, Michael Evans. Life File 50-51t,
Photolink 103cl, Squared Studios 102cl; **Photoshot Holdings Limited:**
72tl, 98c, AllCanadaPhotos 98tr, LFI 73, NHPA 98cr; **Press Association
Images:** Amy Sancetta / AP 60cr (Tara Lipinski), Chris Pizzello / AP
35, Jacquelyn Martin / AP 11tl, Tim Ireland / PA Archive 134; **John
Quintero:** John Quintero 123t; **Reuters:** Fadi Al-Assaad 81bc; **Rex
Features:** 19tl, Jeff Blackler 51bl, Paul Brown 80br, c.MGM / Everett
70tr, c.Universal / Everett 70cr, Chameleons Eye 42bl, 46br, 47b,
Courtesy Everett Collection 70cl, John Rahim / Music Pics Ltd. 37, Nils
Jorgensen 72bl, Lou Linwei 11cr, Luke Marsden / Newspix 8b (Delta
Goodrem), Moviestore Collection 60cl (Tatum O'neal), 70br, Startraks
Photo 11tr, 21tc, The World of Sports SC 60t; **Shutterstock.com:**
Andresr 46bl, Andrey Arkusha 9tr, 88bl, 95cl, artjazz 16c (Mobile
phone), Iuliia Azarova 78tc, bioraven 16bl, Brandon Blinkenberg 85cr,
Artur Bogacki 27tr (Istanbul), DD Coral 28tr (Main), Phil Date 23t, lev
dolgachov 34cr (Using laptop), fotohunter 65b, Goodluz 9tl, Joe Gough
29br, grivet 43tr (Background), Laszlo Halasi 81br, Tom Hirtreiter 99,
Oliver Hoffmann 16c (Coins), JaySi 101tl, JNT Visual 16c (ID card),
jocic 16cr (Camera), Dmitry Kalinovsky 116t, kezza 30tr, lavitrei 30br,
Aija Lehtonen 75b, leungchopan 27br (Hong Kong), Lucky Business
95b, Oleksiy Mark 42c (Cruise liner), Mazzzur 85cl, michaeljung 114tr,
Michaelpuche 82/E, Phillip Minnis 27br (Canberra), MJTH 6t, dora
modly-paris 79tl, Monkey Business Images 66br, Naughty Nut 38tr,
Pelham James Mitchinson 13, Oksana Perkins 44tl, PhotoNAN 79c
(Gold dress), Rido 12tr, Thorsten Rust 12br, 132, Rustamir 84cr, Fedor
Selivanov 41cl, Ljupco Smokovski 42c (Motorbike), sokolovsky 115b,
Standret 17tl (Watch), Supri Suharjoto 23b, Tupungato 31c, V. J.
Matthew 62b, Vitchanan Photography 41cr, Tatyana Vychegzhanina
20tc, wavebreakmedia 118b, 125, Carlos Yudica 92-93, Andrew Zarivny
27cr (San Francisco), Alberto Zornetta 20tl; **SuperStock:** age fotostock
47cr, 95cr, 120b, age fotostock 47cr, 95cr, 120b, age fotostock 47cr,
95cr, 120b, Antoine Juliette / Oredia / Oredia Eurl 34cr (Reading),
Cultura Limited 117br, Eye Ubiquitous 25, Ian Murray / Loop Images
48br, imagebroker.net 54bl, JTB Photo 15bl, Juice Images 82/D, Keith
Morris / age fotostock 114tc, Lucenet Patrice / Oredia Eurl 82/F, Marka
54cl, Nordic Photos 24bl, 31t, Stock Connection 86-87t, Tim Oram /
age fotostock 29cl (Main), Tips Images 6bl, 15tr, 18, Tips Images 6bl,
15tr, 18, Ton Koene / age fotostock 14-15t; **The Art Archive:** Ragab
Papyrus Institute Cairo / Dagli Orti 70bl, 71; **The Kobal Collection:**
Lorimar / Warner Bros 60cl (Olsen Twins); **The Red Consultancy Ltd:**
8c (Samsung); **TopFoto:** © 2002 Credit: Topham Picturepoint 102bl;
**Veer/Corbis:** Deklofenek 75cr (TV), Robert Kneschke 121, leaf 7cl,
Morgan Lane Photography 84l, PT Images 12l, Ivan Synieokov 38tl,
yanc 120t; **www.imagesource.com:** 7br (UAE flag), 8b (Bocelli Flag),
27cr (Paris), 29cl (Inset)

Cover image: © *Front:* Fotolia.com: Kushnirov Avraham

All other images © Pearson Education

**Illustrated by:** In-house p.19, p.22, p.26, p.40, p.59, p.76, p.94, p.113,
p.128, p.130; Andrew Lyons (Handsome Frank) p.88; Julian Mosedale
p.10, p.17, p.36, p.108; Peskimo (Synergy Art) p.28